McDougal Littell
Algebra 2
Concepts and Skills

Larson   Boswell   Kanold   Stiff

Notetaking Guide

The Notetaking Guide contains a lesson-by-lesson framework that allows
students to take notes on and review the main concepts of each lesson in the
textbook. Each Notetaking Guide lesson features worked-out examples and
Checkpoint exercises. Each example has a number of write-on lines for students
to complete, either in class as the example is discussed or at home as part of a
review of the lesson. Each chapter concludes with a review of the main vocabulary of the chapter. Upon completion, each chapter of the Notetaking Guide can
be used by students to help review for the test on that particular chapter.

McDougal Littell
A DIVISION OF HOUGHTON MIFFLIN COMPANY
Evanston, Illinois • Boston • Dallas

Printed in the U.S.A.

ISBN-13 978-0-618-57470-4
ISBN-10 0-618-57470-0

 7 8 9   0982   18 17 16 15 14 13 12 11

4500331846   D E

Contents

ALGEBRA 2 CONCEPTS AND SKILLS NOTETAKING GUIDE

1.1 Real Numbers and Number Operations

Goal • Graph, order, and use real numbers.

VOCABULARY

Origin _____

Graph _____

Coordinate _____

Opposite _____

Reciprocal _____

REAL NUMBERS

The real numbers consist of the _____ numbers
and the _____ numbers. Two subsets of the
rational numbers are the _____ (0, 1, 2, …)
and the _____ (…, −3, −2, −1, 0, 1, 2, 3, …).

Rational Numbers

• _____ be written as the
  ratios of integers

• Can be written as
  _____ that
  terminate or repeat

Irrational Numbers

• _____ be written
  as the ratios of integers

• Cannot be written as
  decimals that
  _____
  or _____

Example 1   *Graph Real Numbers on a Number Line*

Graph the real numbers $-\frac{13}{5}$, 1.4, and $\sqrt{6}$ on a number line.

Solution

Note that $-\frac{13}{5} =$ _____. Use a calculator to approximate $\sqrt{6}$ to the nearest tenth: $\sqrt{6} \approx$ _____. So, graph $-\frac{13}{5}$ between _____ and _____, graph 1.4 between ___ and ___, and graph $\sqrt{6}$ between ___ and ___.

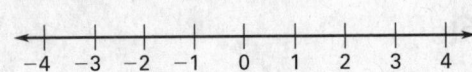

Example 2   *Compare Real Numbers*

Compare the numbers -3 and 2 using the symbol $<$ or $>$.

Solution

Graph both numbers on a real number line.

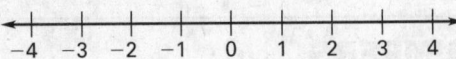

Because -3 is to the _____ of 2, it follows that -3 is _____ than 2, which is written using symbols as -3 __ 2.

✔ *Checkpoint* **Complete the following exercises.**

1. Graph the numbers $\sqrt{5}$, -2, $-\frac{1}{2}$, and 3.2.

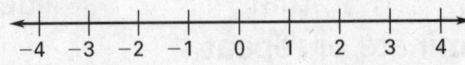

2. Write the numbers above in order from least to greatest.

PROPERTIES OF ADDITION AND MULTIPLICATION

Let a, b, and c be real numbers.

Property	Addition	Multiplication
Commutative	$a + b =$ ___ $+$ ___	$ab =$ ____
Associative	$(a + b) + c =$ ___ $+ ($___ $+$ ___$)$	$(ab)c =$ ___$($___$)$
Identity	$a + 0 =$ ___, $0 + a =$ ___	$a \cdot 1 =$ ___, $1 \cdot a =$ ___
Inverse	$a + ($____$) = 0$	$a \cdot$ ___ $= 1, a \neq$ ___

The following property involves both addition and multiplication.

Distributive $a(b + c) =$ ____ $+$ ____

Example 3   *Use Properties of Real Numbers*

Use the distributive property to evaluate $7 \cdot 302$.

$7 \cdot 302 = 7(300 +$ ___$)$ Rewrite 302 as ____ $+$ ___.

$= 7($____$) + 7($___$)$ Distributive property

$=$ _____ $+$ ____   Multiply.

$=$ _____   Simplify.

Example 4   *Operations with Real Numbers*

a. Find the difference of -11 and 3.

$-11 - 3 = -11 + ($___$)$ Add ____, the opposite of ___.

$= -14$ Simplify.

b. Find the quotient of -20 and $\frac{1}{5}$.

$-20 \div \frac{1}{5} = -20 \cdot$ ___   Multiply by ___, the reciprocal of ___.

$=$ _____   Simplify.

1.2 Algebraic Expressions and Models

Goal • Define and use algebraic expressions.

VOCABULARY

Exponent

Power

Base

Numerical expression

Algebraic expression

Variable

Example 1 *Evaluate Powers*

a. $(-3)^2 = (\underline{\hspace{1cm}}) \cdot (\underline{\hspace{1cm}}) = \underline{\hspace{1cm}}$

b. $-3^2 = -(\underline{\hspace{0.5cm}} \cdot \underline{\hspace{0.5cm}}) = \underline{\hspace{1cm}}$

✔ *Checkpoint* **Evaluate the power.**

1. 5^4	**2.** -5^4
3. $(-5)^4$	**4.** 5^1

ORDER OF OPERATIONS

Step 1 Perform operations that occur within

_____.

Step 2 Evaluate _____.

Step 3 Perform multiplications and _____ from

_____.

Step 4 Perform _____ and subtractions from

_____.

Example 2   *Use Order of Operations*

$$12 \div 6 - 4 \times 2^2 = 12 \div 6 - 4 \times \underline{}$$ **Evaluate power.**

$$= \underline{} - 4 \times 4$$ **Divide.**

$$= 2 - \underline{}$$ **Multiply.**

$$= \underline{}$$ **Subtract.**

Example 3   *Evaluate an Algebraic Expression*

a. Evaluate $3(x - 1) + 5x$ when $x = 2$.

$3(x - 1) + 5x$

$= 3(\underline{} - 1) + 5(\underline{})$ **Substitute 2 for x.**

$= 3(\underline{}) + 5(2)$ **Subtract within parentheses.**

$= \underline{} + \underline{}$ **Multiply.**

$= \underline{}$ **Add.**

b. Evaluate $-6y^2 - 11y + 34$ when $y = -5$.

$-6y^2 - 11y + 34$

$= -6(\underline{})^2 - 11(\underline{}) + 34$ **Substitute −5 for y.**

$= -6(\underline{}) - 11(-5) + 34$ **Evaluate power.**

$= \underline{} + \underline{} + 34$ **Multiply.**

$= \underline{}$ **Add.**

✔ *Checkpoint* **Complete the following exercises.**

5. Evaluate $8 + 3(7 - 5)^2$.	6. Evaluate $2y^2(y - 1)$ when $y = 3$.

Example 4 — *Write and Evaluate a Mathematical Model*

Recreation You have $120 and are buying amusement park tickets that cost $26 each. Write an expression that shows how much money you have left after buying t tickets. Evaluate the expression for $t = 2$ and $t = 4$.

Solution

Verbal Model [Original amount] − [Price per ticket] · [_____]

Labels
Original amount = _____ (dollars)
Price per ticket = _____ (dollars per ticket)
Number of tickets bought = t (tickets)

Algebraic Model _____ − _____

When you buy 2 tickets, you have $120 - 26(\_) = \$\_\_\_$ left.
When you buy 4 tickets, you have $120 - 26(\_) = \$\_\_\_$ left.

✔ *Checkpoint* **Complete the following exercise.**

Homework

7. In Example 4, write an expression that shows how much money you have left after buying t tickets if you have $180 and the tickets cost $39 each. Then evaluate the expression when $t = 2$ and $t = 4$.

1.3 Simplifying Algebraic Expressions

Goal • Simplify algebraic expressions.

VOCABULARY

Terms

Coefficient

Like terms

Constant term

Simplified expression

Example 1 *Identify Terms in an Expression*

Identify the terms in the expression $6 - 5x + x^2$.

Write the expression as a _____.

$6 - 5x + x^2 = 6 + (\underline{\hspace{1cm}}) + \underline{\hspace{0.5cm}}$

The terms of the expression are ___, _____, and ___.

Example 2 *Identify Coefficients and Like Terms*

Identify the coefficients and like terms in the expression $4x^2 - 6x + 3 + 8x - 5$.

Write the expression as a sum.

$4x^2 - 6x + 3 + 8x - 5 = 4x^2 + (\underline{\hspace{1cm}}) + 3 + 8x + (\underline{\hspace{1cm}})$

The coefficients of the expression are ___, _____, and 8.

The terms $-6x$ and _____ are like terms. The terms 3 and _____ are also like terms.

Your Notes

> **1.** Identify the terms, coefficients, and like terms in the expression $2x^3 - 6x^2 + 4 + 5x^2 - 2x - 4x^3$.

Example 3 *Simplify by Combining Like Terms*

Simplify the expression.

a. $11x - 5x$ **b.** $14x - 6y + 5x + 13y$

Solution

a. $11x - 5x = ($ ____ $- $ ____ $)x$ **Distributive property**

             $=$ ____   **Subtract.**

b. $14x - 6y + 5x + 13y$

     $= ($ ____ $+ 5x) + (-6y + $ ____ $)$ **Group like terms.**

     $= ($ ___ $+$ ___ $)x + ($ ____ $+$ ____ $)y$ **Distributive property**

     $=$ ____ $+$ ____   **Add.**

Example 4 *Simplify Expressions with Grouping Symbols*

Simplify the expression $2(y + 5) - 3(y - 9)$**.**

$2(y + 5) - 3(y - 9)$

     $=$ ____ $+ 10 - 3y + $ ____   **Distributive property**

     $= ($ ____ $- $ ____ $) + ($ ____ $+ $ ____ $)$ **Group like terms.**

     $= ($ ___ $- $ ___ $)y + (10 + 27)$ **Distributive property**

     $=$ ____ $+ 37$ **Add or subtract.**

Homework

✓ **Checkpoint** Simplify the expression.

2. $11n - 6 + 14 - 2n$	**3.** $6(x - 4) - 3(x - 11)$

1.4 Solving Linear Equations

Goal • Solve linear equations.

VOCABULARY

Equation

Linear equation in one variable

Solution of an equation

PROPERTIES OF EQUALITY

Addition Property	**Add** the same number to each side: If $a = b$, then ___ $+ c =$ ___ $+ c$.
Subtraction Property	**Subtract** the same number from each side: If $a = b$, then ___ $- c =$ ___ $- c$.
Multiplication Property	**Multiply** each side by the same nonzero number: If $a = b$ and $c \neq 0$, then ___ $=$ ___.
Division Property	**Divide** each side by the same nonzero number: If $a = b$ and $c \neq 0$, then $a \div$ ___ $= b \div$ ___.

Example 1   *Solve a One-Step Equation*

Solve $x + 3 = 7$.

Solution

$$x + 3 = 7 \qquad \text{Write original equation.}$$
$$x + 3 - \underline{} = 7 - \underline{} \qquad \text{Subtract 3 from each side.}$$
$$x = \underline{} \qquad \text{Simplify.}$$

Example 2   *Solve a Multi-Step Equation*

Solve $-2x - 4 = -18$.

Solution

$-2x - 4 = -18$	Write original equation.
$-2x = \underline{\hspace{1cm}}$	Add ___ to each side to isolate the variable.
$x = \underline{\hspace{0.5cm}}$	Divide each side by ____ .

Example 3   *Solve an Equation with Variables on Both Sides*

Solve $2y + 4 = 5y - 2$.

Solution

$2y + 4 = 5y - 2$	Write original equation.
$4 = \underline{\hspace{1cm}} - 2$	Subtract _____ from each side.
$\underline{\hspace{0.5cm}} = 3y$	_____ 2 to each side.
$\underline{\hspace{0.5cm}} = \underline{\hspace{0.5cm}}$	Divide each side by ___ .

✔ *Checkpoint* **Solve the equation. Check your solution.**

1. $x - 5 = -2$

2. $15a - 6 = 9$

3. $x - 4 = 3x + 14$

Example 4   *Use the Distributive Property*

Solve $3(4x - 3) = 7(4x + 3) - 31x$.

$3(4x - 3) = 7(4x + 3) - 31x$	Write original equation.
$\underline{} - \underline{} = \underline{} + \underline{} - 31x$	Distributive property
$12x - 9 = \underline{} + 21$	Combine like terms.
$\underline{} - 9 = 21$	Add ___ to each side.
$\underline{} = \underline{}$	Add ___ to each side.
$x = \underline{}$	Divide each side by ___.

Example 5   *Solve an Equation with Fractions*

Solve $\frac{2}{3}y + \frac{1}{2} = y - \frac{3}{4}$.

$\frac{2}{3}y + \frac{1}{2} = y - \frac{3}{4}$	Write original equation.
$\underline{}\left(\frac{2}{3}y + \frac{1}{2}\right) = \underline{}\left(y - \frac{3}{4}\right)$	Multiply each side by the LCD, ___.
$\underline{} + \underline{} = \underline{} - \underline{}$	Distributive property
$6 = \underline{} - 9$	Subtract ___ from each side.
$\underline{} = \underline{}$	Add ___ to each side.
$\underline{} = y$	Divide each side by ___.

✔ **Checkpoint** Solve the equation. Check your solution.

4. $3(x + 3) = -2(x - 7) - 5x$	**5.** $3 - \frac{1}{3}x = \frac{7}{12}x + \frac{2}{3}$

Homework

1.5 Rewriting Equations and Formulas

Goal • Rewrite common formulas and equations that have more than one variable.

Your Notes

COMMON FORMULAS

	FORMULA	VARIABLES
Distance	$d =$ ____	$d =$ _____, $r =$ rate, $t =$ time
Simple Interest	$I =$ ____	$I =$ interest, $P =$ _____, $r =$ rate, $t =$ time
Temperature	$F =$ _____	$F =$ degrees Fahrenheit, $C =$ degrees Celsius

GEOMETRY FORMULAS

RECTANGLE

Perimeter $P =$ _____

Area $A =$ ____

TRIANGLE

Perimeter $P =$ _____

Area $A =$ ____

TRAPEZOID

Area $A =$ _____

CIRCLE

Circumference $C =$ ____ or

$C =$ ____

Area $A =$ ____

Example 1 | *Rewrite a Common Formula*

Solve $C = 2\pi r$ for r.

Solution

$C = 2\pi r$ Write original formula.

$ = r$ Divide each side by ____.

Your Notes

Example 2   *Use a Rewritten Formula*

Find the radius of a circular pool with a circumference of 26 meters.

$r = \dfrac{C}{2\pi}$ Use the rewritten formula from Example 1.

$r = $ _____   Substitute _____ for C.

$= \dfrac{13}{\pi} \approx$ _____   Divide. Use the π key on a calculator.

The radius of the pool is about _____ meters.

Example 3   *Calculate the Value of a Variable*

Find the value of y in the equation $3x + 4y = 8$ when $x = -4$ and when $x = 12$.

Solution

Method 1: First substitute for x. Then solve for y.

When $x = -4$:

$3x + 4y = 8$

$3(\underline{\quad}) + 4y = \underline{\quad}$

$\underline{\quad} + 4y = \underline{\quad}$

$\underline{\quad} = \underline{\quad}$

$y = \underline{\quad}$

When $x = 12$:

$3x + 4y = 8$

$3(\underline{\quad}) + 4y = \underline{\quad}$

$\underline{\quad} + 4y = \underline{\quad}$

$\underline{\quad} = \underline{\quad}$

$y = \underline{\quad}$

Method 2: First solve for y. Then substitute for x.

$3x + 4y = 8$ Write original equation.

$4y = \underline{\quad} + 8$ Subtract _____ from each side.

$y = \underline{\quad} + \underline{\quad}$ Divide each side by ___.

When $x = -4$: $y = \underline{\quad}(\underline{\quad}) + 2 = \underline{\quad}$

When $x = 12$: $y = \underline{\quad}(\underline{\quad}) + 2 = \underline{\quad}$

> When dividing each side of an equation by the same number, remember to divide every term by the number.

Copyright © McDougal Littell/Houghton Mifflin Company   Lesson 1.5 • Algebra 2 C&S Notetaking Guide   13

✓ **Checkpoint** **Complete the following exercises.**

1. Solve the formula $P = 2\ell + 2w$ for w. Then find the width of a rectangle with length 9 meters and perimeter 32 meters.

---

2. Find the value of y in the equation $5x - 4y = 9$ when $x = -3$ and $x = 9$.

Example 4   *Use an Equation with Two Variables*

Postage Sam is buying some 41-cent stamps and some 58-cent stamps. Write an equation with more than one variable to represent the total cost of the stamps. What is the total cost of twelve 41-cent stamps and ten 58-cent stamps?

Solution

Verbal Model

Total cost	=	Cost	·	Number of 41¢ stamps	+	Cost	·	

Labels   Total cost = T (dollars)

Cost = _____   (dollars)

Number of 41¢ stamps = x (stamps)

Cost = _____   (dollars)

Number of 58¢ stamps = y (stamps)

Algebraic Model   ___ = _____x + _____y

$T = 0.41(\_\_\_) + 0.58(\_\_\_)$ **Substitute** ____ for x and ____ for y.

$= \$\_\_\_\_$ **Simplify.**

Homework

1.6 Problem Solving Using Algebraic Models

Goal • Use problem solving strategies to solve real-life problems.

Your Notes

VOCABULARY

Verbal model

Algebraic model

Example 1   Write and Use a Formula

Travel A bus travels at an average rate of 55 miles per hour. The distance between Chicago and San Francisco is 2130 miles. How many hours of driving will it take for the bus to travel from Chicago to San Francisco?

Solution

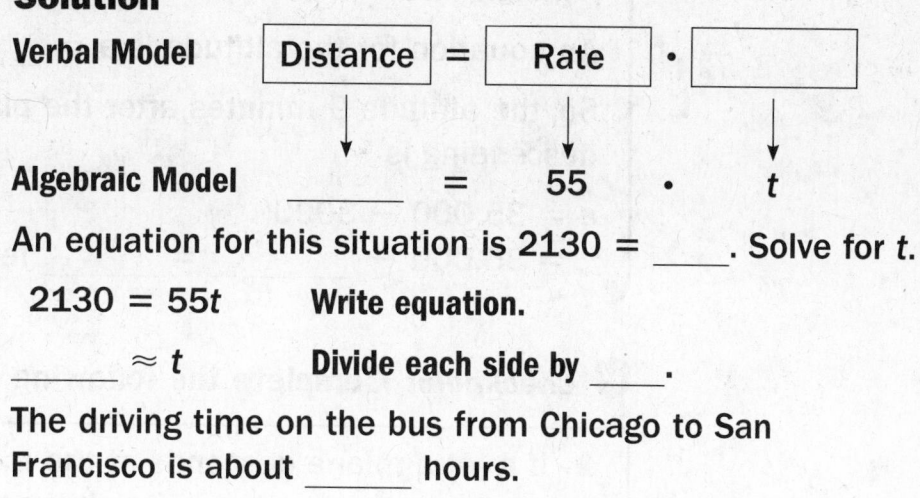

Verbal Model | Distance | = | Rate | · | _____ |

Algebraic Model   _____ = 55 · t

An equation for this situation is 2130 = _____. Solve for t.

$2130 = 55t$ Write equation.

_____ ≈ t   Divide each side by _____.

The driving time on the bus from Chicago to San Francisco is about _____ hours.

✔ **Checkpoint** Complete the following exercise.

1. In Example 1, what is the average rate for the bus if it takes 22 hours to travel from San Francisco to Colorado Springs, a distance of 1335 miles?

Example 2 *Look for a Pattern*

Travel The table gives the altitude *a* of a jet airplane *t* minutes after beginning its descent. Find the altitude of the airplane 9 minutes after it begins descending.

Time, *t* (min)	0	1	2	3	4
Altitude, *a* (ft)	35,000	32,000	29,000	26,000	23,000

Solution

The altitude decreases by _____ feet per minute.

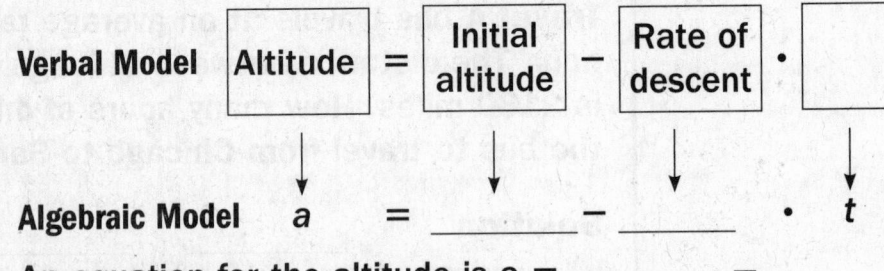

35,000   32,000   29,000   26,000   23,000

−3000   −3000   −3000   −3000

Use the pattern to write a verbal model for the altitude.

Verbal Model   Altitude = Initial altitude − Rate of descent • [   ]

Algebraic Model   *a*   =   _____   −   _____ • *t*

An equation for the altitude is *a* = _____ − _____.

So, the altitude 9 minutes after the plane begins descending is

$a = 35{,}000 − 3000(\_\_)$
$ = 35{,}000 − _____ = _____$ feet.

✔ *Checkpoint* **Complete the following exercise.**

2. If a jet airplane descends at the rate indicated in the table below, what is its altitude 8 minutes after beginning its descent?

Time, *t* (min)	0	1	2	3	4
Altitude, *a* (ft)	36,000	32,800	29,600	26,400	23,200

Example 3 *Draw a Diagram*

Home Improvement You want to paint five 1-foot wide vertical stripes on a wall. There is to be an equal amount of space between the ends of the wall and the stripes and between each pair of stripes. The wall is 14 feet long. How far apart should the stripes be?

Solution

Begin by drawing and labeling a diagram.

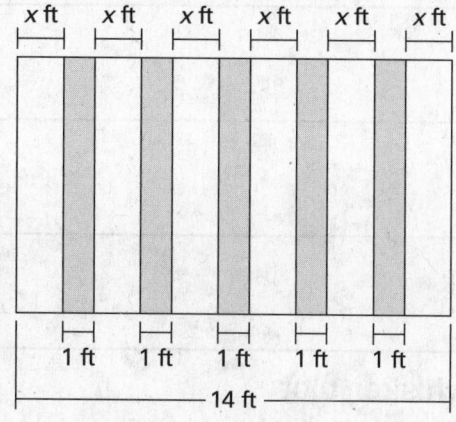

From the diagram, write and solve an equation to find x.

___x + ___(1) = ____	**Write an equation.**
____ + 5 = ____	**Simplify.**
$6x$ = ___	**Subtract ___ from each side.**
x = ____	**Divide each side by ___.**

The stripes should be painted _____ feet apart.

✔ *Checkpoint* **Complete the following exercise.**

3. In Example 3, how far apart would the stripes need to be if you were only going to paint 4 stripes on the wall?

Homework

1.7 Analyzing and Displaying Data

Goal • Use statistical measures and data displays to represent data.

Your Notes

VOCABULARY

Mean

Median

Mode

Range

Box-and-whisker plot

Lower quartile

Upper quartile

Example 1   *Find Measures of Central Tendency and Range*

Find the mean, median, mode(s), and range of these 14 quiz scores: 7, 16, 17, 19, 20, 20, 21, 22, 23, 24, 24, 24, 25, 25.

Mean: $\dfrac{7+16+17+19+20+20+21+22+23+24+24+24+25+25}{14}$

$= \dfrac{287}{14} = $ _____

> Remember that the numbers must be in order before finding the median. Here, the numbers are given in order.

Median: The median is between the 7th and 8th numbers, so the median is $\dfrac{21 + 22}{2} = $ _____ .

Mode: The number that occurs most frequently is _____ .

Range: $25 - $ _____ $= $ _____

   Copyright © McDougal Littell/Houghton Mifflin Compan

✔ *Checkpoint* **Complete the following exercise.**

---

1. Find the mean, median, mode, and range of these numbers of points scored by one team's players in a basketball game: 24, 19, 15, 12, 12, 10, 8, 7, 4, 1.

Example 2 *Find Lower and Upper Quartiles*

Find the lower and upper quartile of the data in Example 1.

Solution

The values are already in order. The median is between ____ and ____ . Each half of the data has ___ items.

Lower quartile: The median of 7, 16, 17, 19, 20, 20, and 21 is ____ .

Upper quartile: The median of 22, 23, 24, 24, 24, 25, and 25 is ____ .

✔ *Checkpoint* **Complete the following exercise.**

---

2. Find the lower and upper quartiles of the data in Checkpoint Exercise 1 above.

DRAWING A BOX-AND-WHISKER PLOT

Step 1 Order the data from least to _____ .

Step 2 Find the _____ and maximum values, the median, and the _____ and _____ quartiles.

Step 3 Plot the five numbers below a _____ .

Step 4 Draw the _____ , the whiskers, and a line segment through the _____ .

Example 3 **Draw a Box-and-Whisker Plot**

Towers The height, in feet, of the world's ten tallest towers are listed below. Show how the heights are distributed by making a box-and-whisker plot.

| 1214 | 1535 | 1230 | 1149 | 1815 |
| 1369 | 1403 | 1362 | 1762 | 1198 |

Solution

1. **Order** the data from least to greatest.

   1149, _____, _____, 1230, 1362, _____, 1403, _____, _____, 1815

2. **Find** the significant values for this data set.

   The *minimum* is _____ and the *maximum* is _____.

   $$median = \frac{1362 + 1369}{2} = \underline{\qquad}$$

   lower half of data   upper half of data

   1149, _____, _____, 1230, 1362, _____, 1403, _____, _____, 1815

   lower quartile = _____   *upper quartile* = _____

3. **Plot** these five numbers below a _____.

4. **Draw** the box, the _____, and a _____ through the median.

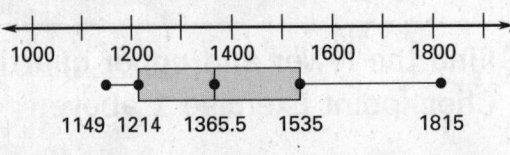

1149 1214 1365.5 1535   1815

> Draw a box whose sides are at the two quartiles; draw a vertical line through the box at the median; and draw the "whiskers" from the sides of the box to the minimum and maximum values.

✔ *Checkpoint* **Complete the following exercise.**

3. Draw a box-and-whisker plot for the data in Checkpoint Exercise 1.

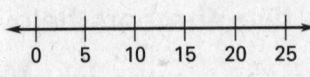

Homework

1.8 Frequency Distributions and Histograms

Goal • Display data in frequency distributions and histograms.

Your Notes

VOCABULARY
Histogram
Frequency distribution

Example 1 Make a Frequency Distribution

Weather The average annual inches of precipitation in 20 United States cities is 16, 47, 54, 13, 44, 35, 31, 9, 48, 98, 50, 8, 36, 45, 66, 13, 51, 11, 21, 29. Make a frequency distribution of this data. Use five intervals beginning with the interval 1–20.

1. Write the five intervals.

The second interval extends from ____ to ____.

2. Tally the data values by _____.

3. Count the tally marks to obtain the _____.

Annual Average Rainfall in 20 U.S. Cities (inches)		
Interval		Frequency
1–20		
21–40		

Be sure your intervals have the same size.

Example 2 **Draw a Histogram**

Draw a histogram for the rainfall data in Example 1.

1. Divide the horizontal axis into _____ equal sections. Label the sections with the _____ shown in the frequency distribution.

2. Draw a scale on the vertical axis to measure the _____.

3. Draw _____ of the appropriate heights to represent the frequencies of the intervals. Label the _____, and include a title.

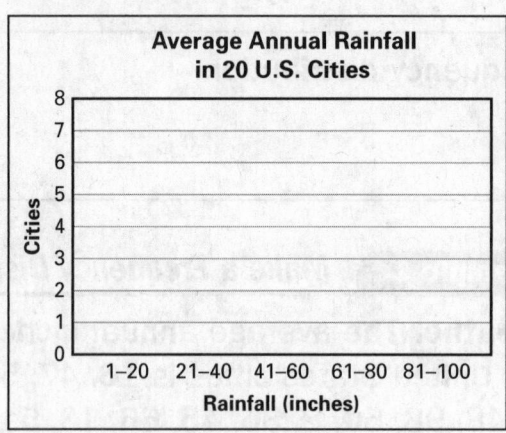

✔ *Checkpoint* **Complete the following exercises.**

A dog show has the following number of dogs of various breeds entered in competition: 2, 5, 17, 22, 15, 19, 12, 29, 30, 36, 52, 26, 34, 37, 37, 40, 45, 56, 50, 51.

1. Make a frequency distribution beginning with the interval 0–9.

2. Draw a histogram.

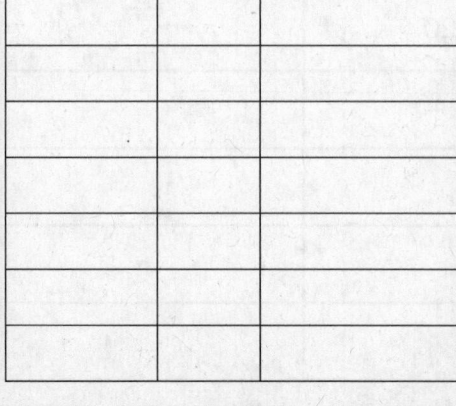

Words to Review

Use your own words and/or an example to explain the vocabulary word.

Origin	Graph
Coordinate	Opposite
Reciprocal	Base
Exponent	Power
Numerical expression	Variable
Algebraic expression	Term
Coefficient	Like terms
Constant term	Simplified expression

Equation	Linear equation
Solution	Verbal model
Algebraic model	Mean
Median	Mode
Range	Box-and-whisker plot
Lower quartile	Upper quartile
Histogram	Frequency distribution

Review your notes and Chapter 1 by using the Chapter Review on pages 57–60 of your textbook.

2.1 Functions and Their Graphs

Goal • Identify and graph functions.

Your Notes

VOCABULARY

Relation

Domain

Range

Function

Equation in two variables

Independent variable

Dependent variable

Example 1 *Identify Functions*

Identify the domain and range. Then tell whether the relation is a function. Explain.

a. Input   Output

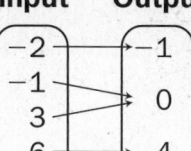

b. Input   Output

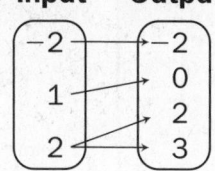

Solution

a. The domain consists of the inputs: −2, −1, ___, and ___. The range consists of the outputs: −1, ___, and ___. The relation ___ a function because each input is mapped onto _____ output.

b. The domain consists of the inputs: −2, ___, and ___. The range consists of the outputs: ____, ___, 2, and ___. The relation _____ a function because the input ___ is mapped onto both 0 and ___.

VERTICAL LINE TEST FOR FUNCTIONS

A relation is a function if and only if no _____ line intersects the graph at more than _____.

Function	**Not a function**
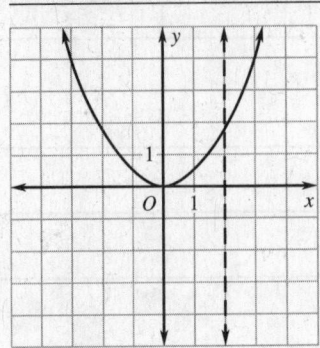	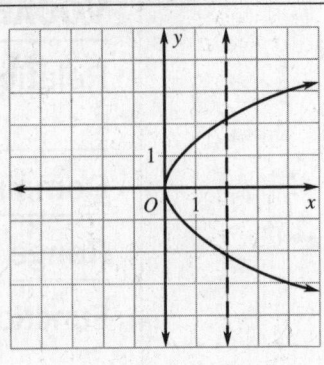

Example 2 *Apply the Vertical Line Test*

Graph the relations from Example 1. Use the vertical line test to tell whether the relations are functions.

a. First, write the relation as a set of ordered pairs.

(–2, –1), _____,
(3, 0), _____

Then plot the points.

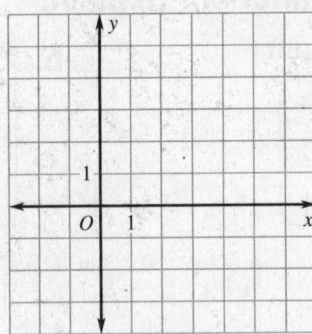

_____ vertical line contains more than _____ so the relation is a _____.

b. First, write the relation as a set of ordered pairs.

_____, (1, 0),
_____, _____

Then plot the points.

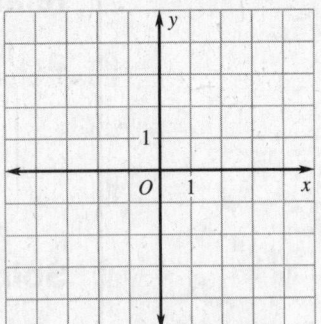

The vertical line at x = ___ contains _____ _____ points in the relation. So, the relation is _____ a function.

GRAPHING EQUATIONS IN TWO VARIABLES

Step 1 **Make** a table of values. Write the _____.

Step 2 **Plot** enough solutions to recognize a _____.

Step 3 **Connect** the points with a _____ or a _____.

Example 3 — *Graph an Equation*

Graph $y = -2x - 2$.

Solution

1. **Make** a _____. Write the _____.

Choose x	−2	−1	0	1	2
Evaluate y	___	___	___	___	___

(x, y): $(-2, $ ___$)$, $(-1, $ ___$)$, $(0, $ ____$)$, $(1, $ ____$)$, $(2, $ ____$)$

2. **Plot** the points. Notice that all the points lie on a _____.

3. **Connect** the points with a _____. Observe that the graph represents a _____.

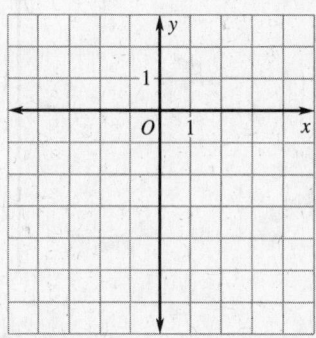

✔ *Checkpoint* **Complete the following exercises.**

1. Graph $y = x + 2$.

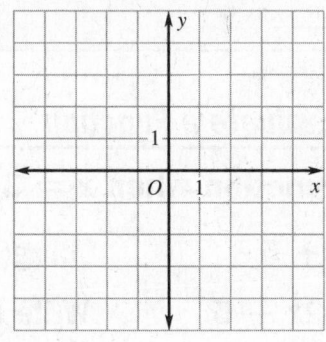

2. Graph $y = 3x - 1$.

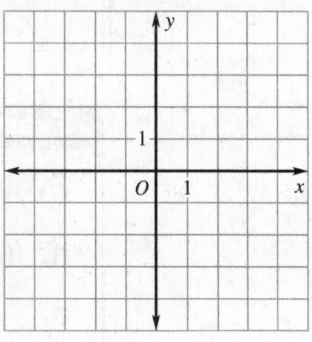

Homework

Linear Functions and Function Notation

Goal • Identify, evaluate, and graph linear functions.

Your Notes

> **VOCABULARY**
>
> Linear function
>
> Function notation

Example 1 *Identify a Linear Function*

Tell whether the function is linear. Explain.

a. $f(x) = 2x^3 + 6 - x$ **b.** $g(x) = 9 + 4x$

a. f _____ a linear function because it has an
_____.

b. g ____ a linear function because it can be rewritten as
_____, so $m =$ ___ and $b =$ ___.

✔ *Checkpoint* **Tell whether the function is linear. Explain.**

1. $f(x) = 6x + 10$	**2.** $g(x) = 2x^2 + 4x - 1$

Example 2 *Evaluate a Function*

Evaluate the function when $x = 3$.

a. $f(x) = -2x + 5$ **b.** $g(x) = x^2 - x - 1$

a. $f(x) = -2x + 5$ Write original function.

$f(\underline{}) = -2(\underline{}) + 5$ Substitute ___ for x.

$= \underline{} + 5$ Multiply.

$= \underline{}$ Simplify.

---

b.　$g(x) = x^2 - x - 1$ **Write original function.**

　　$g(\underline{}) = (\underline{})^2 - \underline{} - 1$ **Substitute ___ for x.**

　　　　$= \underline{} - \underline{} - 1$ **Multiply.**

　　　　$= \underline{}$ **Simplify.**

✔ *Checkpoint* **Evaluate the function when x = −4.**

3. $f(x) = 2x - 3$	4. $g(x) = 2x^2 + 3x$

Example 3　*Graph a Linear Function*

Graph $f(x) = -x + 2$.

Solution

Rewrite the function as ___ $= -x + 2$. Find a point on the graph by substituting a _____ value for ___.

$y = -x + 2$ **Write equation.**

$y = -(\underline{}) + 2$ **Substitute ___ for x.**

$y = \underline{}$ **Simplify.**

One point is _____. Find a second point.

$y = \underline{}$ **Substitute 1 for ___.**

$y = \underline{}$ **Simplify.**

A second point is _____. Draw a line through the two points.

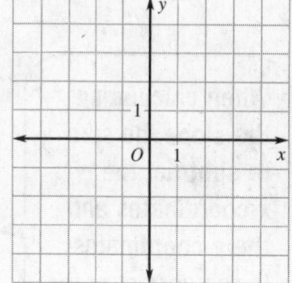

✔ *Checkpoint* **Complete the following exercise.**

5. Graph $h(x) = -2x + 1$.

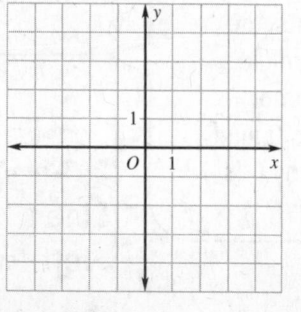

2.3 Slope and Rate of Change

Goal • Find and use the slope of a line.

Your Notes

VOCABULARY

Slope

THE SLOPE OF A LINE

The slope _____ of the nonvertical line passing through the points (x_1, y_1) and (x_2, y_2) is given by the formula

$$m = \frac{}{}.$$

Example 1 | *Find the Slope of a Line*

Find the slope of the line through (1, 3) and (6, 7).

Solution

> When calculating the slope, be sure to subtract the *x*-coordinates and the *y*-coordinates in the correct order.

Let $(x_1, y_1) = (1, 3)$ and $(x_2, y_2) = $ _____.

$$m = \frac{y_2 - y_1}{x_2 - x_1} = \frac{}{} = \underline{}$$

The _____ of the line is ____ .

CLASSIFYING LINES BY SLOPE

> A vertical line has "undefined slope" because for any two points, the slope formula's denominator becomes 0, and division by 0 is undefined.

| Positive | Negative | Zero | Undefined |

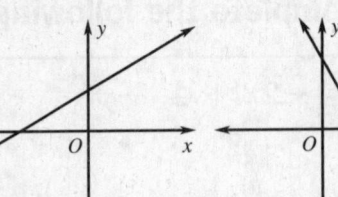
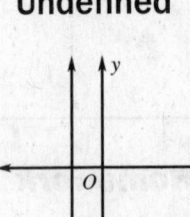

Line _____ from left to right. Line falls from _____ . Line is _____ . Line is _____ .

Example 2   *Classify Lines Using Slope*

Without graphing, tell whether the line through the given points *rises*, *falls*, *is horizontal*, or *is vertical*.

a. $(-6, -2), (1, 3)$ b. $(2, -1), (2, 2)$

Solution

a. $m = \dfrac{3 - (-2)}{1 - (-6)} = \underline{\qquad}$ Because m ____ 0, the line _____ .

b. $m = \dfrac{\underline{\qquad}}{\underline{\qquad}} = \underline{\qquad}$ Because m is _____ , the line is _____ .

✔ *Checkpoint* **Complete the following exercises.**

1. Find the slope of the line through $(4, 2)$ and $(7, 9)$.

2. Without graphing, tell whether the line through the points $(-3, 2)$ and $(1, 4)$ *rises*, *falls*, *is horizontal*, or *is vertical*.

Example 3   *Compare Steepness of Lines*

Tell which line is steeper.

Line 1: through $(2, 3)$ and $(-1, 4)$
Line 2: through $(-7, -2)$ and $(-4, -5)$

Solution

Slope of line 1: $m = \dfrac{4 - 3}{-1 - 2} = \underline{\qquad}$ or $\underline{\qquad}$

Slope of line 2: $m = \dfrac{\underline{\qquad}}{\underline{\qquad}} = \underline{\qquad} = \underline{\qquad}$

Both lines have _____ slope.

Because $|m_1|$ ____ $|m_2|$, line ____ is steeper than line ____ .

✔ *Checkpoint* **Tell which line is steeper.**

> **3.** Line 1: through (3, 5) and (6, 8)
>   Line 2: through (−2, 4) and (10, 12)

Example 4   *Slope as a Rate of Change*

Census The population of Smalltown was **10,000** in 2001 and **12,500** in 2006. Find the average rate of change in the population.

Solution

Let $(x_1, y_1) = (2001, \underline{\hspace{2cm}})$ and
$(x_2, y_2) = (\underline{\hspace{1cm}}, \underline{\hspace{2cm}})$.

$$\text{Average rate of change} = \frac{\text{Change in population}}{\text{Change in time}}$$

$$= \frac{\underline{\hspace{3cm}}}{}$$

$$= \frac{\underline{\hspace{1.5cm}}}{}$$

$$= \underline{\hspace{1cm}}$$

The average rate of change is _____ people per _____.

✔ *Checkpoint* **Complete the following exercise.**

> **4. Census** Suppose the population of Smalltown will be 20,000 in 2011. Use the information in Example 4 to find the average rate of change in the population from 2001 to 2011.

Homework

Quick Graphs of Linear Equations

Goal • Use slope-intercept form and standard form to graph equations.

Your Notes

VOCABULARY

y-intercept

_____

Slope-intercept form

_____

_____

x-intercept

_____

Standard form of a linear equation

GRAPHING EQUATIONS IN SLOPE-INTERCEPT FORM

Step 1 **Write** the equation in slope-intercept form by solving for ___ .

Step 2 **Find** the _____ and plot the corresponding point.

Step 3 **Find** the _____ and use it to plot a _____ _____ on the line.

Step 4 **Draw** a _____ through the _____ .

Your Notes

| Example 1 | *Use Slope-Intercept Form to Graph a Line* |

Graph $y + \frac{3}{2}x = 1.$

Solution

1. **Solve** the equation for y by subtracting ____ from each side:

   $y = 1 - $ ____ or $y = $ _____

2. **Find** the y-intercept. Comparing $y = -\frac{3}{2}x + 1$ to $y = mx + b$, you can see that $b = $ ___. Plot a point at (___, ___).

3. **Find** the slope. The slope is $m = $ _____, so $\frac{rise}{run} = \frac{-3}{2}.$

   From $(0, 1)$, move _____ ___ units and _____ ___ units. Plot a second point at (___, _____).

4. **Draw** a line through the two points.

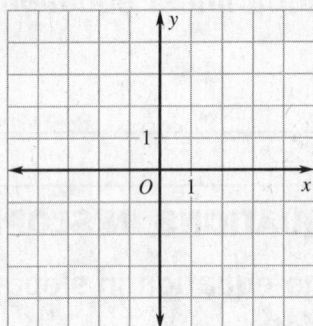

GRAPHING EQUATIONS IN STANDARD FORM

Step 1 **Write** the equation in _____.

Step 2 **Find** the x-intercept by letting ___ = ___ and solving for ___. Plot the corresponding point.

Step 3 **Find** the _____ by letting $x = $ ___ and solving for ___. Plot the corresponding point.

Step 4 **Draw** a _____ through the _____.

34 Lesson 2.4 • **Algebra 2 C&S Notetaking Guide**   Copyright © McDougal Littell/Houghton Mifflin Company

Example 2 **Draw Quick Graphs**

Graph 4*x* + 5*y* = 20.

1. The equation is already in _____.

2. Find the *x*-intercept. $4x + 5(\underline{}) = 20$ **Let *y* = 0.**

$x = \underline{}$ Solve for *x*.

The *x*-intercept is ___, so plot the point _____.

3. Find the *y*-intercept. $4(\underline{}) + 5y = 20$ **Let *x* = ___.**

$y = \underline{}$ Solve for *y*.

The *y*-intercept is ___, so plot the point _____.

4. Draw a line through the intercepts.

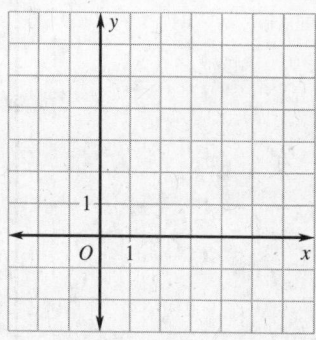

SLOPES OF PARALLEL AND PERPENDICULAR LINES

Consider two different _____ lines ℓ_1 and ℓ_2 with slopes m_1 and m_2.

Two lines are parallel if and only if they have the _____.

$m_1 = \underline{}$

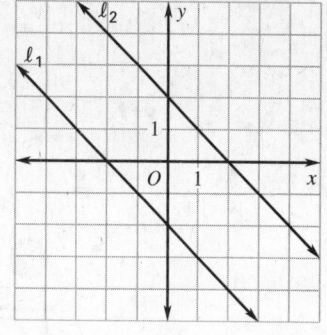

Two lines are perpendicular if and only if their slopes are _____ _____ of each other.

$m_1 = \underline{}$ or $m_1 \cdot m_2 = \underline{}$

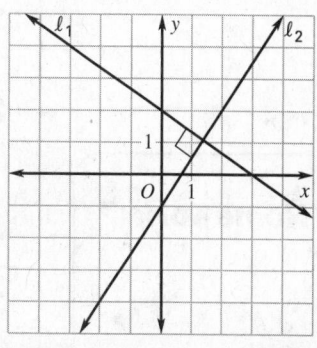

Example 3   *Graph Parallel and Perpendicular Lines*

a. Draw the graph $y = 2x - 3$.

b. Graph the line that passes through (0, 2) and is parallel to the graph of $y = 2x - 3$.

c. Graph the line that passes through (0, 2) and is perpendicular to the graph of $y = 2x - 3$.

Solution

a. Draw the graph $y = 2x - 3$ using the *y*-intercept _____ and slope ___.

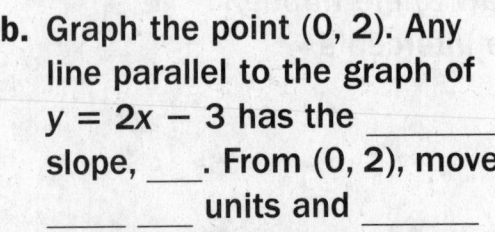

b. Graph the point (0, 2). Any line parallel to the graph of $y = 2x - 3$ has the _____ slope, ___. From (0, 2), move _____ _____ units and _____ 1 unit. Plot a second point at _____. Draw a line through the two points.

c. The slope of any line _____ to the graph of $y = 2x - 3$ is the _____ of 2, or _____. So, from (0, 2), move down 1 unit and _____ _____ units. Plot a second point at _____. Draw the line.

✔ *Checkpoint* **On the same grid, draw each graph.**

1. $y = -\frac{1}{3}x + 1$

2. The line parallel to $y = -\frac{1}{3}x + 1$ through the point (0, 4)

3. The line perpendicular to $y = -\frac{1}{3}x + 1$ through the point (0, 4)

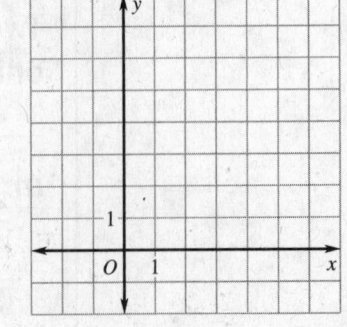

Homework

2.5 Writing Equations of Lines

Goal • Write linear equations.

VOCABULARY

Point-slope form

WRITING AN EQUATION OF A LINE

Slope-Intercept Form Given the slope _____ and the y-intercept _____, use slope-intercept form: $y = $ _____.

Point-Slope Form Given the slope _____ and a point _____, use point-slope form: _____.

Example 1 *Write an Equation Given Slope and y-Intercept*

Write an equation of the line shown.

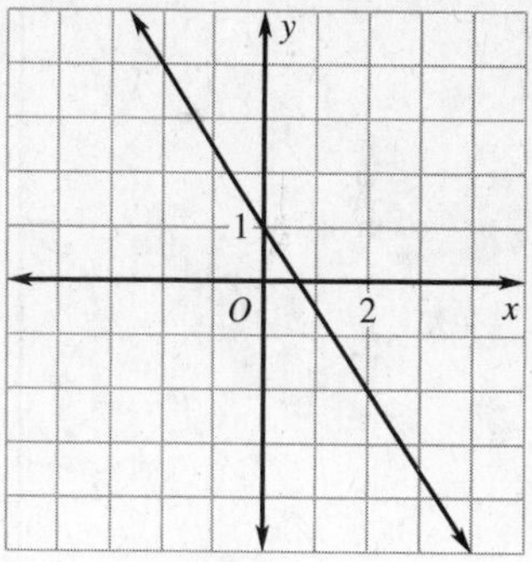

Solution

From the graph, you can see

that the slope is $m = $ _____.

Because the line intersects the y-axis at (_____), the y-intercept is $b = $ ___.

Use the _____ form to write an equation of the line.

$y = mx + b$ Use slope-intercept form.

$y = $ ___ $x + $ ___   Substitute ___ for m and ___ for b.

Example 2   *Write an Equation Given Slope and a Point*

Write an equation of the line that passes through (2, 1) and has a slope of 2.

Solution

Because you know the slope and a point on the line, use the _____ form with $(x_1, y_1) = $ _____ and $m = $ ___.

$$y - y_1 = m(x - x_1)$$ **Use point-slope form.**

$$y - \_\_\_ = \_\_\_(x - \_\_\_)$$ **Substitute for *m*, x_1, and y_1.**

Rewrite the equation in slope-intercept form.

$$y - \_\_\_ = _____$$ **Distributive property**

$$y = _____$$ **Slope-intercept form**

✓ *Checkpoint* **Write an equation of the line.**

1.
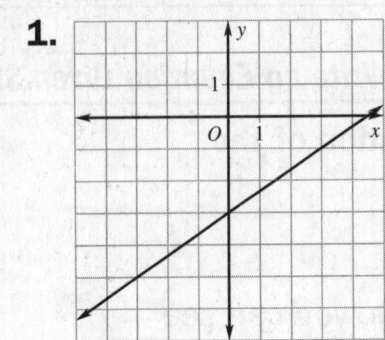

2. The line through (1, 5) with a slope of −2

Example 3   *Write Equations of Parallel Lines*

Write an equation of the line that passes through (−1, 1) and is parallel to the line $y = -2x + 3$.

Solution

The given line has a slope of _____. Any line _____ to this line must also have a slope of _____. Use point-slope form with $(x_1, y_1) = $ _____ and $m = $ _____ to write the equation of the line.

   Copyright © McDougal Littell/Houghton Mifflin Compan

$$y - y_1 = m(x - x_1)$$ Use point-slope form.

$$y - \underline{\quad} = \underline{\quad}[x - \underline{\quad\quad}]$$ Substitute ___ for y_1, ____ for m, and ____ for x_1.

$$y - \underline{\quad} = \underline{\quad\quad\quad}$$ _____ property

$$y = \underline{\quad\quad\quad}$$ Slope-intercept form

Example 4 *Write Equations of Perpendicular Lines*

Write an equation of the line that passes through $(-3, 5)$ and is perpendicular to the line $y = 4x - 1$.

Solution

The given line has a slope of ___. The slope of any line _____ to this line will be the _____ _____ of ___, which is _____ .

Use point-slope form with $(x_1, y_1) = $ _____ and $m = $ _____ to write the equation of the line.

$$y - y_1 = m(x - x_1)$$ Use point-slope form.

$$y - \underline{\quad} = \underline{\quad\quad}[x - \underline{\quad\quad}]$$ Substitute ___ for y_1, ___ for m, and ____ for x_1.

$$y - \underline{\quad} = \underline{\quad\quad\quad}$$ Distributive property

$$y = \underline{\quad\quad\quad}$$ Slope-intercept form

✔ *Checkpoint* Write an equation of the line.

3. The line through $(-2, 3)$ parallel to $y = 4x - 6$	4. The line through $(-2, 3)$ perpendicular to $y = 4x - 6$

Homework

2.6 Direct Variation

Goal • Write and graph direct variation equations.

Your Notes

VOCABULARY

Direct variation

_____

Constant of variation

Example 1   *Graph a Direct Variation Equation*

Graph $y = \dfrac{5}{3}x$.

Solution

Plot a point at the _____.

Find a second point by substituting
a _____ value for ___.

$y = \dfrac{5}{3}x$ **Write equation.**

$y = \dfrac{5}{3}(\underline{})$ **Substitute ___ for x.**

$y = \underline{}$ **Simplify.**

A second point is _____.

Plot the second point. Then draw a _____ through the
two points.

✔ **Checkpoint** Graph the equation.

1. $y = -3x$

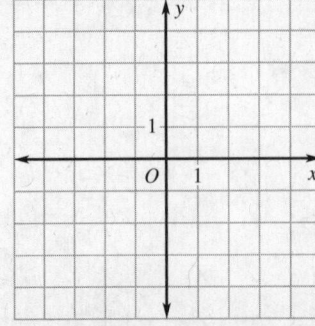

    Copyright © McDougal Littell/Houghton Mifflin Company

Example 2   *Write a Direct Variation Equation*

Physics According to Hooke's law, the amount that a spring is stretched varies directly with the force that is applied to the spring. If 64 pounds of force F stretches a spring a distance d of 8 inches, write an equation so that F varies directly with d. How many pounds of force are needed to stretch the spring to a distance of 14 inches?

Solution

Find the constant of variation.

> The value of k is called the *spring constant*. This constant is unique for each spring.

$F = kd$ Write a _____ equation.

____ $= k(\_\_)$ Substitute ____ for F and ____ for d.

___ $= k$ Simplify.

An equation is $F =$ ____. To find how many pounds of force is needed to stretch the spring 14 inches, substitute ____ for d.

$F = \_\_(\_\_\_) = \_\_\_\_$

A force of _____ pounds will stretch the spring 14 inches.

✔ *Checkpoint* **Complete the following exercise.**

2. Suppose that a force of 92 pounds is applied to the spring discussed in Example 2. How far will the spring be stretched?

Example 3 *Identify Direct Variation*

The table gives sample cell phone bills, showing the total monthly cost and the number of minutes used per month. Tell whether total cost and the number of minutes show direct variation. If so, write an equation relating c and m.

Total cost, c (dollars)	35	45	80	15	28
Minutes used, m	100	129	229	43	80

Solution

Find the ratio of c to m for each data pair.

$$\frac{35}{100} = \underline{\qquad} \qquad \frac{45}{129} \approx \underline{\qquad} \qquad \frac{80}{229} \approx \underline{\qquad}$$

$$\frac{15}{43} \approx \underline{\qquad} \qquad \frac{28}{30} = \underline{\qquad}$$

The ratio of c to m in each pair is nearly the _____, so the data show _____. Substituting _____ for k in c = km gives the direct variation equation c = _____ m, which relates the total cost to number of minutes used.

✔ *Checkpoint* **Complete the following exercise.**

3. Tell whether the data $(-1, -2)$, $(1, 2)$, $(3, 6)$, $(5, 10)$, $(7, 14)$ show direct variation. If so, write an expression relating x and y.

Homework

2.7 Scatter Plots and Correlation

Goal • See correlation in a scatter plot and find a best-fitting line.

VOCABULARY

Scatter plot

_____

Positive correlation

_____

Negative correlation

_____

Relatively no correlation

_____

Best-fitting line

_____

Example 1 *Identify Correlation*

Describe the correlation shown by each plot.

a.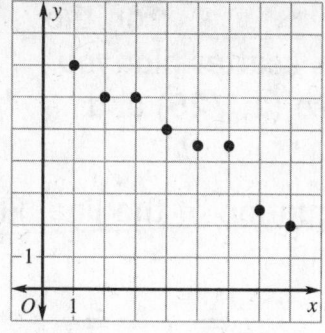

b.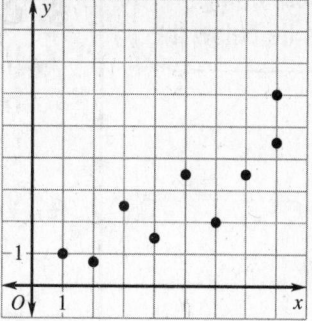

Solution

a. The scatter plot shows a _____ correlation: as
   x increases, *y* _____.

b. The scatter plot shows a _____ correlation: as
   x _____, *y* also _____.

APPROXIMATING A BEST-FITTING LINE

Step 1 Draw a scatter plot of the _____.

Step 2 Sketch a _____ that follows the _____ of the data points.

Step 3 Choose _____ that appear to ____ on the line, and estimate their _____.

Step 4 Write an _____ of the line that passes through the _____ from Step 3. This equation gives a _____ for the data.

Example 2 *Find a Best-Fitting Line*

Football Attendance The table gives the number of people *y* who attended each of the first seven football games *x* of the season. Approximate the best-fitting line for the data.

x	1	2	3	4	5	6	7
y	722	763	772	826	815	857	897

Solution

1. **Draw** a _____ plot.

2. **Sketch** the _____ that _____ fits the data.

> Be sure that about the same number of points lie above your best-fitting line as lie below it.

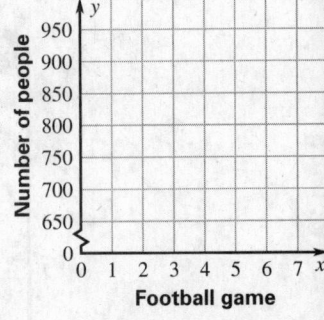

3. **Choose** _____ on the line. For this scatter plot you might choose (1, 725) and (___, 750).

4. **Write** an equation of the line. First find the slope using the two points:

$$m = \frac{}{} = \frac{}{} = \_\_\_$$

Now use point-slope form. Choose $(x_1, y_1) = (1, 725)$.

$y - y_1 = m(x - x_1)$	**Point-slope form**
$y - \_\_\_ = \_\_\_(x - \_\_\_)$	**Substitute for y_1, m, and x_1.**
$y = _____$	**Solve for *y*.**

Example 3   *Use a Best-Fitting Line*

Use the equation of the best-fitting line from **Example 2** to predict the number of people that will attend the tenth football game.

Solution

Substitute _____ for *x* in the equation from Example 2.

$y = 25(\underline{\quad}) + \underline{\quad\quad} = \underline{\quad\quad} + \underline{\quad\quad} = \underline{\quad\quad}$

You can predict that _____ people will attend the game.

✔ *Checkpoint* **Complete the following exercises.**

For each scatter plot, tell whether the data show a positive correlation, negative correlation, or relatively no correlation.

1.

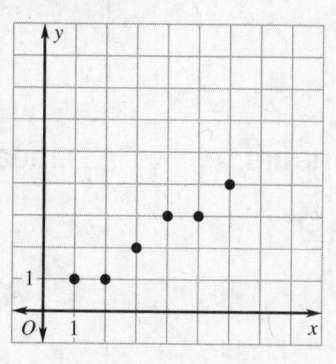

2.

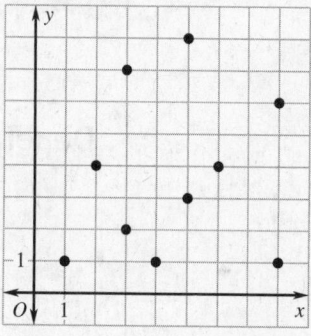

3. School The table gives the average class score *y* on each test for the first six chapters *x* of the textbook.

x	1	2	3	4	5	6
y	84	83	86	88	87	90

a. Approximate the best-fitting line for the data.

b. Use your equation to predict the test score for the 9th test that the class will take.

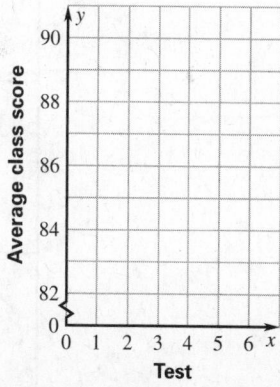

Words to Review

Use your own words and/or an example to explain the vocabulary word.

Relation	Domain
Range	Function
Equation in two variables	Independent variable
Dependent variable	Linear function
Function notation	Slope
y-intercept	Slope-intercept form
x-intercept	Standard form of a linear equation

Point-slope form	Direct variation
Constant of variation	Scatter plot
Positive correlation	Negative correlation
Relatively no correlation	Best-fitting line

Review your notes and Chapter 2 by using the Chapter Review on pages 115–118 of your textbook.

3.1 Solving Linear Systems by Graphing

Goal • Solve a system of linear equations in two variables by graphing.

Your Notes

VOCABULARY

System of two linear equations

Solution of a system of two linear equations

Example 1   *Solve a System by Graphing*

Solve the system by graphing. Then check your solution algebraically.

$4x + 2y = 4$	**Equation 1**
$2x - 3y = 10$	**Equation 2**

Solution

Graph both equations. From the graph, you can see the lines appear to intersect at (___, ____).

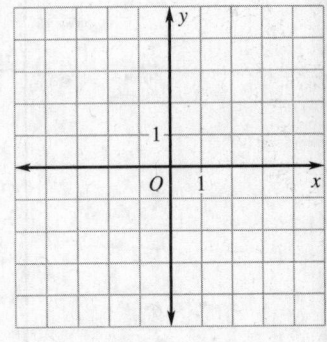

You can check the solution by substituting ___ for x and ____ for y into the original equations.

Equation 1	Equation 2
$4x + 2y = 4$	$2x - 3y = 10$
$4(\underline{}) + 2(\underline{}) \overset{?}{=} 4$	$2(\underline{}) - 3(\underline{}) \overset{?}{=} 10$
$\underline{} + (\underline{}) \overset{?}{=} 4$	$\underline{} + \underline{} \overset{?}{=} 10$
$4 = 4 \checkmark$	$10 = 10 \checkmark$

   Copyright © McDougal Littell/Houghton Mifflin Company

✅ *Checkpoint* **Solve the system by graphing. Then check your solution.**

1. $4x + y = -2$
$-6x - 3y = 12$

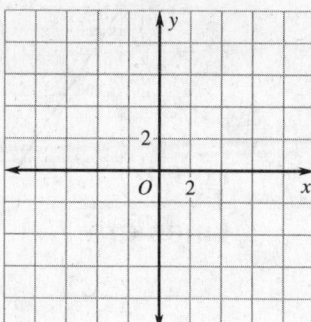

Example 2   *Systems with Many or No Solutions*

Tell how many solutions the linear system has.

a. $-2x + y = 4$
$4x - 2y = -8$

b. $-2x + 4y = 8$
$-2x + 4y = -4$

Solution

a. Because the graphs of the equations are _____, each point on the _____ is a solution. So, the system has _____ solutions.

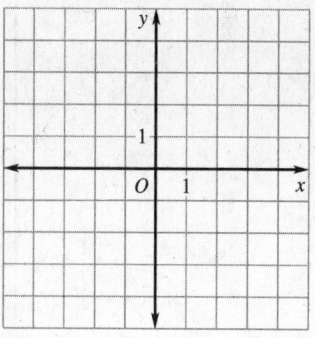

b. Because the graphs of the equations are _____ _____, the two lines have ____ point of _____. So, the system has ____ solutions.

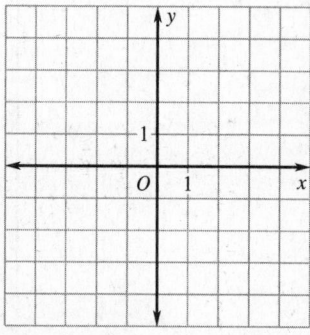

NUMBER OF SOLUTIONS OF A LINEAR SYSTEM

EXACTLY ONE SOLUTION	INFINITELY MANY SOLUTIONS	NO SOLUTION

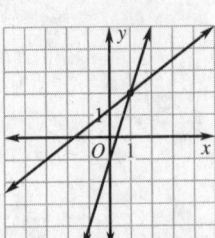 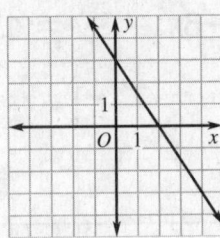 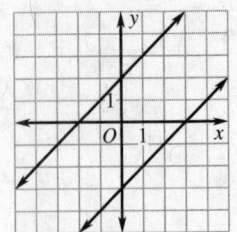

Lines intersect in _____.	Lines are _____.	Lines are _____.

✓ *Checkpoint* **Tell how many solutions the system has.**

2. $3x - 2y = -6$
$-5x + 4y = 8$

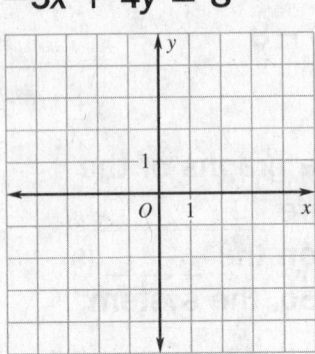

3. $-x - 2y = -5$
$-2x - 4y = -10$

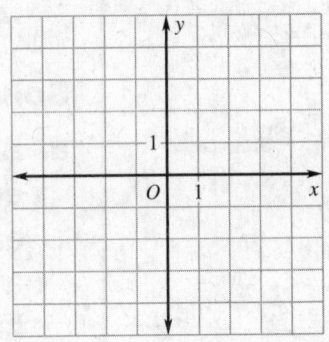

4. $6x - 3y = 12$
$6x - 3y = -6$

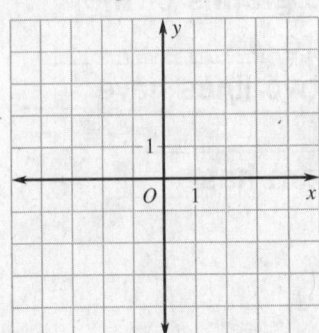

5. $x + y = 2$
$4x - 3y = 1$

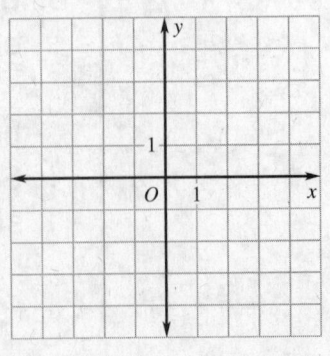

Example 3   *Write and Use a Linear System*

Ice Cream Shop At an ice cream shop, one customer pays $9 for 2 sundaes and 2 milkshakes. A second customer pays $13 for 2 sundaes and 4 milkshakes. How much does each sundae and milkshake cost?

Verbal model

Total cost (dollars)	=	Number of sundaes	·	Cost per sundae (dollars/ sundae)	+	Number of shakes	·	Cost per shake (dollars/ shake)

___ = ___ · x + ___ · y   **Equation 1 (Customer 1)**

____ = ___ · x + ___ · y   **Equation 2 (Customer 2)**

Graph the equations

___x + ___y = ___ and

___x + ___y = ____.

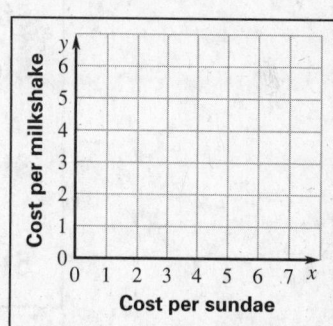

The lines appear to intersect at about the point (____, ____).

Check this algebraically.

__(____) + __(__) = __ + __ = __ ✓   **Equation 1 checks.**

__(____) + __(__) = __ + __ = ____ ✓   **Equation 2 checks.**

The solution is (____, ___). So, each sundae costs $_____ and each milkshake costs $_____.

✔ *Checkpoint* **Complete the following exercise.**

6. In Example 4, how much does each sundae and milkshake cost if the first customer pays $7 and the second customer pays $10?

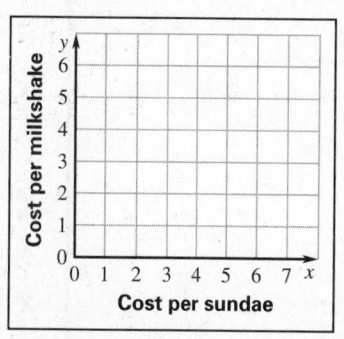

3.2 Solving Linear Systems by Substitution

Goal • Solve a system of linear equations by substitution.

Your Notes

VOCABULARY

Substitution method

SOLVING A LINEAR SYSTEM BY SUBSTITUTION

Step 1 Solve one equation for one of its _____ .

Step 2 Substitute the _____ from _____ into the other _____ and solve for the variable.

Step 3 Substitute the _____ from _____ into the revised equation from Step 1 and solve.

Step 4 Check the _____ in both original equations.

Example 1   *Use Substitution*

Solve the system using substitution.

$x = 4y + 7$ **Equation 1**

$2x - 6y = 12$ **Equation 2**

Solution

Substitute _____ for *x* in Equation 2. Solve for *y*.

$2(\underline{\hspace{1cm}}) - 6y = 12$ **Substitute** _____ **for** *x*.

$\underline{\hspace{1.5cm}} - 6y = 12$ **Use the distributive property.**

$\underline{\hspace{1cm}} + 14 = 12$ **Combine like terms.**

$2y = \underline{\hspace{0.7cm}}$ **Subtract** ____ **from each side.**

$y = \underline{\hspace{0.5cm}}$ **Solve for** *y*.

Substitute _____ for *y* in Equation 1. Solve for *x*.

$x = 4(\underline{\hspace{0.7cm}}) + 7$ **Substitute** _____ **for** *y*.

$x = \underline{\hspace{0.5cm}}$ **Simplify.**

The solution is (___ , _____).

Example 2 · Use Substitution

Solve the system using substitution.

$x + 2y = -2$ **Equation 1**

$3x + 4y = 6$ **Equation 2**

Solution

1. Solve Equation ___ for x.

$x + 2y = -2$ Choose Equation ___ because the coefficient of x is ___.

$x = $ _____ $- 2$ Solve for x to get revised Equation 1.

2. Substitute into Equation ___ and solve for y.

$3($_____$) + 4y = 6$ Substitute _____ for x.

_____ $-$ __ $+ 4y = 6$ Use the distributive property.

_____ $- 6 = 6$ Combine like terms.

$2y = $ _____   Add ___ to each side.

$y = $ _____   Solve for y.

3. Substitute ____ for y in revised Equation 1. Solve for x.

$x = -2($____$) - 2$ Substitute _____ for y.

$x = $ ____   Simplify.

4. Check by substituting _____ for x and _____ for y in the original equations.

The solution is (____, _____).

✔ *Checkpoint* Solve the system using substitution.

1. $y = x + 9$ $3x + 8y = -5$	2. $2x + y = -2$ $5x + 3y = -8$

Example 3 *Write and Use a Linear System*

Shopping David bought 3 DVDs and 4 books for $40 at a yard sale. Anna bought 1 DVD and 6 books for $18. How much did each DVD and each book cost?

Verbal Model

Labels

Number of DVDs $= x$

Number of books $= y$

Algebraic Model

___ • $x +$ ___ • $y =$ ____   **Equation 1 (David)**

___ • $x +$ ___ • $y =$ ____   **Equation 2 (Anna)**

Use substitution to solve the linear system.

$x =$ _____   **Solve Equation 2 for x; revised Equation 2.**

3(_____) + 4y = 40   **Substitute _____ for x in Equation 1.**

_____ + 4y = 40   **Use the distributive property.**

_____ = 40   **Combine like terms.**

_____ = ____   **Subtract ____ from each side.**

$y =$ ___   **Divide each side by _____.**

$x =$ _____   **Write revised Equation 2.**

$x =$ _____   **Substitute ___ for y.**

$x =$ ____   **Simplify.**

Each DVD costs $____ and each book costs $___.

✔ *Checkpoint* **Complete the following exercise.**

3. In Example 3, suppose David had spent $38 and Anna had spent $22. What would the cost of a DVD and the cost of a book have been then?

3.3 Solving Linear Systems by Linear Combinations

Goal • Solve a system of linear equations in two variables by the linear combination method.

Your Notes

VOCABULARY

Linear combination method

USING THE LINEAR COMBINATION METHOD

Step 1 **Multiply** one or both of the equations by a _____, if necessary, to obtain coefficients that differ only in sign for one of its variables.

Step 2 **Add** the _____ from Step 1. Combining like terms will eliminate one variable. Solve for the remaining variable.

Step 3 **Substitute** the _____ obtained in Step 2 into either of the original equations and solve for the other variable.

Step 4 **Check** the _____ in each of the original equations.

Example 1 *Multiply One Equation*

Solve the system using the linear combination method.

$2x + 5y = 14$ **Equation 1**

$4x + 2y = -4$ **Equation 2**

Solution

1. **Multiply** Equation 1 by _____ so that the coefficients of x differ only in sign.

   $2x + 5y = 14$ × _____   _____
   $4x + 2y = -4$ _____

2. **Add** the revised equations.   _____

   And solve for y. $y =$ ___

3. **Substitute** ___ for y in one of the original equations and solve for x.

   $2x + 5y = 14$ **Write Equation 1.**
   $2x + 5(\_\_) = 14$ **Substitute** ___ **for y.**
   $2x + \_\_ = 14$ **Simplify.**
   $2x = \_\_\_$ **Subtract** ___ **from each side.**
   $x = \_\_\_$ **Solve for x.**

4. **Check** by substituting _____ for x and ___ for y in the original equations.

   The solution is (_____, ___).

✓ **Checkpoint** **Solve the system using the linear combination method.**

1. $2x + y = -2$	**2.** $3x + 8y = -5$
$5x + 3y = -8$	$-2x + 2y = 18$

| **Example 2** | *Multiply Both Equations* |

Solve the system using the linear combination method.

$3x - 4y = -37$ **Equation 1**

$-5x + 3y = 14$ **Equation 2**

Solution

1. **Multiply** Equation 1 by ____ and Equation 2 by ____ so that the coefficients of *x* differ only in sign.

$3x - 4y = -37$ × ____   _____

$-5x + 3y = 14$ × ____   _____

2. **Add** the revised equations.   _____

And solve for *y*. $y =$ ____

3. **Substitute** ____ for *y* in one of the original equations and solve for *x*.

$3x - 4y = -37$ **Write Equation 1.**

$3x - 4(\_\_\_\_) = -37$ **Substitute** ____ **for** *y*.

$3x - \_\_\_\_ = -37$ **Multiply.**

$3x = \_\_\_\_$ **Add** ____ **to each side.**

$x = \_\_\_$ **Solve for** *x*.

4. **Check** by substituting ____ for *x* and ____ for *y* in the original equations.

The solution is (____, ____).

Example 3 — *A Linear System with No Solution*

Solve the system using the linear combination method.

a. $x - 3y = 7$

$2x - 6y = 12$

b. $2x - 6y = 12$

$-5x + 15y = -30$

Solution

a. Multiply the first equation by _____ to eliminate x.

$x - 3y = 7$ _____ × _____ _____

$2x - 6y = 12$ _____

Add the revised equations. _____

Because the statement ___ = ____ is false, there is _____ solution.

b. Multiply the first equation by ___ and the second equation by ___ to eliminate x.

$2x - 6y = 12$ ×___ _____

$-5x + 15y = -30$ ×___ _____

Add the revised equations. _____

Because the statement ___ = ___ is true, there are _____ solutions.

✔ *Checkpoint* Solve the system using the linear combination method.

3. $2x - y = 6$	**4.** $2x + 3y = 7$
$8x - 4y = 13$	$5x + 7y = 15$

Homework

Graphing Linear Equations in Three Variables

Goal • Graph linear equations in three variables.

Your Notes

VOCABULARY

Three-dimensional coordinate system

_____

z-axis

_____

Ordered triple

_____

Octants

_____

Linear equation in three variables

Example 1 — *Plot Points in Three Dimensions*

Plot the ordered pair (7, 1, −3) in a three-dimensional coordinate system.

Solution

To plot (7, 1, −3), first find the point (_____) in the *xy*-plane. The point (7, 1, −3) lies ____ units _____ it.

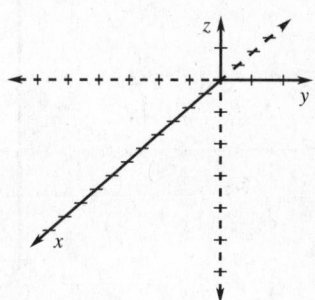

Example 2 *Graph a Linear Equation in Three Variables*

Sketch the graph of $2x - y + 4z = 8$. Label the points where the graph crosses the x-, y-, and z-axes.

Solution

Find the points where the graph intersects the axes.

First let $x =$ ___ and $y =$ ___, and then solve for ___.

$2(\_\_) - \_\_ + 4z = 8$ **Substitute 0 for x and y.**

$\qquad\qquad 4z = 8$ **Simplify.**

$\qquad\qquad z =$ ___ **Solve for z.**

The z-intercept is ___, so plot the point $(0, 0, \_\_)$.

Next, let $y =$ ___ and $z =$ ___, and then solve for ___.

$2x - \_\_ + 4(\_\_) = 8$ **Substitute 0 for y and z.**

$\qquad\qquad 2x = 8$ **Simplify.**

$\qquad\qquad x =$ ___ **Solve for x.**

The x-intercept is ___, so plot the point $(\_\_, 0, 0)$.

Finally, let $x =$ ___ and $z =$ ___, and then solve for ___.

$2(\_\_) - y + 4(\_\_) = 8$ **Substitute 0 for x and z.**

$\qquad\qquad -y = 8$ **Simplify.**

$\qquad\qquad y =$ ___ **Solve for y.**

The y-intercept is ___, so plot the point $(0, \_\_, 0)$.

Connect the points with _____ to show the _____ region of the plane that lies in the first _____.

> A point on the z-axis has the form $(0, 0, z)$.
>
> A point on the x-axis has the form $(x, 0, 0)$.
>
> A point on the y-axis has the form $(0, y, 0)$.

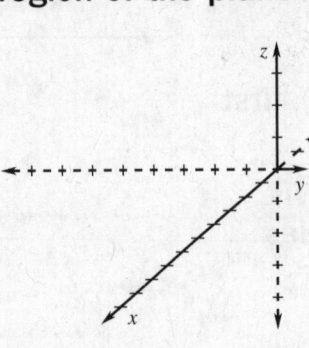

✔ *Checkpoint* **Plot the ordered triple in a three-dimensional system.**

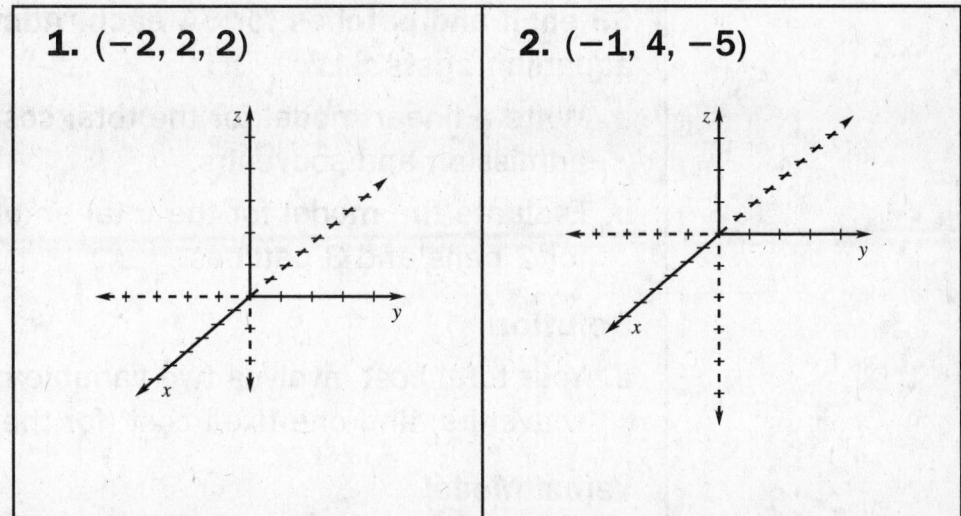

1. $(-2, 2, 2)$

2. $(-1, 4, -5)$

Sketch the graph of the equation. Label the points where the graph crosses the x-, y-, and z-axes.

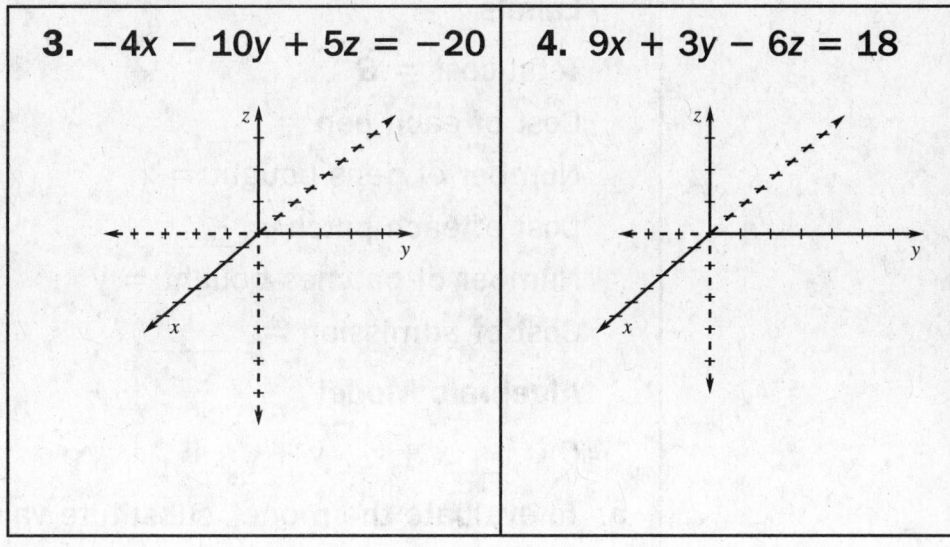

3. $-4x - 10y + 5z = -20$

4. $9x + 3y - 6z = 18$

Example 3   *Model a Real-Life Situation*

Souvenirs At an aquarium, you can buy pens for $3 each and patches for $4 each. Admission to the aquarium costs $12.

a. Write a linear model for the total cost you will spend for admission and souvenirs.

b. Evaluate the model for the total amount you will spend for 2 pens and 3 patches.

Solution

a. Your total cost involves two variable costs (for the souvenirs) and one fixed cost (for the admission).

Verbal Model

Total cost	=	Cost of each pen	$\cdot$	Number of pens bought	+	Cost of each patch	$\cdot$	Number of patches bought	+	Cost of admission

Labels

Total cost = C   (dollars)

Cost of each pen = ____   (dollars)

Number of pens bought = x   (pens)

Cost of each patch = ____   (dollars)

Number of patches bought = y   (patches)

Cost of admission = ____   (dollars)

Algebraic Model

C = ___x + ___y + ____

b. To evaluate the model, substitute values for ___ and ___.

C = ___x + ___y + ____

C = ___(___) + ___(___) + ____

C = ___ + ___ + ____

C = ____

The total cost will be _____.

Homework

Solving Systems of Linear Equations in Three Variables

Goal • Solve systems of linear equations in three variables.

VOCABULARY

System of three linear equations

Solution of a system of three linear equations

LINEAR COMBINATION METHOD (3-VARIABLE SYSTEMS)

Step 1 Rewrite the linear system in three variables as a linear system in _____ variables using the _____ method.

Step 2 Solve the new linear system for _____ of its variables.

Step 3 Substitute the _____ found in Step 2 into one of the _____ equations and solve for the remaining variable.

Step 4 Check the solution in _____ of the _____ equations.

Example 1	*Use the Linear Combination Method*

Solve the system.

$3x - 2y + 4z = 20$ **Equation 1**
$-x + 5y + 12z = 73$ **Equation 2**
$x + 3y - 2z = 1$ **Equation 3**

1. **Rewrite** the system as a system in two variables. Add _____ times Equation 3 to Equation 1 to eliminate *x*.

$3x - 2y + 4z = 20$ $3x - 2y + 4z = 20$
$x + 3y - 2z = 1$ × _____   _____

New Eq. 1 _____

Now add Equation 3 to Equation 2 to eliminate ___.

$-x + 5y + 12z = 73$
$x + 3y - 2z = 1$

New Eq. 2 _____

2. **Solve** the new system. First, add _____ times new Equation 2 to new Equation 1 to eliminate ___.

$-11y + 10z = 17$ $-11y + 10z = 17$
$8y + 10z = 74$ × _____   _____

_____

Solve for *y*. $y = $ ___

Substitute ___ for *y* in new Equation 1 or new Equation 2 and solve for *z* to get $z = $ ___.

3. **Substitute** ___ for *y* and ___ for *z* in one of the original equations and solve for *x*.

$x + 3y - 2z = 1$ **Equation 3**
$x + 3(\underline{\ \ }) - 2(\underline{\ \ }) = 1$ **Substitute ___ for y and ___ for z.**
$x + \underline{\ \ } - \underline{\ \ } = 1$ **Multiply.**
$x = $ ___   **Solve for x.**

4. **Check** by substituting ___ for *x*, ___ for *y*, and ___ for *z* in each of the original equations.

The solution is the ordered triple (___, ___, ___).

Example 2 **Solve a System with No Solution**

Solve the system.

$2x + 4y + 10z = 14$ **Equation 1**
$x + 2y + 5z = -4$ **Equation 2**
$3x - 4y - 3z = 15$ **Equation 3**

Multiply Equation 2 by -2 and add the result to Equation **1.**

     $2x + 4y + 10z = 14$ Add _____ times Equation 2

_____   to Equation 1.

       _____   _____ statement

Because solving the system resulted in the _____
statement _____, the original system of equations
has _____.

Example 3 **Solve a System with Infinitely Many Solutions**

Solve the system.

$2x - 2y + 4z = 6$ **Equation 1**
$4x + 2y + 8z = 12$ **Equation 2**
$4x - 2y + 8z = 12$ **Equation 3**

1. Rewrite the system as a system in two variables.

     $2x - 2y + 4z = 6$ **Add Equation 1 to Equation 2.**
     $4x + 2y + 8z = 12$

     _____   **New Equation 1**

     $4x + 2y + 8z = 12$ **Add Equation 2 to Equation 3.**
     $4x - 2y + 8z = 12$

     _____   **New Equation 2**

2. Solve the new system of equations in two variables.

     _____ $= -72$ Add _____ times new Equation 1
     _____ $= 72$ to ___ times new Equation 2.

       _____

Because solving the system resulted in the _____
statement _____, the original system of equations
has _____. The three planes
intersect in a _____.

✔ *Checkpoint* **Tell how many solutions the linear system has. If the system has one solution, solve the system. Then check your solution.**

1. $x + 2y + 3z = 17$

$-4x + 2y - z = 24$

$3x - 6y - 8z = -67$

2. $4x + 3y - 2z = 8$

$4x + 3y + 2z = 24$

$4x + 3y + z = 20$

3. $2x - 2y + z = 7$

$4x - 4y + 2z = 17$

$3x + 2y - 6z = -2$

Homework

Words to Review

Use your own words and/or an example to explain the vocabulary word.

System of two linear equations	Solution of a system of two linear equations
Substitution method	Linear combination method
Three-dimensional coordinate system	z-axis
Ordered triple	Octants
Linear equation in three variables	System of three linear equations
Solution of a system of three linear equations	

Review your notes and Chapter 3 by using the Chapter Review on pages 160–162 of your textbook.

 **Solving Linear Inequalities**

Goal • Solve and graph simple and compound inequalities in one variable.

VOCABULARY

Linear inequality in one variable

_____

Solution of an inequality in one variable

_____

Graph of an inequality in one variable

_____

Compound inequality

PROPERTIES OF INEQUALITIES

To write an _____ inequality:

Add the _____ number to _____ side.

Subtract the _____ number from _____ side.

Multiply or **divide** _____ side by the same _____ number.

Multiply or **divide** _____ side by the same _____ number and _____ the inequality _____.

Example 1 *Inequality with a Variable on One Side*

Solve the inequality.

a. $x + 2 \leq 6$ **b.** $-3z - 7 < 8$

Solution

a. $x + 2 \leq 6$ Write original inequality.

   $x \leq$ ____   Subtract ____ from each side.

The solution is all real numbers _____ or

_____ ____ ____.

b. $-3z - 7 < 8$ Write original inequality.

   $-3z <$ ____   Add ____ to each side.

   $z >$ ____   Divide each side by ____; _____
                        the inequality.

The solution is all real numbers _____ ____.

Example 2 *Inequality with a Variable on Both Sides*

Solve $4x + 5 > 9x - 10$. **Graph the solution.**

Solution

   $4x + 5 > 9x - 10$ Write original inequality.

   ____ $+ 5 > -10$ Subtract ____ from each side.

   ____ $>$ ____   Subtract ____ from each side.

   $x <$ ____   Divide each side by ____;
                        _____ the inequality.

The solution is all real numbers _____ ____.
The graph is shown below.

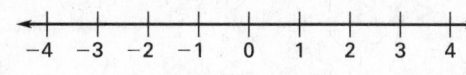

✔ *Checkpoint* **Solve the inequality. Then graph your solution.**

1. $x - 2 \le 4x - 8$

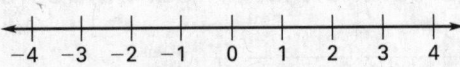

2. $-7x + 6 > -1$

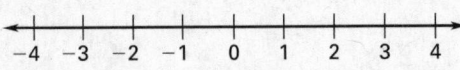

Example 3 *Solve an "and" Compound Inequality*

Solve $-7 < 5x - 2 \le 8$. Then graph the solution.

Solution

$-7 < 5x - 2 \le 8$	Write original inequality.
$-7 + \underline{} < 5x - 2 + \underline{} \le 8 + \underline{}$	Add ___ to each expression.
$\underline{} < 5x \le \underline{}$	Simplify.
$\underline{} < x \le \underline{}$	Divide each expression by ___.

The solution is all real numbers _____ _____ **and** _____ **or** _____ ___.

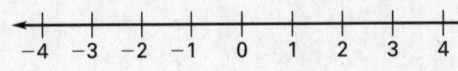

Example 4   *Solve an "or" Compound Inequality*

Solve **4x − 7 ≤ 5 or 3x + 2 ≥ 23. Then graph the solution.**

Solution

Solve each part separately.

First Inequality		Second Inequality	
$4x - 7 \le 5$	Write inequality.	$3x + 2 \ge 23$	Write inequality.
$4x \le \underline{\quad}$	Add ___ to each side.	$3x \ge \underline{\quad}$	Subtract ___ from each side.
$x \le \underline{\quad}$	Divide each side by ___.	$x \ge \underline{\quad}$	Divide each side by ___.

The solution is all real numbers _____

or _____.

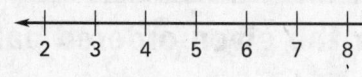

✔ *Checkpoint* **Solve the inequality. Then graph your solution.**

3. −3 < 4x + 5 < 21

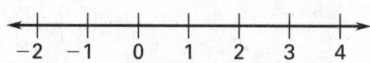

---

4. 2x − 6 ≤ −2 or 5x + 1 > 26

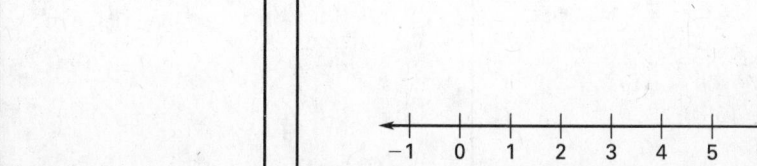

4.2 Linear Inequalities in Two Variables

Goal • Solve and graph linear inequalities in two variables.

Your Notes

> **VOCABULARY**
>
> Linear inequality in two variables
>
> _____
>
> Half-plane

Example 1 *Check Solutions of Inequalities*

Check whether the given ordered pair is a solution of $4x + 2y > 6$.

a. (3, 2)   b. (−1, 4)

Solution

ORDERED PAIR	SUBSTITUTE	CONCLUSION
a. (3, 2)	4(__) + 2(__) = ___ > 6	(3, 2) ___ a solution.
b. (−1, 4)	4(__) + 2(__) = __ > 6	(−1, 4) _____ a solution.

✔ **Checkpoint** Check whether the given ordered pair is a solution of $2x - y \leq 8$.

1. (6, 2)	2. (3, −1)

GRAPHING A LINEAR INEQUALITY

Step 1 **Graph** the boundary line of the inequality. Use a _____ line for < or >. Use a _____ line for ≤ or ≥.

Step 2 **Test** a point that is _____ on the boundary line to see whether it is a _____ of the inequality. Then shade the _____ half-plane.

Example 2   *Graph Linear Inequalities in One Variable*

Graph y ≥ −1 in a coordinate plane.

Solution

1. **Graph** the boundary line y = −1. Use a _____ line because y ≥ −1.

2. **Test** the point (0, 0). It ____ a solution, so shade the _____ that _____ contain (0, 0).

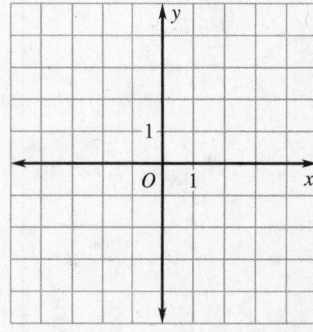

Example 3   *Graph Linear Inequalities in Two Variables*

Graph 3x − 2y < −6 in a coordinate plane.

Solution

1. **Graph** the boundary line 3x − 2y = −6. Use a _____ line because 3x − 2y < −6.

2. **Test** the point (0, 0). Because (0, 0) _____ a solution, shade the _____ that _____ contain (0, 0).

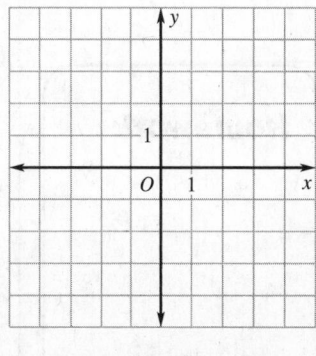

✔ *Checkpoint* **Graph the inequality in a coordinate plane.**

3. $x < -2$

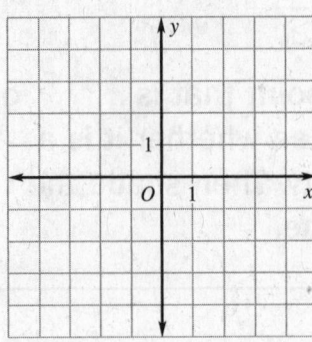

4. $y \geq 1$

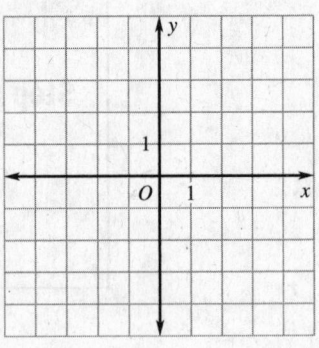

5. $y \leq -x + 2$

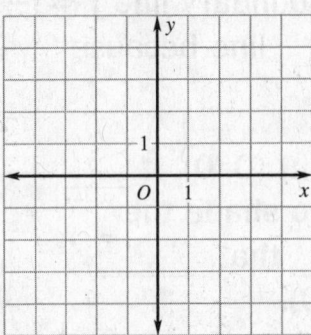

6. $9x + 3y > 9$

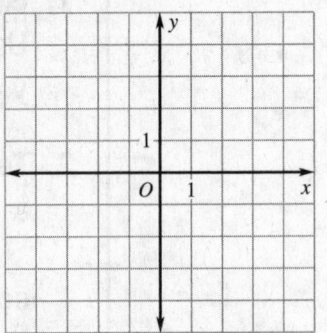

7. $5x - y \geq 2$

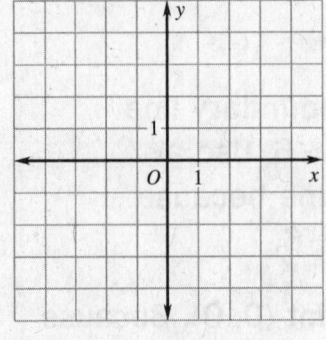

8. $x - 4y < -8$

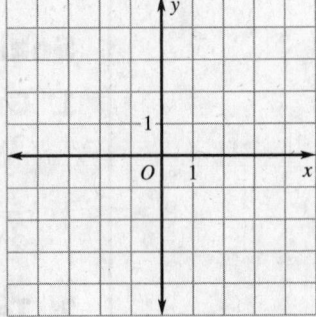

Homework

Systems of Linear Inequalities

Goal • Graph, write, and use a system of linear inequalities.

Your Notes

> **VOCABULARY**
>
> System of linear inequalities in two variables
>
> Solution of a system of linear inequalities
>
> Graph of a system of linear inequalities

Example 1 *Check Solutions of Inequalities*

Check whether (3, −2) is a solution of the system of inequalities.

a. $x + y < 5$
$2x \le 8$

b. $4x + y \ge 1$
$-x - y < -9$

Solution

ORDERED PAIR	SUBSTITUTE	CONCLUSION
a. (3, −2)	__ + (____) = __ < 5	(3, −2) ___ a
	2(__) = __ ≤ __	solution.
b. (3, −2)	4(__) + (____) = ___ ≥ 1	(3, −2) _____
	−__ − (____) = ___ < ____	a solution.

✔ *Checkpoint* Check whether (−5, 4) is a solution of the system of inequalities.

1. $2y > 7$	**2.** $-x + 1 > 10$
$x - y < 10$	$3y - 2 \le 10$

GRAPHING A SYSTEM OF LINEAR INEQUALITIES

Step 1 **Graph** the _____
lines of the inequalities.
Use a _____ line for an
inequality with < or ___.
Use a _____ line for an
inequality with ___ or ___.

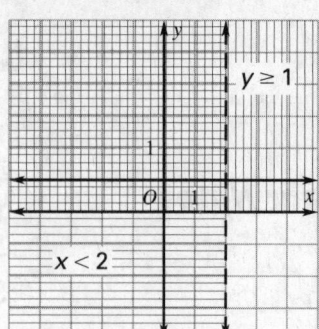

Step 2 **Shade** the _____
for the inequalities. The
graph of the system is the
region _____ to
all the half-planes.

The double-shaded region shown above is the graph
of $x < 2$ and $y \geq 1$.

Example 2 *Graph a System of Two Inequalities*

Graph the system.

$y < 2x + 1$ **Inequality 1**
$y \leq -x - 3$ **Inequality 2**

Solution

1. **Graph** the _____ line of
   each inequality. Use a _____
   line for Inequality 1. Use a
   _____ line for Inequality 2.

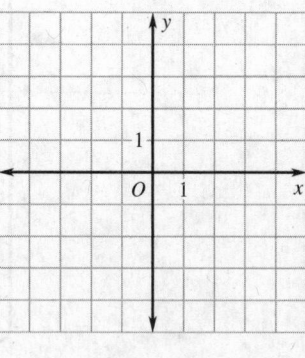

2. **Shade** the half-plane _____
   $y = 2x + 1$ with horizontal lines
   to represent _____.

   Shade the half-plane _____ and _____ $y = -x - 3$
   with vertical lines to represent _____.

The graph of the system is the _____, or intersection,
of the two shaded areas.

Example 3 | *Graph a System of Three Inequalities*

Graph the system.

$x > -2$ **Inequality 1**
$y \leq 3$ **Inequality 2**
$-3x + 2y > 6$ **Inequality 3**

Solution

> Beginning here in Example 3, it is only necessary to show the solution region in your graphs of the systems of inequalities.

The inequality $x > -2$ implies that the region is to the _____ of the _____ line $x =$ ____.

The inequality $y \leq 3$ implies that the region is ____ and _____ the line $y =$ ___.

The inequality $-3x + 2y > 6$ implies that the region is _____ the _____ line _____.

The graph of the system is the shaded _____ region shown above.

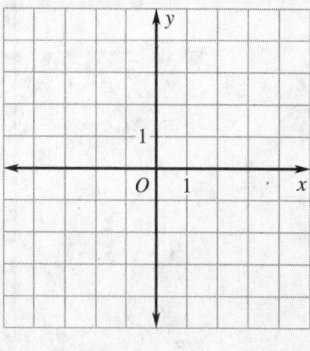

✔ *Checkpoint* **Graph the system.**

3. $y < 2x - 3$
$x + 3y \leq -6$

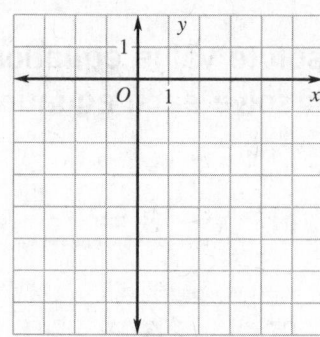

4. $x \leq -1$
$y \leq 2$
$y > x - 2$

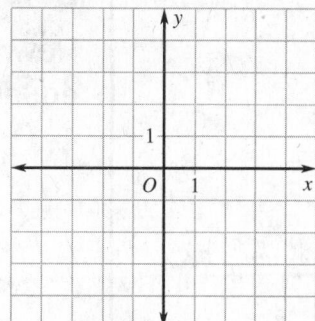

Homework

4.4 Solving Absolute Value Equations

Goal • Solve and write absolute value equations in one variable.

VOCABULARY

Absolute value

_____

Absolute value equation

SOLVING AN ABSOLUTE VALUE EQUATION

The absolute value equation $|ax + b| = c$ where $c > 0$ is _____ to the compound statement ____ $+ b = c$ ____ $ax +$ ___ $=$ ____.

EXAMPLE	EQUIVALENT FORM	SOLUTIONS
$|x + 5| = 8$	$x + 5 =$ _ or $x + 5 =$ ___	_, ____

So, the _____ of $|x + 5| = 8$ are ___ and _____.

Example 1   Solve an Absolute Value Equation

Solve $|x - 3| = 6.$

Solution

Rewrite the absolute value equation in _____ _____ equations. Then solve each equation.

$|x - 3| = 6$ Write original equation.

$x - 3 =$ _   or $x - 3 =$ ___   Expression can equal ___ or ____.

$x =$ _   or $x =$ ___   Add to ___ each side.

The equation has _____ solutions: ___ and _____.

CHECK $|$___ $- 3| \stackrel{?}{=} 6$ $|$___ $- 3| \stackrel{?}{=} 6$

          $|$___$| \stackrel{?}{=} 6$ $|$___$| \stackrel{?}{=} 6$

          $6 = 6$ ✓ $6 = 6$ ✓

     Copyright © McDougal Littell/Houghton Mifflin Company

Example 2   *Solve an Absolute Value Equation*

Solve $|2x + 4| + 2 = 14$.

Solution

First isolate the absolute value _____ on one side of the _____ .

$\|2x + 4\| + 2 = 14$	Write original equation.
$|2x + 4| = $ ____	Subtract ____ from each side.

Rewrite $|2x + 4| = $ ____ as two _____ equations.
Then solve each equation.

$|2x + 4| = $ ____	Write original equation.
$2x + 4 = $ ____ or $2x + 4 = $ _____	Expression can equal ____ or _____ .
$2x = $ ____ or $2x = $ _____	Subtract ____ from each side.
$x = $ ____ or $x = $ ____	Divide each side by ____ .

> **Both solutions should be checked in the original absolute value equation.**

The equation has _____ solutions: ____ and ____ .

☑ *Checkpoint* Solve the equation.

1. $|3 - x| = 15$

2. $|2x + 3| - 6 = 7$

Example 3 *Write an Absolute Value Equation*

Write an absolute value equation that has −2 and 8 as its solutions.

Solution

Graph the _____ on a number line. Then locate the _____ of the graph.

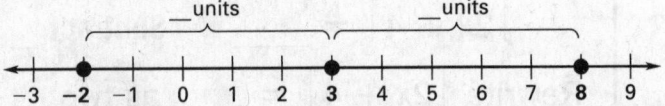

The graph of each solution is ___ units from the midpoint, ___. The distance between a number x and ___ on a number line is $|x - \underline{}|$. You can use the _____ and the _____ to write an absolute value equation.

$$|x - \underline{}| = \underline{}$$

An equation that has ___ and ___ as its solutions is $|x - \underline{}| = \underline{}$.

CHECK $\quad |-2 - \underline{}| = |\underline{}| = \underline{}$ ✓

$\qquad\qquad |8 - \underline{}| = |\underline{}| = \underline{}$ ✓

✔ **Checkpoint** Write an absolute value equation that has the given solutions.

3. −5 and −1	4. −2 and 6

Homework

4.5 Solving Absolute Value Inequalities

Goal • Solve and graph absolute value inequalities.

Your Notes

VOCABULARY

Absolute value inequality

SOLVING ABSOLUTE VALUE INEQUALITIES

In the inequalities below, $c > 0$.

INEQUALITY	EQUIVALENT FORM	GRAPH
$\lvert ax + b \rvert < c$	$-c < \underline{\hspace{2cm}} < c$	
$\lvert ax + b \rvert \leq c$	$\underline{\hspace{1cm}} \leq ax + b \leq \underline{\hspace{1cm}}$	
$\lvert ax + b \rvert > c$	$ax + b \ \underline{\hspace{0.5cm}}\ -c$ or $ax + b \ \underline{\hspace{0.5cm}}\ c$	
$\lvert ax + b \rvert \geq c$	$ax + b \ \underline{\hspace{0.5cm}}\ -c$ or $ax + b \ \underline{\hspace{0.5cm}}\ c$	

Example 1 — Solve an Inequality of the Form $\lvert x + b \rvert \leq c$

Solve $\lvert x - 1.5 \rvert \leq 4.5$. Then graph the solution.

Solution

$\lvert x - 1.5 \rvert \leq 4.5$	Write original inequality.
$\underline{\hspace{1.5cm}} \leq x - 1.5 \leq \underline{\hspace{1.5cm}}$	Write equivalent compound inequality.
$\underline{\hspace{1.5cm}} \leq x \leq \underline{\hspace{1cm}}$	Add $\underline{\hspace{1cm}}$ to each expression.

The solution is all $\underline{\hspace{1.5cm}}$ numbers $\underline{\hspace{1.5cm}}$ than or equal to $\underline{\hspace{1cm}}$ and less than or $\underline{\hspace{1.5cm}}$ to $\underline{\hspace{0.5cm}}$.

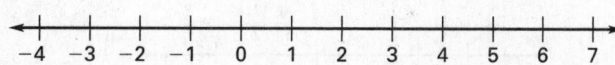

Example 2 | *Solve an Inequality of the Form* $|ax + b| < c$

Solve $|2x + 8| < 2$. Then graph the solution.

Solution

$\|2x + 8\| < 2$	Write original inequality.
_____ $< 2x + 8 <$ ___	Write equivalent compound inequality.
_____ $< 2x <$ _____	Subtract ___ from each expression.
_____ $< x <$ _____	Divide each expression by ___.

The solution is all _____ numbers greater than _____ and _____ than _____.

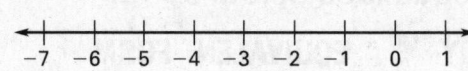

✔ *Checkpoint* **Solve the inequality. Then graph your solution.**

1. $|x + 3| \le 7$

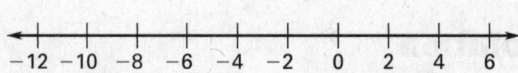

2. $|4x - 1| < 9$

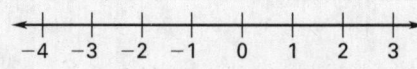

Example 3 *Solve an Inequality of the Form $|ax + b| \geq c$*

Solve $|2x + 5| \geq 3$. Then graph the solution.

The absolute value inequality is equivalent to
$2x + 5$ ___ -3 or $2x + 5 \geq$ ___ .

First Inequality		**Second Inequality**
$2x + 5$ ___ -3	Write inequalities.	$2x + 5 \geq$ ___
$2x$ ___ ___	Subtract ___ from each side.	$2x \geq$ ___
x ___ ___	Divide each side by ___ .	$x \geq$ ___

The solutions are all real numbers _____ or equal
to _____ or greater than or equal to _____ .

$$-8 \quad -7 \quad -6 \quad -5 \quad -4 \quad -3 \quad -2 \quad -1 \quad 0 \quad 1 \quad 2 \quad 3$$

Example 4 *Write a Model for Tolerance*

Manufacturing A manufacturer of sewing machine
needles uses a tolerance of 0.01 millimeter for a needle
that is designed to be 3.8 millimeters long. Write and
solve an absolute value inequality that describes the
acceptable lengths for the needles.

$$|x - \underline{\quad}| \leq \underline{\quad\quad}$$ Write algebraic model.

$$\underline{\quad\quad} \leq x - \underline{\quad} \leq 0.01$$ Write equivalent compound inequality.

$$\underline{\quad\quad} \leq x \leq \underline{\quad\quad}$$ Add _____ to each side.

The acceptable lengths for the needles is between
_____ millimeters and _____ millimeters, inclusive.

✔ **Checkpoint** Complete the following exercise.

3. Solve $|5x - 2| > 12$. Then graph the solution.

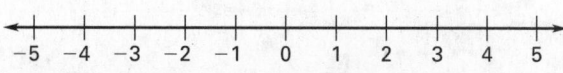

$$-5 \quad -4 \quad -3 \quad -2 \quad -1 \quad 0 \quad 1 \quad 2 \quad 3 \quad 4 \quad 5$$

4.6 Absolute Value Functions

Goal • Evaluate, graph, and use simple absolute value functions.

Your Notes

VOCABULARY

Vertex

Example 1 *Evaluate Absolute Value Functions*

Evaluate the function when $x = -4$ and $x = 7$.

a. $f(x) = |x + 3|$ **b.** $g(x) = |x| - 5$

Solution

a. When $x = -4$:

$f(x) = |x + 3|$ **Write function.**

$f(-4) = |\_\_ + 3|$ **Substitute ____ for x.**

$= |\_\_\_|$ **Simplify.**

$= \_\_\_$

When $x = 7$:

$f(x) = |x + 3|$ **Write function.**

$f(7) = |\_\_ + 3|$ **Substitute ___ for x.**

$= |\_\_\_|$ **Simplify.**

$= \_\_\_$

b. When $x = -4$:   When $x = 7$:

$g(x) = |x| - 5$ $g(x) = |x| - 5$

$g(-4) = |\_\_\_\_| - 5$ $g(7) = |\_\_\_| - 5$

$= \_\_\_ - 5$ $= \_\_\_ - 5$

$= \_\_\_$ $= \_\_\_$

     Copyright © McDougal Littell/Houghton Mifflin Company

✔ *Checkpoint* **Evaluate the function when x = −2 and when x = 5.**

1. $f(x) = |x - 7|$	**2.** $g(x) = |x| + 10$

Example 2   *Graph an Absolute Value Function*

Graph $y = \dfrac{1}{3}|x|$.

Solution

1. **Plot** the vertex at the _____.

2. **Find** a second point by substituting an _____.

$y = \dfrac{1}{3}|x|$ **Write original equation.**

$= \dfrac{1}{3}|\underline{\quad}|$ **Substitute 3 for x.**

$= \dfrac{1}{3}(\underline{\quad})$ **Evaluate** $|\underline{\quad}|$.

$= \underline{\quad}$ **Multiply.**

A second point is (____, ____).

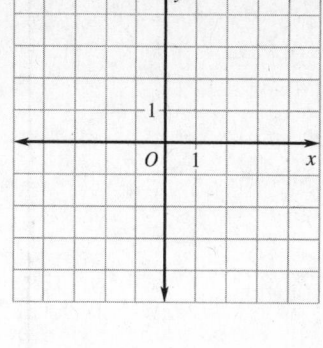

3. **Plot** the second point and use symmetry to plot a third point at (____, ____).

4. **Connect** these three points with a ____-shaped graph.

Example 3 **Graph an Absolute Value Function**

Graph $y = -3|x|$.

Solution

1. **Plot** the _____ at the origin.

2. **Find** a second point by _____ an x-value.

$y = -3|x|$ Write original equation.

$ = -3|\underline{}|$ Substitute 1 for x.

$ = -3(\underline{})$ Evaluate $|\underline{}|$.

$ = \underline{}$ Multiply.

A second point is (___, _____).

3. **Plot** the second point and use _____ to plot a third point at (_____, _____).

4. **Connect** these three points with a _____ graph.

✔ *Checkpoint* **Graph the function.**

3. $y = 4|x|$

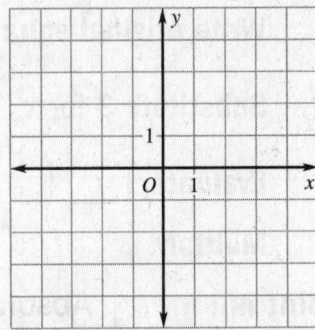

4. $y = -\frac{1}{4}|x|$

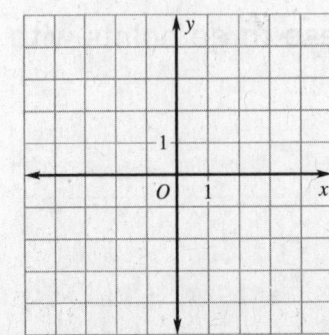

Homework

Words to Review

Use your own words and/or an example to explain the vocabulary word.

Linear inequality in one variable	Solution of an inequality in one variable
Graph of an inequality in one variable	Compound inequality
Linear inequality in two variables	Half-plane
System of linear inequalities	Solution of a system of linear inequalities
Graph of a system of linear inequalities	Absolute value of x
Absolute value equation	Absolute value inequality
Vertex	

Review your notes and Chapter 4 by using the Chapter Review on pages 212–214 of your textbook.

Graphing Quadratic Functions in Standard Form

Goal • Graph quadratic functions in the form $y = ax^2 + bx + c$.

Your Notes

VOCABULARY

Quadratic function

Parabola

Vertex

Axis of symmetry

Monomial

Binomial

STANDARD FORM OF A QUADRATIC FUNCTION

STEPS FOR GRAPHING $y = ax^2 + bx + c$

Step 1 **Draw** the _____. It is the line
$x = \underline{\quad}$.

Step 2 **Find** and plot the _____. The ___-coordinate
of the vertex is _____ . Substitute this value
for x in the function and evaluate to find the
___-coordinate of the vertex.

Step 3 **Plot** two points on one side of the _____
_____. Use symmetry to plot _____ more
points on the _____ side.

Step 4 **Draw** a _____ through the points.

Example 1 **Graph a Quadratic Function in Standard Form**

Graph $y = 3x^2 + 6x - 1$.

Solution

The function is in standard form $y = ax^2 + bx + c$ where $a = \underline{\hspace{1cm}}$, $b = \underline{\hspace{1cm}}$, and $c = \underline{\hspace{1cm}}$. Because $a \underline{\hspace{1cm}} 0$, the parabola opens $\underline{\hspace{1cm}}$.

1. **Draw** the axis of symmetry.

   $x = -\dfrac{b}{2a} = \underline{\hspace{2cm}} = \underline{\hspace{1cm}}$

2. **Find** and plot the vertex. The x-coordinate of the vertex is $\underline{\hspace{1cm}}$. Find the y-coordinate.

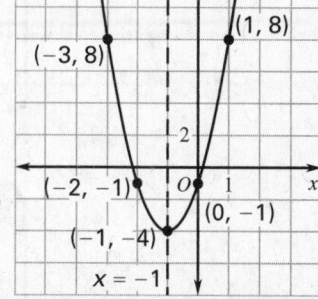

   $y = 3x^2 + 6x - 1$

   $ = 3(\underline{\hspace{1cm}})^2 + 6(\underline{\hspace{1cm}}) - 1 = \underline{\hspace{1cm}}$

   The vertex is $(\underline{\hspace{1cm}}, \underline{\hspace{1cm}})$.

3. **Plot** two points to the left of the axis of symmetry. Evaluate the function for two x-values that are less than $\underline{\hspace{1cm}}$, such as -2 and -3.

   $y = 3(\underline{\hspace{1cm}})^2 + 6(\underline{\hspace{1cm}}) - 1 = \underline{\hspace{1cm}}$

   $y = 3(\underline{\hspace{1cm}})^2 + 6(\underline{\hspace{1cm}}) - 1 = \underline{\hspace{1cm}}$

   Plot the points $(-2, \underline{\hspace{1cm}})$ and $(-3, \underline{\hspace{1cm}})$. Plot their $\underline{\hspace{3cm}}$ by counting the distance to the axis of symmetry and then counting the $\underline{\hspace{2cm}}$ distance beyond the axis of symmetry.

4. **Draw** a parabola through the points.

✔ *Checkpoint* **Complete the following exercise.**

1. **Graph** the function $y = 2x^2 + 4x - 3$. Label the vertex and the axis of symmetry.

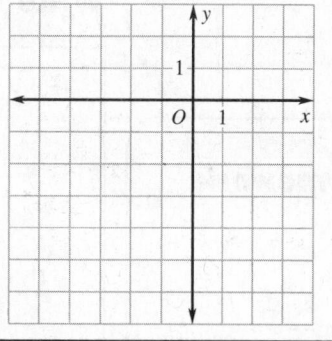

Your Notes

Example 2 *Multiply Binomials*

Find the product $(x + 3)(x + 5)$.

Solution

$(x + 3)(x + 5)$

$= x(\underline{}) + x(5) + \underline{}(x) + 3(5)$ Write products of terms.

$= x^2 + \underline{} + \underline{} + \underline{}$ Multiply.

$= x^2 + \underline{} + \underline{}$ Combine like terms.

Example 3 *Write a Quadratic Function in Standard Form*

Write $y = 3(x + 2)(x + 1)$ in standard form.

Solution

$y = 3(x + 2)(x + 1)$ Write original function.

$= 3(x^2 + 1x + \underline{} + \underline{})$ Multiply using _____.

$= 3(\underline{})$ Combine _____ terms.

$= \underline{}$ Use the distributive property.

✔ *Checkpoint* Find the product.

2. $(x - 6)(x + 8)$	3. $(4x + 1)(x - 3)$

Write the function in standard form.

4. $y = 6(x - 4)(x + 5)$	5. $y = 5(x + 2)^2 + 4$

Homework

5.2 Graphing Quadratic Functions in Vertex or Intercept Form

Goal • Graph quadratic functions in different forms.

Your Notes

VOCABULARY

Vertex form

_____

Intercept form

_____

Minimum value

_____

Maximum value

VERTEX FORM OF A QUADRATIC FUNCTION

STEPS FOR GRAPHING $y = a(x - h)^2 + k$

Step 1 Draw the _____. It is the line
$x =$ ___.

Step 2 Plot the _____, (___, ___).

Step 3 Plot two points on one side of the _____
_____. Use symmetry to plot _____ more
points on the _____ side.

Step 4 Draw a _____ through the points.

opyright © McDougal Littell/Houghton Mifflin Company

Lesson 5.2 • **Algebra 2 C&S Notetaking Guide** 91

Example 1 **Graph a Quadratic Function in Vertex Form**

Graph $y = 2(x - 3)^2 + 2$.

Solution

The function is in _____ $y = (x - h)^2 + k$ where $a =$ ___, $h =$ ___, and $k =$ ___. Because $a >$ ___, the parabola opens ___.

1. **Draw** the axis of symmetry, $x = h =$ ___.

2. **Plot** the vertex $(h, k) =$ (___, ___).

3. **Plot** points. The x-values 1 and 2 are to the right of the axis of symmetry.

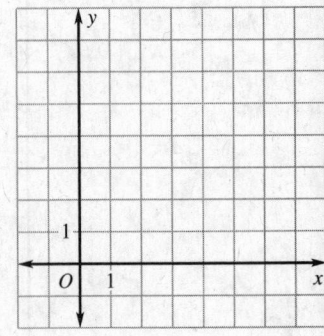

$x = 1$: $y = 2($___ $- 3)^2 + 2 =$ ___

$x = 2$: $y = 2($___ $- 3)^2 + 2 =$ ___

Plot the points (1, ___) and (2, ___). Then plot their _____ across the axis of symmetry.

4. **Draw** a parabola through the points.

INTERCEPT FORM OF A QUADRATIC FUNCTION

STEPS FOR GRAPHING $y = a(x - p)(x - q)$

Step 1 Draw the _____. It is the line
$x =$ _____.

Step 2 Find and plot the _____. The ___-coordinate of the vertex is _____. Substitute this value for x in the function to find the ___-coordinate of the vertex.

Step 3 Plot the points where the _____, p and q, occur.

Step 4 Draw a _____ through the points.

Example 2 *Graph a Quadratic Function in Intercept Form*

Graph $y = -(x - 2)(x - 4)$.

Solution

The function is in _____ $y = a(x - p)(x - q)$
where $a =$ ____, $p =$ ___, and $q =$ ___. Because $a <$ ___,
the parabola opens _____.

1. **Draw** the axis of symmetry.
   The axis of symmetry is:

   $x = \dfrac{p + q}{2} =$ _____ $=$ ___

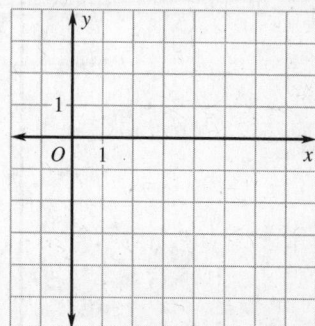

2. **Find** and plot the vertex.
   The x-coordinate of the vertex
   is $x =$ ___. Calculate the
   y-coordinate of the vertex.

   $y = -(x - 2)(x - 4)$

   $= -(\rule{1cm}{0.4pt} - 2)(\rule{1cm}{0.4pt} - 4) =$ ___

   Plot the vertex (___, ___).

3. **Plot** the points where the x-intercepts occur. The
   x-intercepts are ___ and ___. Plot the points (___, 0)
   and (___, 0).

4. **Draw** a parabola through the points.

✔ *Checkpoint* **Complete the following exercises.**

1. Graph the function
   $y = (x - 4)^2 - 2$.
   Label the vertex and
   axis of symmetry.

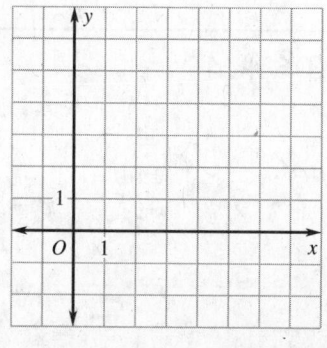

2. Graph the function
   $y = (x - 3)(x + 1)$.
   Label the vertex and
   the x-intercepts.

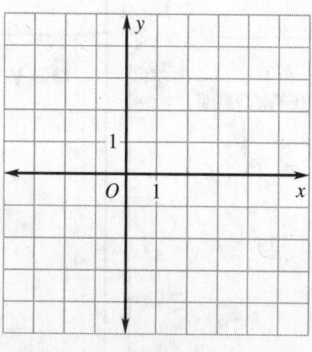

Example 3   *Find the Minimum or Maximum Value*

Tell whether the function $y = 2(x + 4)(x - 2)$ has a minimum value or a maximum value. Then find the minimum or maximum value.

Solution

The function is in _____ $y = a(x - p)(x - q)$ where $a =$ ___, $p =$ _____, and $q =$ ___ . Because a ___ 0, the function has a _____ value. Find the y-coordinate of the vertex.

$$x = \frac{p + q}{2} = \underline{\hspace{2cm}} = \underline{\hspace{1cm}}$$

$$y = \underline{\hspace{1cm}}(\underline{\hspace{1.5cm}} + 4)(\underline{\hspace{1.5cm}} - 2) = \underline{\hspace{1.5cm}}$$

The _____ value of the function is _____ .

✔ *Checkpoint* **Tell whether the function has a minimum or maximum value. Find the minimum or maximum value of the functions.**

3. $y = -(x + 6)(x - 2)$

4. $y = 3(x - 1)(x - 5)$

5. $y = 4(x - 3)^2 + 4$

5.3 Factoring $x^2 + bx + c$

Goal • Factor trinomials of the form $x^2 + bx + c$.

VOCABULARY

Trinomial

Quadratic equation

Example 1 *Factor $x^2 + bx + c$ when c is Positive*

Factor $x^2 - 7x + 6$.

Solution

You want $x^2 - 7x + 6 = (x + m)(x + n)$ where $mn =$ ___ and $m + n =$ ____. When mn is _____, m and n must have the _____ sign. Since, $mn =$ ___, find the factors of ___ that have a sum of _____.

Factors of 6: m, n	1, __	−1, ___	2, __	−2, ____
Sum of factors: $m + n$	__	____	__	____

Notice that $m =$ _____ and $n =$ _____. So, $x^2 - 7x + 6 =$ (_____)(_____). Check your answer by multiplying.

Example 2 *Factor $x^2 + bx + c$ when c is Negative*

Factor $x^2 + 3x - 10$.

Solution

You want $x^2 + 3x - 10 = (x + m)(x + n)$ where $mn =$ _____ and $m + n =$ ___. When mn is _____, m and n must have _____ signs. Since, $mn =$ _____, find the factors of _____ that have a sum of ___.

Factors of −10: m, n	1, _____	−1, ____	2, ____	−2, ____
Sum of factors: $m + n$	____	__	____	__

Notice that $m =$ _____ and $n =$ ___. So, $x^2 + 3x - 10 =$ (_____)(_____). Check your answer by multiplying.

✓ *Checkpoint* **Factor the expression.**

1. $x^2 + 8x + 15$	**2.** $x^2 - 7x + 12$
3. $x^2 + 11x - 12$	**4.** $x^2 - 3x - 4$

ZERO PRODUCT PROPERTY

Words   When the _____ of two expressions
is _____, then at least _____ of the
expressions must equal zero.

Algebra   Let A and B be expressions.
If $AB = $ ____, then $A = $ ____ or $B = $ ____.

Example   If $(x + 9)(x + 3) = 0$, then $x + 9 = $ ____ or
$x + 3 = $ ____.

Example 3   *Solve a Quadratic Equation by Factoring*

Solve the equation $x^2 + 9x + 20 = 0$.

Solution

$x^2 + 9x + 20 = 0$ **Original equation**

(_____)(_____) = 0   **Factor.**

_____ = 0 or _____ = 0   **Zero product property**

$x = $ ____ $x = $ ____   **Solve for** x.

The solutions are ____ and ____.

| Example 4 | *Solve a Quadratic Equation by Factoring* |

Solve the equation $x^2 + 9x = -8$.

Solution

$$x^2 + 9x = -8 \qquad \text{Original equation}$$

$$x^2 + 9x + 8 = 0 \qquad \text{Standard form}$$

$$(\underline{\hspace{1cm}})(\underline{\hspace{1cm}}) = 0 \qquad \text{Factor.}$$

$$\underline{\hspace{1.5cm}} = 0 \quad \text{or} \quad \underline{\hspace{1.5cm}} = 0 \qquad \text{Zero product property}$$

$$x = \underline{\hspace{0.8cm}} \qquad\qquad x = \underline{\hspace{0.8cm}} \qquad \text{Solve for } x.$$

The solutions are _____ and _____.

✔ **Checkpoint** **Solve the equation.**

5. $x^2 + 13x + 12 = 0$

6. $y^2 - 5y = 14$

Homework

7. $x^2 - 3 = 2x$

5.4 Factoring $ax^2 + bx + c$

Goal • Factor trinomials of the form $ax^2 + bx + c$.

VOCABULARY

Zero of a function

Example 1 *Factor $ax^2 + bx + c$ when c is Positive*

Factor $2x^2 + 23x + 11$.

Solution

You want $2x^2 + 23x + 11 = (kx + m)(jx + n)$ where $kj = $ ____ and $mn = $ ____. Because mn is _____, m and n have the _____ sign.

Factors of 2: k, j	Factors of 11: m, n	$(kx + m)(jx + n)$	$ax^2 + bx + c$
1, 2	1, ___	$(x + 1)($_____$)$	_____
1, 2	11, ___	$(x + 11)($_____$)$	_____

$2x^2 + 23x + 11 = ($_____$)($_____$)$

✔ *Checkpoint* **Factor the expression.**

1. $2x^2 + 15x + 7$	**2.** $3x^2 + 5x + 2$

Example 2   *Factor ax² + bx + c when c is Negative*

Factor 6x² + x − 5.

Solution

You want $6x^2 + x - 5 = (kx + m)(jx + n)$ where $kj =$ ___
and $mn =$ ___ . Because mn is _____, m and n
have _____ signs.

Factors of 6: k, j	Factors of −5: m, n	(kx + m)(jx + n)	ax² + bx + c
2, 3	1, ___	(2x + 1)(_____)	_____
2, 3	−1, ___	(2x − 1)(_____)	_____
2, 3	5, ___	(2x + 5)(_____)	_____
2, 3	−5, ___	(2x − 5)(_____)	_____
1, 6	1, ___	(x + 1)(_____)	_____
1, 6	−1, ___	(x − 1)(_____)	_____
1, 6	5, ___	(x + 5)(_____)	_____
1, 6	−5, ___	(x − 5)(_____)	_____

$6x^2 + x - 5 = ($_____$)($_____$)$

Example 3   *Factor Out a Common Constant*

Factor 8x² + 28x + 12.

Solution

The coefficients of $8x^2 + 28x + 12$ have a common
factor of ___ . Factor out ___ .

___(___x² + 7x + ___)

Now factor ___(___x² + ___x + ___). You want
$2x^2 + 7x + 3 = (kx + m)(jx + n)$ where $kj =$ ___ and
$mn =$ ___ . Because mn is _____, m and n have
the _____ sign.

Factors of 2: k, j	Factors of 3: m, n	(kx + m)(jx + n)	ax² + bx + c
1, 2	1, ___	(x + 1)(_____)	_____
1, 2	3, ___	(x + 3)(_____)	_____

$8x^2 + 28x + 12 = $ ___$($_____$)($_____$)$

✓ *Checkpoint* **Factor the expression.**

3. $4x^2 + 6x + 2$	4. $7x^2 - 8x + 1$	5. $3x^2 + 18x + 15$

Example 4   *Find the Zeros of a Quadratic Function*

Find the zeros of $y = x^2 + 2x - 8$.

Solution

To find the zeros of the function, let $y = 0$. Solve for x.

$y = x^2 + 2x - 8$	**Write original function.**
$0 = x^2 + 2x - 8$	**Let $y = 0$.**
$0 = (\underline{\hspace{1cm}})(\underline{\hspace{1cm}})$	**Factor the right side.**
$\underline{\hspace{1cm}} = 0$ or $\underline{\hspace{1cm}} = 0$	**Use the zero product property.**
$x = \underline{\hspace{1cm}}$ $x = \underline{\hspace{0.5cm}}$	**Solve for x.**

The zeros of the function are
_____ and ___.

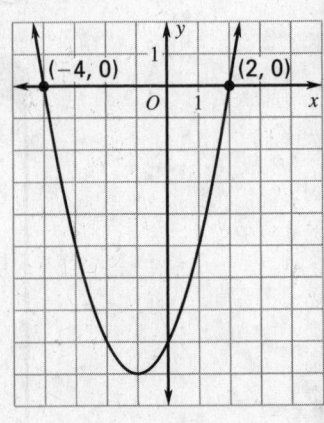

The zeros of the function are
also the *x*-intercepts of the graph
of the function. So the answer
can be checked by graphing
$y = x^2 + 2x - 8$. The *x*-intercepts
of the graph are _____ and ___,
so the answer is correct.

✓ *Checkpoint* **Find the zeros of the function.**

Homework	6. $y = 2x^2 + x - 3$	7. $y = 3x^2 + x - 10$

5.5 Factoring Using Special Patterns

Goal • Factor using special patterns.

VOCABULARY

Trinomial _____

DIFFERENCE OF TWO SQUARES PATTERN

Algebra $a^2 - b^2 = (\underline{} + \underline{})(\underline{} - \underline{})$

Example $x^2 - 9 = (\underline{} + \underline{})(\underline{} - \underline{})$

Example 1 *Factor a Difference of Two Squares*

Factor the expression.

a. $x^2 - 16$ b. $p^2 - 144$ c. $4y^2 - 81$

Solution

a. $x^2 - 16 = x^2 - \underline{}^2$ Write as $a^2 - b^2$.

  $= (\underline{} + \underline{})(\underline{} - \underline{})$ Difference of two squares pattern

b. $p^2 - 144 = p^2 - \underline{}^2$ Write as $a^2 - b^2$.

  $= (\underline{} + \underline{})(\underline{} - \underline{})$ Difference of two squares pattern

c. $4y^2 - 81 = (2y)^2 - \underline{}^2$ Write as $a^2 - b^2$.

  $= (\underline{})(\underline{})$ Difference of two squares pattern

---

✔ *Checkpoint* **Factor the expression.**

1. $x^2 - 49$	2. $k^2 - 121$	3. $9m^2 - 25$

PERFECT SQUARE TRINOMIAL PATTERNS

Algebra	Example
$a^2 + 2ab + b^2$	$x^2 + 12x + 36$
$= (\underline{} + \underline{})^2$	$= (\underline{} + \underline{})^2$
$a^2 - 2ab + b^2$	$x^2 - 6x + 9$
$= (\underline{} - \underline{})^2$	$= (\underline{} - \underline{})^2$

Example 2 *Factor a Perfect Square Trinomial*

Factor the expression.

a. $h^2 + 20h + 100$
b. $16g^2 + 40g + 25$
c. $4w^2 - 36w + 81$

Solution

a. $h^2 + 20h + 100$

$= h^2 + 2(h)(\underline{}) + \underline{}^2$ **Write as $a^2 + 2ab + b^2$.**

$= (\underline{} + \underline{})^2$ **Perfect square trinomial**

b. $16g^2 + 40g + 25$

$= (4g)^2 + 2(4g)(\underline{}) + \underline{}^2$ **Write as $a^2 + 2ab + b^2$.**

$= (\underline{} + \underline{})^2$ **Perfect square trinomial**

c. $4w^2 - 36w + 81$

$= (2w)^2 - 2(2w)(\underline{}) + \underline{}^2$ **Write as $a^2 - 2ab + b^2$.**

$= (\underline{} - \underline{})^2$ **Perfect square trinomial**

Example 3 *Factor Out a Common Constant*

Factor $4x^2 - 32x + 64$.

Solution

$4x^2 - 32x + 64$

$= \underline{}(x^2 - \underline{}x + \underline{})$ **Factor out $\underline{}$.**

$= \underline{}[x^2 - 2(x)(\underline{}) + \underline{}^2]$ **Write as $a^2 - 2ab + b^2$.**

$= \underline{}(\underline{} - \underline{})^2$ **Perfect square trinomial**

✔ *Checkpoint* **Factor the expression.**

4. $x^2 + 26x + 169$

_____

5. $16x^2 - 8x + 1$

_____

6. $3x^2 + 12x + 12$

Example 4   *Solve a Quadratic Equation*

Solve $49x^2 + 9 = -42x$.

Solution

$49x^2 + 9 = -42x$	Write original equation.
$49x^2 + 42x + 9 = 0$	Write in standard form.
$(\underline{\quad})^2 + 2(\underline{\quad})(\underline{\quad}) + \underline{\quad}^2 = 0$	Write as $a^2 + 2ab + b^2$.
$(\underline{\quad} + \underline{\quad})^2 = 0$	Perfect square trinomial pattern
$\underline{\qquad} = 0$	Use the zero product property.
$x = \underline{\qquad}$	Solve for x.

The solution is ____ .

Homework

✔ *Checkpoint* **Solve the equation.**

7. $a^2 + 4 = 260$	**8.** $4p^2 + 44p = -121$

5.6 Solving Quadratic Equations by Finding Square Roots

Goal • Solve quadratic equations by finding square roots.

VOCABULARY

Square root
_____

Radical
_____

Radicand
_____

Rationalizing the denominator

PROPERTIES OF SQUARE ROOTS ($a > 0$, $b > 0$)

Product Property

$\sqrt{ab} =$ _____ • _____

$\sqrt{27} = \sqrt{9} \cdot$ _____ $= 3\sqrt{3}$

Quotient Property

$\sqrt{\dfrac{a}{b}} =$ _____

$\sqrt{\dfrac{5}{36}} =$ _____ $= \dfrac{\sqrt{5}}{6}$

Example 1   *Use Properties of Square Roots*

a. $\sqrt{40} =$ _____ • _____ $=$ _____

b. $\sqrt{3} \cdot \sqrt{15} =$ _____ $=$ _____ • _____ $=$ _____

c. $\sqrt{\dfrac{49}{81}} =$ ___ $=$ _____

d. $\sqrt{\dfrac{7}{144}} =$ ___ $=$ _____

Example 2 **Rationalize the Denominator of a Fraction**

Simplify $\sqrt{\dfrac{2}{3}}$.

Solution

$\sqrt{\dfrac{2}{3}} = $ _____   Quotient property of square roots

$= $ _____ $\cdot$ _____   Multiply by _____.

$= $ _____   Simplify.

✔ **Checkpoint** **Simplify the expression.**

1. $\sqrt{50}$	2. $\sqrt{6} \cdot \sqrt{10}$	3. $\sqrt{\dfrac{5}{6}}$

Example 3 **Solve a Quadratic Equation**

Solve $x^2 + 3 = 21$.

Solution

$x^2 + 3 = 21$ Write original equation.

$x^2 = $ _____   Subtract ____ from each side.

$x = \pm$ _____   Take the _____ of each side.

$x = \pm$ _____ $\cdot$ _____   Product property of square roots

$x = $ _____   Simplify.

The solutions are _____ and _____.

✅ **Checkpoint** Solve the equation.

4. $x^2 - 6 = 14$	5. $x^2 + 9 = 53$	6. $6y^2 = 72$

Example 4   *Use a Quadratic Equation as a Model*

Physics A penny is dropped from the top of a building 240 feet above the ground. How many seconds does it take for the penny to be 80 feet above the ground?

Solution

$h = -16t^2 + h_0$	Write falling object model.
$\underline{\quad} = -16t^2 + \underline{\quad}$	Substitute ____ for h and ____ for h_0.
$\underline{\qquad} = -16t^2$	Subtract ____ from each side.
$\underline{\quad} = t^2$	Divide each side by ____.
$\underline{\quad} = t^2$	Simplify.
$\underline{\quad} = t$	Take the _____ of each side.
$\underline{\quad} \approx t$	Use a calculator.

Reject the solution ____, because time must be _____. The penny falls for about ___ seconds before it is 80 feet above the ground.

✅ **Checkpoint** Complete the following exercise.

7. A bungee jumper leaps from a bridge that is 650 feet high. The jumper falls to within 10 feet of the ground. How many seconds does the jumper fall before he is snapped back up?

5.7 Complex Numbers

Goal • Understand and use complex numbers.

VOCABULARY

Imaginary unit *i*

Complex number

Imaginary number

Complex conjugates

THE SQUARE ROOT OF A NEGATIVE NUMBER

Property   **Example**

1. If *r* is a positive real   = _____
number, then $\sqrt{-r} = i\sqrt{r}$.

2. By Property (1), it follows $(i\sqrt{7})^2 = $ ____ $\cdot 7 = $ _____
that $(i\sqrt{r})^2 = -r$.

Example 1   *Solve a Quadratic Equation*

Solve the equation $8x^2 = -64$.

Solution

$8x^2 = -64$ Write original equation.

$x^2 = $ _____   Divide each side by ___.

$x = $ _____   Take the square root of each side.

$x = $ _____   Write in terms of *i*.

$x = $ _____   Simplify the radical.

Your Notes

✔ *Checkpoint* **Solve the equation.**

1. $x^2 = -15$	**2.** $2x^2 = -24$	**3.** $3x^2 + 13 = 4$

Example 2   *Add Complex Numbers*

Write $(4 + 6i) + (7 - 4i)$ as a complex number in standard form.

Solution

$(4 + 6i) + (7 - 4i)$

$= (\underline{\hspace{1.5cm}}) + (\underline{\hspace{1.5cm}})i$ **Group real and imaginary terms.**

$= \underline{\hspace{1cm}} + \underline{\hspace{1cm}}$ **Write in standard form.**

Example 3   *Subtract Complex numbers*

Write $(10 + 5i) - (3 - 6i)$ as a complex number in standard form.

Solution

$(10 + 5i) - (3 - 6i)$

$= (\underline{\hspace{1.5cm}}) + (\underline{\hspace{1.5cm}})i$ **Group real and imaginary terms.**

$= \underline{\hspace{1cm}} + \underline{\hspace{1cm}}$ **Write in standard form.**

✔ *Checkpoint* **Write the expression as a complex number in standard form.**

4. $(2 + 2i) +$ $(3 + 7i)$	**5.** $(9 - 3i) +$ $(4 - 5i)$	**6.** $(3 + 6i) -$ $(-4 + 2i)$

Example 4   *Multiply Complex Numbers*

Write $(2 + 3i)(-6 + 4i)$ as a complex number in standard form.

Solution

$(2 + 3i)(-6 + 4i)$

$= \underline{\hspace{1cm}} + \underline{\hspace{0.5cm}} i - 18i + \underline{\hspace{0.5cm}} i^2$ Multiply using \underline{\hspace{1cm}}.

$= \underline{\hspace{1cm}} - \underline{\hspace{0.5cm}} i + \underline{\hspace{0.5cm}} i^2$ Simplify.

$= \underline{\hspace{1cm}} - \underline{\hspace{0.5cm}} i + \underline{\hspace{0.5cm}} (\underline{\hspace{0.5cm}})$ Use $i^2 = \underline{\hspace{0.5cm}}$.

$= \underline{\hspace{1cm}} - \underline{\hspace{0.5cm}} i$ Write in standard form.

Example 5   *Divide Complex Numbers*

Write $\dfrac{4 + 9i}{2 + 3i}$ as a complex number in standard form.

Solution

$\dfrac{4 + 9i}{2 + 3i} = \dfrac{4 + 9i}{2 + 3i} \cdot \dfrac{2 - 3i}{2 - 3i}$ Multiply the numerator and denominator by \underline{\hspace{1cm}}, the complex conjugate of $2 + 3i$.

$= \dfrac{}{}$ Multiply using \underline{\hspace{1cm}}.

$= \dfrac{}{}$ Simplify and use $i^2 = \underline{\hspace{0.5cm}}$.

$= \dfrac{}{}$ Simplify.

$= \underline{\hspace{0.8cm}} + \underline{\hspace{0.8cm}} i$ Write in standard form.

 Checkpoint Write the expression as a complex number in standard form.

7. $4i(5 + 2i)$	**8.** $(3 + i)(6 - i)$	**9.** $\dfrac{5 + 10i}{2 + 5i}$

5.8 Completing the Square

Goal • Solve quadratic equations by completing the square.

VOCABULARY

Completing the square

COMPLETING THE SQUARE

To complete the square for $x^2 + bx$, *add* ____ .

Algebra $x^2 + bx + \underline{} = \left(x + \dfrac{b}{2}\right)\left(x + \dfrac{b}{2}\right) = \underline{}$

Example $x^2 + 16x + 8^2 = (x + \underline{})^2$

Example 1 *Complete the Square*

Find the value of c that makes $x^2 + 10x + c$ a perfect square trinomial. Write the expression as the square of a trinomial.

Solution

To find the value of c, complete the square using $b = \underline{}$.

1. Find half the coefficient of x. $\dfrac{1}{2}(\underline{}) = \underline{}$

2. Square the result of Step 1. $(\underline{})^2 = \underline{}$

3. Replace c with the result of Step 2. $x^2 + 10x + \underline{}$

The trinomial $x^2 + 10x + c$ is a perfect square trinomial when $c = \underline{}$. Then $x^2 + 10x + \underline{} = (\underline{})^2$.

✔ *Checkpoint* **Find the value of c that makes the expression a perfect square trinomial. Then write the expression as the square of a binomial.**

1. $x^2 + 18x + c$	**2.** $x^2 - 20x + c$

Example 2   *Solve a Quadratic Equation*

Solve $3x^2 + 12x + 9 = 0$ by completing the square.

Solution

$3x^2 + 12x + 9 = 0$ Write original equation.

$x^2 + \underline{\quad}x + \underline{\quad} = 0$ Divide each side by the _____ of x^2.

$x^2 + \underline{\quad}x = \underline{\quad}$ Write the left side in the form $x^2 + \underline{\quad}$.

$x^2 + \underline{\quad}x + \underline{\quad} = \underline{\quad} + \underline{\quad}$ Add $\dfrac{\quad}{\quad} = (\underline{\quad})^2 = \underline{\quad}$ to each side.

$(\underline{\qquad})^2 = \underline{\quad}$ Write the left side as the _____ of a binomial.

$\underline{\qquad} = \pm\underline{\quad}$ Take the _____ of each side.

$x = \pm\underline{\quad} - \underline{\quad}$ Subtract ___ from each side.

The solutions are _____ and _____.

✔ *Checkpoint* **Solve the equation by completing the square.**

3. $x^2 - 6x + 4 = 0$	**4.** $x^2 + 4x + 15 = 0$

Example 3 *Write a Quadratic Function in Vertex Form*

Write $y = x^2 - 8x + 20$ in vertex form.

Solution

$y = x^2 - 8x + 20$	Write original equation.
$y + ? = (x^2 - 8x + ?) + 20$	Prepare to complete the square.
$y + \underline{\quad} = (x^2 - 8x + \underline{\quad}) + 20$	Add _____ to each side.
$y + \underline{\quad} = (\underline{\qquad})^2 + 20$	Write $x^2 - 8x + \underline{\quad}$ as $(\underline{\qquad})^2$.
$y = (\underline{\qquad})^2 + \underline{\quad}$	Solve for y.

The vertex form is $y = (\underline{\qquad})^2 + \underline{\quad}$.

Example 4 *Use a Quadratic Equation to Model Area*

Landscaping An architect is planning a garden. The garden will be a rectangle with an area of 240 square feet. The architect has 64 feet of fence to use along the sides. Each side will be at least 10 feet long. What should the length and width of the garden be?

Solution

$x(32 - x) = 240$	length · width = area
$\underline{\qquad} - x^2 = 240$	Distributive property
$\underline{\qquad\qquad} = -240$	Divide each side by -1.
$x^2 - 32x + \underline{\quad} = -240 + \underline{\quad}$	Add 256 to each side.
$(\underline{\qquad})^2 = \underline{\quad}$	Write left side as a square of a binomial.
$x - \underline{\quad} = \pm\underline{\quad}$	Take the square root of each side.
$x = \underline{\quad}$ or $\underline{\quad}$	Solve for x.

The dimensions of the garden are _____ feet by _____ feet.

5.9 The Quadratic Formula and the Discriminant

Goal • Solve quadratic equations using the quadratic formula.

Your Notes

VOCABULARY

_____

Quadratic formula

_____

Discriminant

THE QUADRATIC FORMULA

Let a, b and c be _____ numbers with $a \neq 0$.
The _____ of the quadratic equation
$ax^2 + bx + c = 0$ are:

$$x = \frac{-b \pm \sqrt{b^2 - 4ac}}{2a}$$

Example 1   *Solve an Equation with Two Real Solutions*

Solve $x^2 + 4x + 3 = 0$.

Solution

$x^2 + 4x + 3 = 0$ **Write original equation.**

$x = \dfrac{-b \pm \sqrt{b^2 - 4ac}}{2a}$ **Quadratic formula**

$x = $ _____   **Substitute values in the quadratic formula: $a = $ __, $b = $ __, and $c = $ __.**

$x = $ _____   **Simplify.**

The solutions are _____ = ____ and _____ = ____.

✔ *Checkpoint* **Use the quadratic formula to solve.**

1. $x^2 + 3x - 10 = 0$	**2.** $2x^2 + 8x + 4 = 0$

Example 2   *Solve an Equation with One Real Solution*

Solve $x^2 - 12x = -36$.

Solution

$x^2 - 12x = -36$ **Original equation**

$x^2 - 12x + 36 = 0$ **Standard form**

$x = \dfrac{-b \pm \sqrt{b^2 - 4ac}}{2a}$ **Quadratic formula**

$x =$ _____   **Substitute $a =$ ___,**
                                           $b =$ _____, $c =$ ____.

$x =$ _____   **Simplify.**

$x =$ ___   **Simplify.**

The solution is ___.

Example 3   *Solve an Equation with Imaginary Solutions*

Solve $x^2 - 5x + 7 = 0$.

Solution

$x^2 - 5x + 7 = 0$ **Original equation**

$x = \dfrac{-b \pm \sqrt{b^2 - 4ac}}{2a}$ **Quadratic formula**

$x =$ _____   **Substitute $a =$ ___,**
                                           $b =$ ____, $c =$ ___.

$x =$ _____   **Simplify and rewrite using i.**

The solutions are _____ and _____.

✔ **Checkpoint** Use the quadratic formula to solve.

3. $x^2 - 8x + 10 = 0$	**4.** $x^2 + 7x + 14 = 0$

DISCRIMINANT OF A QUADRATIC EQUATION

The discriminant determines the _____ and _____ of solutions.

$b^2 - 4ac > 0$ _____ solutions

$b^2 - 4ac = 0$ _____ solution

$b^2 - 4ac < 0$ _____ solutions

Example 4   *Use the Discriminant*

Find the discriminant of the quadratic equation and give the number and type of solutions of the equation.

a. $x^2 + 12x + 15 = 0$
b. $x^2 - 24x + 144 = 0$
c. $x^2 - 3x + 9 = 0$

Solution

DISCRIMINANT	**SOLUTION TYPE(S)**
$b^2 - 4ac$	$x = \dfrac{-b \pm \sqrt{b^2 - 4ac}}{2a}$
a. (___)^2 − 4(__)(__) = ____	_____
b. (____)^2 − 4(__)(____) = __	_____
c. _____ = ____	_____

✔ **Checkpoint** Find the discriminant of the quadratic equation and give the number and type of solutions.

5. $x^2 + 6x + 1 = 0$	**6.** $x^2 - 4x + 11 = 0$

Words to Review

Use your own words and/or an example to explain the vocabulary word.

Quadratic function	Parabola
Vertex	Axis of symmetry
Monomial	Binomial
Vertex form	Intercept form
Minimum value	Maximum value
Trinomial	Quadratic equation
Zero of a function	Square root
Radical	Radicand

Rationalizing the denominator	Imaginary unit *i*
Complex number	Imaginary number
Complex conjugates	Completing the square
Quadratic formula	Discriminant

Review your notes and Chapter 5 by using the Chapter Review on pages 285–288 of your textbook.

6.1 Properties of Exponents

Goal • Use properties of exponents to evaluate and simplify expressions involving powers.

VOCABULARY

Scientific notation

PROPERTIES OF EXPONENTS

Let a and b be real numbers and m and n be integers.

	ALGEBRA	EXAMPLE
Product of Powers	$a^m \cdot a^n = a\text{---}$	$5^2 \cdot 5^4 = 5\text{---}$
Power of a Power	$(a^m)^n = a\text{---}$	$(4^5)^2 = 4\text{---} \cdot \text{---}$
Power of a Product	$(ab)^m = a\text{---}b\text{---}$	$(6 \cdot 2)^5 =$ $6\text{---} \cdot 2\text{---}$
Negative Exponent	$a^{-m} = \dfrac{}{\underline{}} , a \neq 0$	$7^{-2} = \underline{}$
Zero Exponent	$a^0 = \underline{} , a \neq 0$	$50^0 = \underline{}$
Quotient of Powers	$\dfrac{a^m}{a^n} = a\text{---} , a \neq 0$	$\dfrac{8^7}{8^5} = 8\text{---}^{-}\text{---}$
Power of a Quotient	$\left(\dfrac{a}{b}\right)^m = \dfrac{}{\underline{}} , b \neq 0$	$\left(\dfrac{9}{10}\right)^2 = \underline{}$

Example 1   *Evaluate Expressions with Negative Exponents*

$(-4)^{-3}(-4)^{-2}$

$= (-4)\underline{}$ **Product of powers property**

$= (-4)\underline{}$ **Simplify exponent.**

$= \dfrac{}{\underline{}}$ **Negative exponent property**

$= \underline{}$ **Evaluate power.**

Example 2   *Evaluate Quotients with Exponents*

Evaluate $\left(\dfrac{2^9}{2^6}\right)^2$.

Solution

$\left(\dfrac{2^9}{2^6}\right)^2 = (\underline{\quad})^2$ **Quotient of powers property**

$\qquad = \underline{\quad}$ **Power of a power property**

$\qquad = \underline{\quad}$ **Evaluate power.**

✔ *Checkpoint* **Evaluate the expression.**

1. $(4^{-1})^3$	2. $\dfrac{9^5}{9^3}$	3. $(2^5)^0$	4. $5^9 \cdot 5^{-10}$

Example 3   *Simplify Algebraic Expressions*

a. $(6y^2)^2 5y^3$

$\qquad = \underline{\qquad\qquad} \cdot 5y^3$ **Power of a product property**

$\qquad = \underline{\quad}y\underline{\quad} \cdot \underline{\quad} \cdot 5y^3$ **Power of a power property**

$\qquad = \underline{\quad}y\underline{\quad} \cdot 5y^3$ **Simplify exponent.**

$\qquad = \underline{\quad}y\underline{\quad} + \underline{\quad}$ **Product of powers property**

$\qquad = \underline{\quad}y\underline{\quad}$ **Simplify exponent.**

b. $\dfrac{x^6 y^8}{x^{-4} y^{12}} = x\underline{\qquad\qquad}y\underline{\qquad}$ **Quotient of powers property**

$\qquad = x\underline{\quad}y\underline{\quad}$ **Simplify exponents.**

$\qquad = \underline{\qquad\qquad}$ **Negative exponent property**

Your Notes

✓ **Checkpoint** Simplify the expression. Tell which properties of exponents you used.

5. $(3c)^2 c^8$	6. $\dfrac{k^{-5}}{k^{-4}m^6}$	7. $\left(\dfrac{h^0}{n^4}\right)^5$

Example 4 *Use Scientific Notation*

Astronomy The average distance from Earth to the sun is approximately 9.3×10^7 miles. The distance from Earth to the moon is approximately 2.4×10^5 miles. Estimate how many trips from Earth to the moon it would take to equal one trip from Earth to the sun.

Solution

Divide the distance to the sun by the distance to the moon.

$\dfrac{\text{Distance to sun}}{\text{Distance to moon}} = \underline{\hspace{2cm}}$ **Divide distances.**

$= \underline{\hspace{0.5cm}} \times 10\underline{\hspace{1cm}}$ **Quotient of powers property**

$= \underline{\hspace{0.5cm}} \times 10\underline{\hspace{0.5cm}}$ **Simplify exponent.**

$\approx \underline{\hspace{0.5cm}} \times 10\underline{\hspace{0.5cm}}$ **Use a calculator.**

$= \underline{\hspace{0.5cm}}$ **Simplify.**

It would take about _____ trips from Earth to the moon to equal one trip from Earth to the sun.

Homework

  Copyright © McDougal Littell/Houghton Mifflin Company

6.2 Polynomial Functions and Their Graphs

Goal • Define, graph, and use polynomial functions.

VOCABULARY

Polynomial

Standard form of a polynomial function

Leading coefficient

Degree of a polynomial

Constant term

End behavior

Example 1 *Identify Polynomial Functions*

Tell whether the function is a polynomial function. If it is, write the function in standard form. Then state its degree, type, and leading coefficient.

a. $f(x) = 8x^4 + 5x^2 - 6x^3 + 2$

b. $f(x) = 2x^2 + 5x - 3 + x^{-1}$

Solution

a. This ____ a polynomial function. Its standard form is
$f(x) =$ _____. It has degree ___, so it
is a _____ function. The leading coefficient is ___.

b. This _____ a polynomial function. The term _____
has an exponent that _____ a _____ number.

Your Notes

✓ *Checkpoint* Tell whether the function is a polynomial function. If it is, write the function in standard form. Then state its degree, type, and leading coefficient.

---

1. $f(x) = 3x^2 + 6x - 2x^3 + 9$

---

2. $f(x) = x^3 + 2x^2 - 4\sqrt{x} + 1$

END BEHAVIOR OF POLYNOMIAL FUNCTIONS

The graph of a polynomial function has the following end behavior.

Degree: even
Leading coefficient: positive

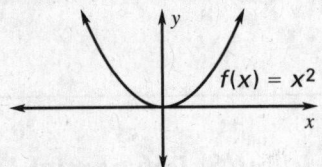

$f(x)$ approaches _____ as x approaches $+\infty$ or $-\infty$.

Degree: even
Leading coefficient: _____

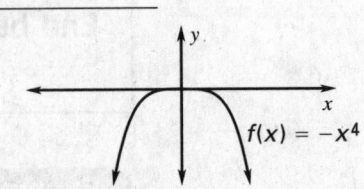

$f(x)$ approaches _____ as x approaches $+\infty$ or $-\infty$.

Degree: odd
Leading coefficient: positive

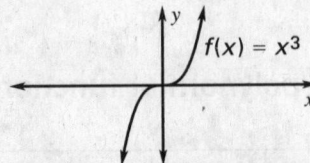

$f(x)$ approaches $-\infty$ as x approaches _____ and $f(x)$ approaches $+\infty$ as x approaches _____.

Degree: _____
Leading coefficient: _____

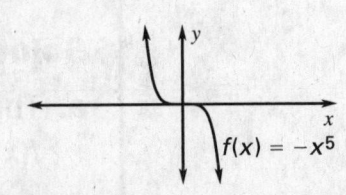

$f(x)$ approaches _____ as x approaches $-\infty$ and $f(x)$ approaches _____ as x approaches $+\infty$.

Copyright © McDougal Littell/Houghton Mifflin Compan

Example 2   *Graph Polynomial Functions*

Graph $f(x) = x^3 + 2x^2 + 3$. Use the domain $x = -3$, $-2, -1, 0, 1, 2, 3$. Then describe the end behavior of the graph.

Solution

First, make a table of values. Plot the corresponding points. Then connect the points with a smooth curve.

x	−3	−2	−1	0	1	2	3
$f(x)$	____	____	____	____	____	____	____

The degree is _____ and the leading coefficient is _____, so $f(x)$ approaches _____ as x approaches $-\infty$ and $f(x)$ approaches _____ as x approaches $+\infty$.

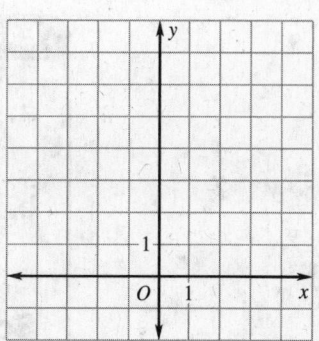

✔ *Checkpoint* Graph the function using the domain $x = -3, -2, -1, 0, 1, 2, 3$.

3. $f(x) = -3x^3 + 2x^2 + 5$	**4.** $f(x) = x^5 - 10x$

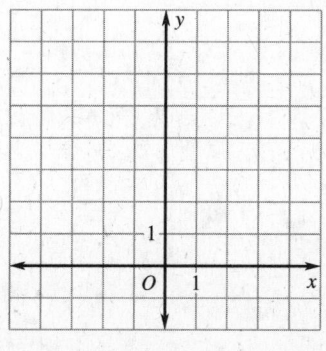

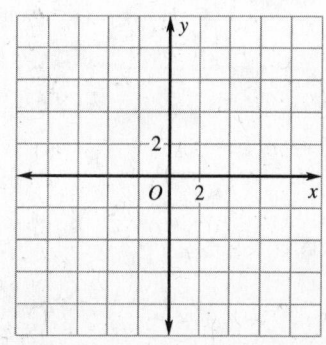

Homework

6.3 Adding and Subtracting Polynomials

Goal • Add and subtract polynomials.

Your Notes

VOCABULARY

Polynomial

Example 1 *Add Polynomials Vertically and Horizontally*

a. Add $3x^3 + 9x^2 + 4x + 7$ and $x^3 - 5x^2 + 6x - 11$ in a vertical format.

b. Add $5x^3 + 2x^2 + 10x$ and $-13x^3 - x^2 + 20x$ in a horizontal format.

Solution

a.
$$3x^3 + 9x^2 + 4x + 7$$
$$+ \quad x^3 - 5x^2 + 6x - 11$$
$$\underline{x^3 + \underline{}x^2 + \underline{}x - \underline{}}$$

b. $(5x^3 + 2x^2 + 10x) + (-13x^3 - x^2 + 20x)$

$= (\underline{}x^3 - \underline{}x^3) + (\underline{}x^2 - \underline{})$
$+ (\underline{}x + \underline{}x)$

$= \underline{}$

Example 2 — Subtract Polynomials Vertically and Horizontally

a. Subtract $5x^3 + 10x^2 + 6x + 14$ from $15x^3 + 11x^2 + 3x - 20$ in a vertical format.

b. Subtract $-8x^3 - x^2 - 25x$ from $-10x^3 - 5x^2 + 16x$ in a horizontal format.

Solution

a. Align _____, then add the _____ of the subtracted polynomial.

$$15x^3 + 11x^2 + 3x - 20$$
$$- (5x^3 + 10x^2 + 6x + 14)$$

$$15x^3 + 11x^2 + 3x - 20$$
$$+ \underline{\hspace{4cm}}$$ **Add the opposite.**
$$\underline{\hspace{4cm}}$$

b. Write the _____ of the subtracted polynomial, then _____ like terms.

$(-10x^3 - 5x^2 + 16x) - (-8x^3 - x^2 - 25x)$

$= -10x^3 - 5x^2 + 16x + \underline{\hspace{3cm}}$

$= (\underline{\hspace{2cm}}) + (\underline{\hspace{2cm}}) + (\underline{\hspace{2cm}})$

$= \underline{\hspace{4cm}}$

✓ *Checkpoint* **Simplify the expression.**

1. $7y^2 + 4y + 2 + (6y^2 - 2y + 5)$

2. $-x^3 - 12x^2 + 17x - (14x^3 + 2x^2 + 11)$

Example 3 **Use the Distributive Property**

Simplify the expression.

a. $3(2x^2 - 3x + 6) + 4(3x^2 + 7x - 8)$

$= \underline{\quad}x^2 - \underline{\quad}x + \underline{\quad\quad}$ **Distributive Property**

$\quad + \underline{\quad}x^2 + \underline{\quad}x - \underline{\quad\quad}$

$= (\underline{\quad}x^2 + \underline{\quad}x^2)$ **Group like terms.**

$\quad + (\underline{\quad}x + \underline{\quad}x)$

$\quad + (\underline{\quad\quad} - \underline{\quad\quad})$

$= \underline{\quad\quad\quad\quad\quad\quad}$ **Combine like terms.**

b. $2x^2(6x^2 - 3x) - 3(5x^3 - 11)$

$= \underline{\quad}x^4 - \underline{\quad}x^3 - \underline{\quad}x^3 + \underline{\quad}$

$= \underline{\quad}x^4 + (\underline{\quad}x^3 - \underline{\quad}x^3) + \underline{\quad}$

$= \underline{\quad\quad\quad\quad\quad\quad}$

✔ *Checkpoint* **Simplify the expression. Write the answer in standard form.**

3. $(x^2 + 13x + 7) + 6(2x^2 + 4x - 3)$

4. $2(x^2 + 2x - 5) + 3(x^2 - 8x - 1)$

5. $(10x^3 + 12x^2 + 2x + 17) - 2(3x^3 + 14x^2 - 20x)$

6. $5(2x^3 - 3x^2 + 4) - 4(x^3 - x^2 + 10)$

Homework

6.4 Multiplying and Dividing Polynomials

Goal • Multiply and divide polynomials.

VOCABULARY

Polynomial long division

Example 1 *Multiply Polynomials Vertically*

Find the product $(x^2 + 2x + 7)(x - 3)$.

Solution

$$
\begin{array}{r}
x^2 + 2x + 7 \\
\times \qquad x - 3 \\
\hline
\underline{\quad}x^2 - \underline{\quad}x - \underline{\quad} \\
\underline{\quad} + \underline{\quad}x^2 + \underline{\quad}x \qquad\qquad \\
\hline
\end{array}
$$

Multiply $x^2 + 2x + 7$ by ____.

Multiply $x^2 + 2x + 7$ by ___.

Combine like terms.

Example 2 *Multiply Polynomials Horizontally*

Find the product $(3x + 4)(2x^2 + x + 3)$.

Solution

$(3x + 4)(2x^2 + x + 3)$

$= $ ____ $(2x^2 + x + 3) + 4($ _____ $)$

$= $ ____ $+$ ____ $+$ ____ $+$ ____ $+$ ____ $+$ ____

$= $ ____ $+ ($ ____ $+$ ____ $) + ($ ___ $+$ ___ $) +$ ____

$= $ ___ $x^3 +$ ___ $x^2 +$ ___ $x +$ ____

✓ **Checkpoint** **Find the product.**

1. $(x + 9)(2x^2 + 5x - 4)$	**2.** $(x - 7)(x - 1)(x + 6)$

SPECIAL PRODUCT PATTERNS

Sum and Difference   **Example**

$(a + b)(a - b) = a^2 - b^2$ $(x + 6)(x - 6) = $ _____

Square of a Binomial   **Example**

$(a + b)^2 = a^2 + 2ab + b^2$ $(x + 5)^2$
                               $= $ _____

$(a - b)^2 = a^2 - 2ab + b^2$ $(2x - 3)^2$
                               $= $ _____

Cube of a Binomial   **Example**

$(a + b)^3 = a^3 + 3a^2b$ $(x + 3)^3 = $ ____ $+$ ____x^2
$\qquad\quad + 3ab^2 + b^3$ $+$ ___$x + $ ___

$(a - b)^3 = a^3 - 3a^2b$ $(x - 4)^3 = $ ___ $-$ ___x^2
$\qquad\quad + 3ab^2 - b^3$ $+$ ___$x - $ ___

Example 3 *Use Special Product Patterns*

Find the product.

a. $(x + 7)(x - 7)$ **b.** $(3x - 2)^2$ **c.** $(4x + 2)^3$

Solution

a. $(x + 7)(x - 7) = ($___$)^2 - $___^{2}

$\qquad\qquad\qquad = $ _____

b. $(3x - 2)^2 = ($___$)^2 - 2($____$)($___$) + $___^{2}

$\qquad\qquad\quad = $ _____

c. $(4x + 5)^3 = ($___$)^3 + 3($____$)^2($___$)$

$\qquad\qquad\qquad + 3($___$)($___$)^2 + $___^{3}

$\qquad\qquad\quad = $ _____

✓ *Checkpoint* Find the product.

3. $(y + 8)(y - 8)$	**4.** $(5h + 1)^2$	**5.** $(x - 2)^3$

Example 4   *Use Polynomial Long Division*

Find the quotient $(x^3 + 7x^2 + 7x - 11) \div (x + 5)$.

Solution

Write the division in the same format you use to divide whole numbers.

$$\dfrac{\underline{\quad} + \underline{\quad} - \underline{\quad}}{x + 5 \,\overline{)\,x^3 + 7x^2 + 7x - 11}}$$

$x^3 \div x =$ _____

$\underline{\qquad\qquad}$
$\underline{\qquad\quad}$

Subtract _____$(x + 5) =$
$\underline{\qquad\qquad}$.

$\underline{\qquad\qquad}$

Simplify and bring down $7x$.

$\underline{\qquad\qquad}$
$\underline{\qquad\qquad}$

Subtract _____$(x + 5) =$
$\underline{\qquad\qquad}$.

$\underline{\qquad\qquad}$

Simplify and bring down -11.

$\underline{\qquad\qquad}$
$\underline{\qquad\qquad}$

Subtract _____$(x + 5) =$
$\underline{\qquad\qquad}$.

$\underline{\qquad}$ **Remainder**

> You can check your result by multiplying the divisor by the quotient.

The result is written as $\underline{\qquad\qquad\qquad\qquad}$.

✓ *Checkpoint* Use long division to find the quotient.

6. $(3x^3 + 15x^2 - 14x - 29) \div (x + 6)$

Homework

6.5 Factoring Cubic Polynomials

Goal • Factor cubic polynomials and solve cubic equations.

Your Notes

> ### VOCABULARY
>
> Factor by grouping

> ### SPECIAL PRODUCT PATTERNS
>
> **Sum of Two Cubes**   **Example**
>
> $a^3 + b^3$ $x^3 + 27 =$
> $= (a + b)(a^2 - ab + b)$ $(x + 3)(\underline{\hspace{3cm}})$
>
> **Difference of Two Cubes**   **Example**
>
> $a^3 - b^3$ $64x^3 - 1 =$
> $= (a - b)(a^2 + ab + b)$ $(4x - 1)(\underline{\hspace{3cm}})$

> **Example 1**   *Factor the Sum or Difference of Two Cubes*
>
> **a.** Factor $x^3 + 125$.   **b.** Factor $343x^3 - 216$.
>
> **Solution**
>
> **a.** $x^3 + 125 = x^3 + \underline{}^3$
>
> $ = (x + \underline{})(\underline{} - \underline{} + \underline{})$
>
> $ = (x + \underline{})(\underline{\hspace{3cm}})$
>
> **b.** $343x^3 - 216 = (\underline{}x)^3 - (\underline{})^3$
>
> $ = (\underline{} - \underline{})[(\underline{})^2 + \underline{}(\underline{}) + \underline{}^2]$
>
> $ = (\underline{} - \underline{})(\underline{\hspace{3cm}})$

✔ *Checkpoint* Factor the polynomial.

1. $x^3 + 512$	**2.** $x^3 - h^3$

Example 2   Factor Polynomials

a. Factor $x^3 + 2x^2 - 8x$.   **b.** Factor $8x^3 + 64$.

Solution

a. $x^3 + 2x^2 - 8x$	Factor common
$= x(\underline{\hspace{2.5cm}})$	monomial.
$= x(\underline{\hspace{1.2cm}})(\underline{\hspace{1.2cm}})$	Factor trinomial.
b. $8x^3 + 64$	Factor common
$= 8(\underline{\hspace{1.5cm}})$	monomial.
$= 8(\underline{\hspace{1.2cm}})(\underline{\hspace{2.5cm}})$	Use special product pattern.

✓ *Checkpoint* **Factor the polynomial.**

3. $2x^3 + 6x^2 - 36x$	**4.** $9x^4 + 72x$

Example 3   Factor by Grouping

Factor the polynomial $x^3 - 3x^2 - 36x + 108$.

Solution

$x^3 - 3x^2 - 36x + 108$	
$= (\underline{\hspace{2cm}}) + (\underline{\hspace{2.5cm}})$	Group terms.
$= x^2(\underline{\hspace{1.5cm}}) + (-36)(\underline{\hspace{1.5cm}})$	Factor each group.
$= (x^2 - 36)(\underline{\hspace{1.5cm}})$	Distributive property
$= (\underline{\hspace{1.2cm}})(\underline{\hspace{1.2cm}})(\underline{\hspace{1.2cm}})$	Difference of two squares

✓ *Checkpoint* **Factor the polynomial by grouping.**

5. $x^2(x - 10) - 49(x - 10)$	**6.** $x^3 - 3x^2 - 81x + 243$

Example 4   *Solve a Cubic Equation by Factoring*

Solve $4x^3 - 36x^2 = -80x$.

Solution

$$4x^3 - 36x^2 = -80x$$ Write original equation.

_____ $= 0$ Rewrite in standard form.

____(_____) $= 0$ Factor common monomial.

____(_____)(_____) $= 0$ Factor trinomial.

____ $= 0$ or   _____ $= 0$
or _____ $= 0$ Use zero product property.

$x =$ ___ , $x =$ ___ , $x =$ ___   Solve for x.

The solutions are ___ , ___ , and ___ .

Example 5   *Solve a Cubic Equation by Factoring*

Solve $x^3 - 7x^2 + 35 = 5x$.

Solution

$$x^3 - 7x^2 + 35 = 5x$$ Write original equation.

_____ $= 0$ Rewrite in standard form.

(_____) + (_____) $= 0$ Group terms.

x^2(_____) + (-5)(_____) $= 0$ Factor each group.

(_____)(_____) $= 0$ Use distributive property.

_____ $= 0$ or   _____ $= 0$ Use zero product property.

$x =$ _____ , $x =$ _____ , $x =$ ___   Solve for x.

The solutions are _____ , _____ , and ___ .

Homework

6.6 Polynomials of Greater Degree

Goal • Factor polynomials and solve polynomial equations of degree greater than three.

VOCABULARY

Quadratic form

Repeated solution

Example 1   *Factor a Common Monomial*

Factor $81x^5 - 3x^2$.

Solution

$81x^5 - 3x^2$

$= \underline{\quad}(\underline{\quad} - \underline{\quad})$ **Factor common** _____.

$= \underline{\quad}[(\underline{\quad})^3 - \underline{\quad}^3]$ **Write as difference of two** _____.

$= \underline{\quad}(\underline{\quad\quad})(\underline{\quad\quad\quad})$ **Use special product pattern.**

Example 2   *Factor Polynomials in Quadratic Form*

Factor the polynomial.

a. $x^4 - 625$ b. $9x^6 - 18x^4 - 27x^2$

Solution

a. $x^4 - 625$

$= (\underline{\quad})^2 - \underline{\quad}^2$ **Write as difference of two squares;** $u = $ ____.

$= (\underline{\quad} + \underline{\quad})(\underline{\quad} - \underline{\quad})$ **Factor difference of two** _____.

$= (\underline{\quad} + \underline{\quad})(\underline{\quad} + \underline{\quad})(\underline{\quad} - \underline{\quad})$

---

b. $9x^6 - 18x^4 - 27x^2$

$= \underline{\hspace{1cm}}(\underline{\hspace{3cm}})$ **Factor common monomial;** $u = \underline{\hspace{1cm}}$.

$= \underline{\hspace{1cm}}(\underline{\hspace{0.6cm}} - \underline{\hspace{0.6cm}})(\underline{\hspace{0.6cm}} + \underline{\hspace{0.6cm}})$

✅ *Checkpoint* **Factor the polynomial.**

1. $64x^5 - x^2$	**2.** $3x^6 - 9x^4 - 30x^2$

Example 3   *Factor a Polynomial*

Factor $5x^6 - 80x^4 + 315x^2$.

Solution

$5x^6 - 80x^4 + 315x^2$

$= \underline{\hspace{1cm}}(\underline{\hspace{3cm}})$ **Factor common** $\underline{\hspace{2cm}}$.

$= \underline{\hspace{1cm}}(\underline{\hspace{0.6cm}} - \underline{\hspace{0.6cm}})(\underline{\hspace{0.6cm}} - \underline{\hspace{0.6cm}})$ **Factor trinomial.**

$= \underline{\hspace{1cm}}(\underline{\hspace{0.6cm}} - \underline{\hspace{0.6cm}})(\underline{\hspace{0.6cm}} + \underline{\hspace{0.6cm}})(\underline{\hspace{0.6cm}} - \underline{\hspace{0.6cm}})$

Example 4 Solve a Polynomial Equation

Solve the polynomial equation.

a. $4x^5 + 80x = 36x^3$ **b.** $x^5 + 6x^4 + 7x^3 = 0$

Solution

a. $4x^5 + 80x = 36x^3$ Write original
                                                    equation.

          _____ = 0   Rewrite in
                                     standard form.

          ____(_____) = 0   Factor common
                                           _____.

          ____(_____)(_____) = 0   Factor trinomial.

     ___(_____)(_____)(_____) = 0   Factor difference
                                           of two _____.

     $x =$ ___, $x =$ ____, $x =$ _____,   Zero product
     $x =$ ___, $x =$ ____   property

The solutions are ___, ____, _____, ___, **and** _____.

b. $x^5 + 6x^4 + 7x^3 = 0$

     ____(_____) = 0   Factor common
                                      _____.

     ___ = 0 or _____ = 0   Zero product property

     $x =$ Substitute $a =$ ___,
     _____ $b =$ ___, and $c =$ ___.

     $x =$ Simplify.
     _____

     $x =$
     _____

     $x =$
     _____

     $x =$ _____

The solutions are ___, _____, **and** _____.

✔ *Checkpoint* **Complete the following exercises.**

3. Factor $x^6 - 62x^4 - 128x^2$.	**4.** Solve $x^4 + 3x^3 + 9x^2 = 0$.

THE FUNDAMENTAL THEOREM OF ALGEBRA

Theorem If $f(x)$ is a polynomial of _____ n where n ___ 0, then the equation $f(x) = 0$ has at least _____ root in the set of _____ numbers.

Corollary If $f(x)$ is a polynomial of _____ n where n ___ 0, then the equation $f(x) = 0$ has exactly ____ solutions provided each _____ solution is counted individually.

Example 5 *Approximate Real Zeros*

Use a graphing calculator to approximate the real zeros of the function $f(x) = -2x^4 - 3x^3 + 2x^2 - x + 5$.

Solution

One way to approximate real zeros is to use the _____ (or _____) feature of a graphing calculator.

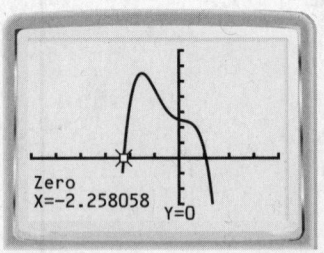

From these screens, you can see that the real zeros are about _____ and _____. By the corollary to the fundamental theorem of algebra, this function also has _____ imaginary roots.

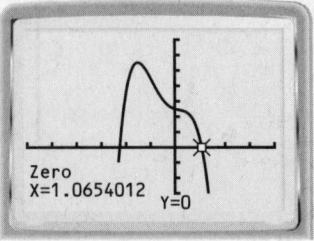

Homework

6.7 Modeling with Polynomial Functions

Goal • Use polynomial functions to model finding a maximum or minimum value in real-life situations.

VOCABULARY

Local maximum _____

_____

Local minimum _____

TURNING POINTS OF POLYNOMIAL FUNCTIONS

The graph of every _____ function of degree *n* has at most _____ turning points.

If a _____ function of degree *n* has *n* _____ real zeros, then its graph has exactly _____ turning points.

Example 1   *Find the Number of Turning Points*

Find the number of turning points for the function $f(x) = x(x - 5)(x + 4)$.

Solution

Rewrite the function $f(x) = x(x - 5)(x + 4)$ as $f(x) = $ _____.

The function has a degree ____, so it can have at most ____ − 1 = ____ turning points. The factored form of the function shows that it has _____ distinct real zeros. So, the function has exactly ____ − 1 = ____ turning points.

Lesson 6.7 • **Algebra 2 C&S Notetaking Guide**

Your Notes

✓ **Checkpoint** Find the exact or maximum number of turning points for the function. Label each number as *exact* or *maximum*.

1. $f(x) = (x^2 - 5)(x + 10)$	**2.** $f(x) = x(x - 8)(x + 14)$

Example 2 **Find Turning Points**

Graph the function $f(x) = x^3 - 2x^2 - 5x + 6$. Identify the *x*-intercepts and the coordinates where the local maximums and local minimums occur.

Solution

Use a graphing calculator to graph the function. Notice that the graph has _____ *x*-intercepts and _____ turning points. Use the graphing calculator's *Zero*, *Maximum*, and *Minimum* features to approximate the *x*-intercepts and the _____ of the local maximum and local minimum.

x-intercepts

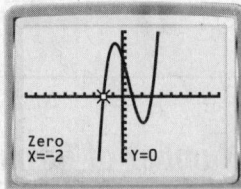 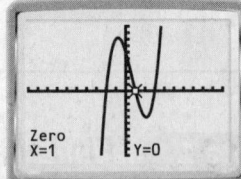 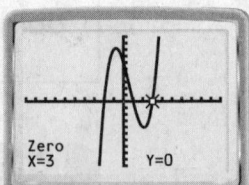

turning points

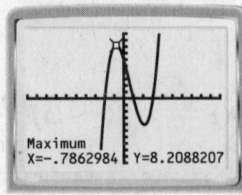 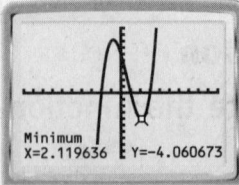

The *x*-intercepts of the graph are $x =$ _____, $x =$ ___, and $x =$ ___. The function has a local maximum at about (_____, _____) and a local minimum at about (_____, _____).

Example 3 *Maximize a Polynomial Model*

Manufacturing Open boxes are being designed to hold mail for the post office. The boxes will be made to have the greatest possible volume.

Each box will be made from a sheet of metal that measures 15 inches by 12 inches. They will be formed by cutting and removing a square from each corner. The sides will then be folded up and welded together along each corner.

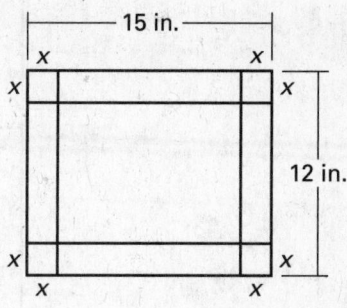

Solution

Verbal Model | Volume | = | Length | · | Width | · | |

Labels   Volume = V Length = 15 − ____

          Width = 12 − ____   Height = ___

Algebraic Model

$V = (15 − $ ____ $)(12 − $ ____ $)$ ___   Write volume equation.

$= ($ _____ $)$ ___   Multiply binomials.

$=$ _____   Distributive property

To find the maximum volume, graph the volume function on a graphing calculator.

Use the *Maximum* feature. Look at the interval $0 < x <$ ___, since ___ inches is the longest possible length for a corner square.

From the graph, you can see that the maximum volume is about _____ cubic inches. It occurs when $x \approx$ _____.

The corner cutouts should be approximately ____ inches square. The dimensions of the finished box will be $x =$ ____ inches by $12 − 2($ ____ $) =$ ____ inches by $15 − 2($ ____ $) =$ _____ inches.

Words to Review

Use your own words and/or an example to explain the vocabulary word.

Scientific notation	Polynomial
Standard form of a polynomial function	Leading coefficient
Degree of a polynomial	Constant term
End behavior	Polynomial long division
Factor by grouping	Quadratic form
Repeated solution	Local maximum
Local minimum	

Review your notes and Chapter 6 by using the Chapter Review on pages 341–344 of your textbook.

*n*th Roots and Rational Exponents

Goal • Evaluate *n*th roots of real numbers.

Your Notes

VOCABULARY

*n*th root of *a*

_____

Index of a radical

NUMBER OF REAL *n*th ROOTS

Let *n* be an integer, (*n* > 1) and let *a* be a real number.

If *n* is an even integer:

- *a* < 0   No real *n*th roots.

- *a* = 0   One real *n*th root:
  $\sqrt[n]{0} =$ ___

- *a* > 0   Two real *n*th roots:
  $\pm\sqrt[n]{a} =$ _____

If *n* is an odd integer:

- *a* < 0   One real *n*th root:
  $\sqrt[n]{a} =$ _____

- *a* = 0   One real *n*th root:
  $\sqrt[n]{0} =$ ___

- *a* > 0   One real *n*th root:
  $\sqrt[n]{a} =$ _____

Example 1   *Find nth Root(s)*

Find the indicated *n*th root(s) of *a*.

a. *n* = 3, *a* = −27   **b.** *n* = 6, *a* = 729

Solution

a. Because *n* = 3 is odd and *a* = −27 ___ 0, −27 has one real _____ root. Because (____)³ = −27, you can write $\sqrt[3]{-27} =$ ____.

b. Because *n* = 6 is even and *a* = 729 ___ 0, 729 has two real _____ roots. Because ___⁶ = 729 and (____)⁶ = 729, you can write $\pm\sqrt[6]{729} =$ ____.

Your Notes

Example 2 — Solve Equations Using nth Roots

Solve the equation.

a. $2x^6 = 1458$ b. $(x - 4)^3 = 64$

Solution

a. $2x^6 = 1458$

$x^6 = $ _____

$x = $ _____

$x = $ _____

b. $(x - 4)^3 = 64$

$x - 4 = \sqrt[3]{64}$

$x - 4 = $ ___

$x = $ ___

✔ **Checkpoint** Find the indicated nth root(s) of a.

1. $n = 4$, $a = 625$	2. $n = 3$, $a = 512$

Solve the equation.

3. $3x^5 = 729$	4. $(x + 6)^4 = 256$

Example 3 — Evaluate Expressions with Rational Exponents

Evaluate the expression.

a. $8^{1/3}$ b. $64^{1/2}$

c. $(-1024)^{1/5}$ d. $(-16)^{1/4}$

Solution

a. $8^{1/3} = \sqrt[3]{8} = $ ___

b. $64^{1/2} = \sqrt{64} = $ ___

c. $(-1024)^{1/5} = \sqrt[5]{-1024} = $ _____

d. $(-16)^{1/4} = $ _____ , no real solution

Copyright © McDougal Littell/Houghton Mifflin Compa

RATIONAL EXPONENTS

Let $a^{1/n}$ be an nth _____ of a ($a > 0$ and $a \neq 1$), and let m be a _____ integer.

$$a^{m/n} = (a^{1/n})^m = (\underline{})^m$$

$$a^{-m/n} = \frac{1}{a^{m/n}} = \frac{1}{(a^{1/n})\underline{}} = \underline{}$$

Example 4   *Rewrite Expressions*

a. Rewrite $\left(\sqrt[3]{7}\right)^4$ using rational exponents.

b. Rewrite $9^{-3/5}$ using radicals.

a. $\left(\sqrt[3]{7}\right)^4 = (7^{1/\underline{}})\underline{} = \underline{}$

b. $9^{-3/5} = \dfrac{1}{9^{3/5}} = \dfrac{1}{(9^{1/5})^3} = \underline{}$

Example 5   *Evaluate Expressions with Rational Exponents*

a. Evaluate $32^{-2/5}$.   b. Evaluate $8^{4/3}$.

a. $32^{-2/5} = \underline{} = \dfrac{1}{(\sqrt[5]{32})^2} = \dfrac{1}{2^2} = \underline{}$

b. $8^{4/3} = \underline{} = 2^4 = \underline{}$

✔ *Checkpoint* **Rewrite the expression.**

5. $\dfrac{1}{(\sqrt[3]{7})^8}$	6. $5^{4/9}$

Evaluate the expression.

7. $(-125)^{-2/3}$	8. $16^{3/2}$

7.2 Properties of Rational Exponents

Goal • Use properties of radicals and rational exponents.

Your Notes

VOCABULARY

Simplest form of a radical

Like radicals

PRODUCT AND QUOTIENT PROPERTIES OF RADICALS

Product Property $\qquad \sqrt[n]{a \cdot b} = $ _____ • _____

Quotient Property $\qquad \sqrt[n]{\dfrac{a}{b}} = $ _____

Example 1 **Use Properties of Radicals**

Use the properties of radicals to simplify the expression.

a. $\sqrt[5]{27} \cdot \sqrt[5]{9} = \sqrt[5]{27 \cdot 9}$ **Product property**

$\qquad\qquad = \underline{\hspace{3cm}} = $ ___

b. $\dfrac{\sqrt[3]{192}}{\sqrt[3]{3}} = \underline{\hspace{2cm}} = \sqrt[3]{64} = $ ___   **Quotient property**

Example 2 **Write Radicals in Simplest Form**

Write $\sqrt[5]{128}$ in simplest form.

$\sqrt[5]{128} = \underline{\hspace{3cm}}$ **Factor out perfect fifth power.**

$\qquad = \underline{\hspace{2cm}} \cdot \sqrt[5]{4}$ **Product property of radicals**

$\qquad = \underline{\hspace{1cm}} \sqrt[5]{4}$ **Simplify.**

144 Lesson 7.2 • **Algebra 2 C&S Notetaking Guide**   Copyright © McDougal Littell/Houghton Mifflin Compan

PROPERTIES OF RATIONAL EXPONENTS

Let a and b be _____ real numbers. Let m and n be _____ numbers.

PROPERTY	EXAMPLE
1. $a^m \cdot a^n = a^{m+n}$	$4^{1/2} \cdot 4^{3/2} = 4^{(\underline{} + \underline{})}$ $= 4^2 = \underline{}$
2. $(a^m)^n = a^{mn}$	$(2^{5/2})^2 = 2^{(\underline{} \cdot \underline{})}$ $= 2^5 = \underline{}$
3. $(ab)^m = a^m b^n$	$(16 \cdot 4)^{1/2} = \underline{}^{1/2} \cdot \underline{}^{1/2}$ $= \underline{} \cdot \underline{} = \underline{}$
4. $a^{-m} = \dfrac{1}{a^m}, a \neq 0$	$25^{-1/2} = \underline{} = \underline{}$
5. $\dfrac{a^m}{a^n} = a^{m-n}, a \neq 0$	$\dfrac{3^{5/2}}{3^{1/2}} = 3^{(\underline{} - \underline{})} = 3^2 = \underline{}$
6. $\left(\dfrac{a}{b}\right)^m = \dfrac{a^m}{b^m}, b \neq 0$	$\left(\dfrac{27}{8}\right)^{1/3} = \underline{} = \underline{}$

Example 3 — Use Properties of Rational Exponents

Simplify the expression.

a. $9^{1/2} \cdot 9^{1/4} = 9^{(\underline{})} = 9^{\underline{}}$

b. $(7^{2/3})^3 = 7^{(\underline{})} = 7^{\underline{}} = \underline{}$

c. $\left(\dfrac{16}{625}\right)^{1/4} = \underline{} = \underline{}$

d. $81^{-1/4} = \underline{} = \underline{}$

e. $\dfrac{3^{5/6}}{3^{1/3}} = 3^{(\underline{})} = 3^{3/6} = 3^{\underline{}} = \underline{}$

Example 4 — Add or Subtract Like Radicals

Perform the indicated operation.

a. $6\sqrt[4]{5} + 8\sqrt[4]{5} = (\underline{})\sqrt[4]{5} = \underline{}\sqrt[4]{5}$

b. $12(4^{3/5}) - 5(4^{3/5}) = (\underline{})4^{3/5} = \underline{}(4^{3/5})$

✓ **Checkpoint** Simplify the expression.

1. $\dfrac{\sqrt{245}}{\sqrt{5}}$	2. $\sqrt[3]{6} \cdot \sqrt[3]{36}$
3. $\sqrt[3]{250}$	4. $14(4^{2/3}) - 12(4^{2/3})$

Example 5　*Simplify Expressions with Variables*

Simplify the expression. Write the answer using positive exponents only. Assume all variables are positive.

a. $\sqrt[5]{32x^{15}} =$ _____　　**Factor out perfect fifth powers.**

　　　　$=$ _____　　**Simplify.**

b. $(36m^4n^{10})^{1/2}$

　　$= 36$___(m^4)___(n^{10})___　　**Power of a product property**

　　$= 36$___$m^{(\underline{\hspace{1cm}})}n^{(\underline{\hspace{1cm}})}$　　**Power of a power property**

　　$=$ _____　　**Simplify.**

c. $\sqrt[3]{\dfrac{a^9}{b^6}} =$　　**Factor out perfect cube powers.**

　　　　_____

　　$=$　　**Simplify.**

　　____

d. $\dfrac{42x^{3/2}z^7}{6x^4y^{-3}z^5}$

　　$= \dfrac{42}{6}x^{(\underline{\hspace{1.5cm}})}y^{[0 - \underline{\hspace{1cm}}]}z^{(\underline{\hspace{1cm}})}$　　**Quotient of powers property**

　　$= 7x$___y___z___ $=$　　**Simplify.**

　　　　　　　　____

Example 6 **Add/Subtract Expressions with Variables**

Simplify the expression. Assume all variables are positive.

a. $10\sqrt[5]{y} - 6\sqrt[5]{y}$

b. $3a^2b^{1/4} + 4a^2b^{1/4}$

Solution

a. $10\sqrt[5]{y} - 6\sqrt[5]{y} = ($_____$)\sqrt[5]{y}$

$= $___$\sqrt[5]{y}$

b. $3a^2b^{1/4} + 4a^2b^{1/4} = ($_____$)a^2b^{1/4}$

$= $_____

✔ *Checkpoint* Simplify the expression. Write your answer using positive exponents only. Assume all variables are positive.

5. $\sqrt[3]{8x^7y^3z^{11}}$	6. $\dfrac{c^5d^{1/2}}{4cd^{5/2}}$

Simplify the expression. Assume all variables are positive.

7. $9\sqrt[7]{5y^4} + 16\sqrt[7]{5y^4}$	8. $8k^{5/9} - 7k^{5/9}$

Homework

7.3 Solving Radical Equations

Goal • Solve equations that contain radicals or rational exponents.

Your Notes

VOCABULARY

Radical equation _____

_____

Extraneous solution

SOLVING RADICAL EQUATIONS

To solve a radical equation, follow these steps:

Step 1 Isolate the radical on _____ of the equation, if necessary.

Step 2 Raise each side of the equation to the same _____ to eliminate the radical.

Step 3 Solve the resulting _____ using techniques that you learned in previous chapters.

Step 4 Check your solution.

Example 1   Solve a Radical Equation

Solve $\sqrt{x} + 6 = 3$.

Solution

$$\sqrt{x} + 6 = 3$$ Write original equation.

$$\underline{} = \underline{}$$ Square each side to eliminate the radical.

$$\underline{} = \underline{}$$ Simplify.

$$x = \underline{}$$ Subtract ____ from each side.

Example 2   *Solve an Equation with Two Radicals*

Solve $\sqrt{2x+1} - \sqrt{10-x} = 0$.

Solution

$$\sqrt{2x+1} - \sqrt{10-x} = 0$$ Original equation

$$\sqrt{2x+1} = \sqrt{10-x}$$ Add _____ to each side.

$$\underline{\hspace{2cm}} = (\sqrt{10-x})^2$$ Square each side.

$$\underline{\hspace{1.5cm}} = \underline{\hspace{1.5cm}}$$ Simplify.

$$2x = \underline{\hspace{1.5cm}}$$ Subtract ___ from each side.

$$\underline{\hspace{1cm}} = \underline{\hspace{0.5cm}}$$ Add x to each side.

$$x = \underline{\hspace{0.5cm}}$$ Solve for x.

Example 3   *Solve an Equation with an Extraneous Solution*

Solve $x - 2 = \sqrt{x+10}$. Check for extraneous solutions.

Solution

$$x - 2 = \sqrt{x+10}$$ Original equation

$$(x-2)^2 = \underline{\hspace{2cm}}$$ Square each side.

$$\underline{\hspace{2cm}} = x + 10$$ Expand left side; simplify right side.

$$\underline{\hspace{2cm}} = 0$$ Standard form

$$(\underline{\hspace{1cm}})(\underline{\hspace{1cm}}) = 0$$ Factor.

$$\underline{\hspace{1cm}} = 0 \quad \text{or} \quad \underline{\hspace{1cm}} = 0$$ Zero product property

$$x = \underline{\hspace{0.5cm}} \quad \text{or} \quad x = \underline{\hspace{1cm}}$$ Solve for x.

CHECK Substitute __ for x and _____ for x in the original equation.

$$6 - 2 \stackrel{?}{=} \underline{\hspace{2cm}} \qquad\qquad -1 - 2 \stackrel{?}{=} \underline{\hspace{2cm}}$$

$$\underline{\hspace{1cm}} \stackrel{?}{=} \underline{\hspace{1cm}} \qquad\qquad \underline{\hspace{1cm}} \stackrel{?}{=} \underline{\hspace{1cm}}$$

$$\underline{\hspace{1cm}} = \underline{\hspace{1cm}} \checkmark \qquad\qquad \underline{\hspace{1cm}} \neq \underline{\hspace{1cm}} \checkmark$$

Because _____ does not satisfy the original equation, the only solution is ___.

| **Example 4** | *Solve an Equation with Rational Exponents* |

Solve $(3x + 4)^{2/3} = 16$. Check for extraneous solutions.

Solution

$$(3x + 4)^{2/3} = 16$$ Write original equation.

$$[(3x + 4)^{2/3}]^{\underline{\quad}} = (16)^{\underline{\quad}}$$ Raise each side to the $\frac{3}{2}$ power.

$$\underline{\qquad} = (\sqrt{16})^3$$ Definition of rational exponents

$$\underline{\quad} = \underline{\quad}$$ Simplify.

$$\underline{\quad} = \underline{\quad}$$ Subtract ___ from each side.

$$x = \underline{\quad}$$ Divide each side by ___.

The solution is ___. Check this in the original equation.

✔ **Checkpoint** Solve the equation. Check for extraneous solutions.

1. $\sqrt[4]{x + 3} = 2$	2. $\sqrt[3]{x - 5} + 1 = -1$
3. $\sqrt{4x + 5} = 3\sqrt{x}$	4. $\sqrt{3x} - \sqrt{x + 14} = 0$
5. $-2x^{4/3} - 21 = -53$	6. $x + 2 = \sqrt{2x + 7}$

Homework

Function Operations and Composition of Functions

Goal • Perform operations with functions, including composition of functions.

Your Notes

VOCABULARY

Composition of functions

OPERATIONS ON FUNCTIONS

Let $f(x)$ and $g(x)$ be any two functions. You can add, subtract, multiply, or divide $f(x)$ and $g(x)$ to form a new function $h(x)$.

Operation	Definition	Example: $f(x) = 3x$, $g(x) = x + 3$
Addition	$h(x) = f(x) + g(x)$	$h(x) = 3x + (x + 3)$ $= \underline{\hspace{2cm}}$
Subtraction	$h(x) = f(x) - g(x)$	$h(x) = 3x - (x + 3)$ $= \underline{\hspace{2cm}}$
Multiplication	$h(x) = f(x) \cdot g(x)$	$h(x) = 3x(x + 3)$ $= \underline{\hspace{2cm}}$
Division	$h(x) = \dfrac{f(x)}{g(x)}$	$h(x) = \dfrac{\underline{\hspace{1.5cm}}}{\underline{\hspace{1.5cm}}}$, $x \neq -3$

The domain of h consists of the x-values that are in the domains of both _____. When h involves division, the domain does _____ include x-values for which the _____ is equal to _____.

Example 1   *Add and Subtract Functions*

Let $f(x) = 3x^2 + 1$ and $g(x) = x - 5$. Find $h(x)$ and state its domain.

a. $h(x) = f(x) + g(x)$ **b.** $h(x) = f(x) - g(x)$

Solution

a. $f(x) + g(x) = 3x^2 + 1 + (x - 5)$

$= \underline{\hspace{3cm}}$

b. $f(x) - g(x) = 3x^2 + 1 - (x - 5)$

$= \underline{\hspace{3cm}}$

In both parts (a) and (b), the domains of f and g are
$\underline{\hspace{3cm}}$. So, the domain of h is
$\underline{\hspace{3cm}}$.

Example 2   *Multiply and Divide Functions*

Let $f(x) = x^3$ and $g(x) = 7x$. Find $h(x)$ and state its domain.

a. $h(x) = f(x) \cdot g(x)$ **b.** $h(x) = \dfrac{f(x)}{g(x)}$

Solution

a. $f(x) \cdot g(x) = (x^3)(7x)$

$= \underline{\hspace{2cm}}$

The domains of both f and g are $\underline{\hspace{3cm}}$.
So, the domain of $h(x)$ is $\underline{\hspace{3cm}}$.

b. $\dfrac{f(x)}{g(x)} = \underline{\hspace{1.5cm}}$

$= \dfrac{x^{(\underline{\hspace{1cm}})}}{\underline{\hspace{1cm}}}$

$= \dfrac{x^{\underline{\hspace{1cm}}}}{\underline{\hspace{1cm}}}$

Because $g(0) = \underline{\hspace{1cm}}$, $\dfrac{f}{g}$ is $\underline{\hspace{2cm}}$ when $x = \underline{\hspace{1cm}}$.
So, the domain of $h(x)$ is $\underline{\hspace{3cm}}$
except $\underline{\hspace{1cm}}$.

✔ *Checkpoint* **Complete the following exercise.**

1. Let $f(x) = 5x^3$ and $g(x) = -2x^3$. Find (a) $f + g$,
(b) $f - g$, (c) $f \cdot g$, (d) $\dfrac{f}{g}$, and (e) the domains.

COMPOSITION OF FUNCTIONS

The composition of a function f with a function g is:

$$h(x) = \underline{\hspace{3cm}}$$

The domain of h is the set of all _____ where x is
in the _____ of g and $g(x)$ is in the domain of ___.

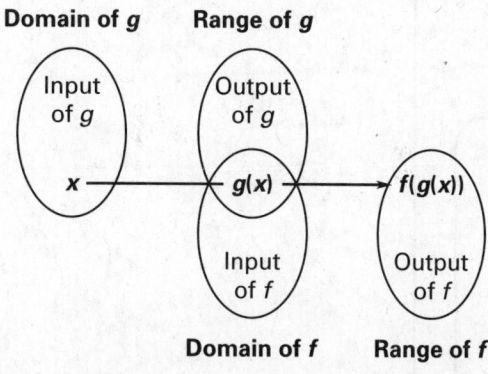

Domain of g Range of g

Input of g Output of g

x — $g(x)$ → $f(g(x))$

Input of f Output of f

Domain of f Range of f

Your Notes

Example 3   *Write a Composition of Functions*

Let $f(x) = 6x$ and $g(x) = 3x + 5$. Find the following.

a. $f(g(x))$ **b.** $g(f(x))$

c. the domain of each composition

Solution

To find the compositions, write the composition, substitute the expression for the _____ function in the _____ function, and simplify.

a. $f(g(x)) = f(\underline{\hspace{1.5cm}}) = 6(\underline{\hspace{1.5cm}}) = \underline{\hspace{2cm}}$

b. $g(f(x)) = g(\underline{\hspace{0.8cm}}) = 3(\underline{\hspace{0.8cm}}) + 5 = \underline{\hspace{1.5cm}}$

c. The domain of each function is _____ , so the domain of each composition is _____ .

Example 4   *Evaluate a Composition of Functions*

Let $f(x) = 6x$ and $g(x) = 3x + 5$. Evaluate $f(g(-2))$.

Solution

To evaluate $f(g(-2))$, first find $g(-2)$:

$g(-2) = 3(\underline{\hspace{1cm}}) + 5 = \underline{\hspace{1cm}} + 5 = \underline{\hspace{1cm}}$

Then substitute $g(-2) = \underline{\hspace{1cm}}$ into $f(g(-2))$:

$f(g(-2)) = f(\underline{\hspace{1cm}}) = 6(\underline{\hspace{1cm}}) = \underline{\hspace{1cm}}$

✓ **Checkpoint** **Complete the following exercise.**

2. Let $f(x) = 5x - 4$ and $g(x) = 3x$. Find
   (a) $f(g(x))$, (b) $g(f(x))$, (c) $f(g(-3))$, and (d) $g(f(4))$.

Homework

1111111111
111

7.5 Inverse Functions

Goal • Find the inverses of linear and nonlinear functions.

VOCABULARY

Inverse relation

_____

Inverse functions

INVERSE FUNCTIONS

Functions f and g are inverses if:

$$f(g(x)) = \underline{\quad} \quad \text{and} \quad g(f(x)) = \underline{\quad}$$

The inverse of f is denoted by _____, which is read as "f_____."

Example 1   *Verify Inverse Functions*

Verify that $f(x) = 7x - 4$ and $g(x) = \frac{1}{7}x + \frac{4}{7}$ are inverse functions.

Solution

To verify $f(x)$ and $g(x)$ are inverse functions, show that $f(g(x)) = \underline{\quad}$ and $g(f(x)) = \underline{\quad}$.

$$f(g(x)) = f\left(\frac{1}{7}x + \frac{4}{7}\right) \qquad\qquad g(f(x)) = g(7x - 4)$$

$$= 7\left(\underline{\qquad}\right) - 4 \qquad\qquad = \frac{1}{7}(\underline{\qquad}) + \frac{4}{7}$$

$$= \underline{\qquad} - 4 \qquad\qquad\qquad = \underline{\qquad} + \frac{4}{7}$$

$$= \underline{\quad} \checkmark \qquad\qquad\qquad\qquad = \underline{\quad} \checkmark$$

FINDING INVERSE FUNCTIONS

You can find the inverse of a function by following these steps.

Step 1   **Replace** $f(x)$ with ____ (if the function is written using _____ notation).

Step 2   **Switch** x and y.

Step 3   **Solve** for ____.

Example 2   *Find the Inverse of a Linear Function*

Find the inverse of the function $f(x) = -3x + 6$.

Solution

$$f(x) = -3x + 6 \qquad \text{Write original function.}$$
$$\underline{} = -3x + 6 \qquad \text{Replace } f(x) \text{ with } y.$$
$$\underline{} = \underline{} \qquad \text{Switch } x \text{ and } y.$$
$$\underline{} = \underline{} \qquad \text{Subtract ___ from each side.}$$
$$\underline{} = y \qquad \text{Divide each side by ____ to solve for ___.}$$

The inverse function is $f^{-1}(x) = $ _____.

✔ *Checkpoint* **Complete the following exercise.**

1. Find the inverse of the function $g(x) = 7x - 3$. Then verify that the two functions are inverses of each other.

HORIZONTAL LINE TEST

The inverse of a function f is also a function if and only if no _____ line intersects the graph of f _____.

Example 3 *Find the Inverse of a Nonlinear Function*

Determine whether the inverse of $f(x) = \frac{1}{4}x^3 + 3$ is a function. Then find the inverse.

Solution

First, graph the function on a graphing calculator. Because no _____ line intersects the graph more than once, the inverse of f is also a _____.

Next, find an equation for f^{-1}.

$$f(x) = \frac{1}{4}x^3 + 3 \qquad \text{Write original function.}$$

$$\underline{} = \frac{1}{4}x^3 + 3 \qquad \text{Replace } f(x) \text{ with } y.$$

$$\underline{} = \underline{} \qquad \text{Switch } x \text{ and } y.$$

$$\underline{} = \underline{} \qquad \text{Subtract } \underline{} \text{ from each side.}$$

$$\underline{} = y^3 \qquad \text{Multiply each side by } \underline{}.$$

$$\underline{} = y \qquad \text{Take the } \underline{} \text{ root of each side.}$$

✔ **Checkpoint** Determine whether the inverse of f is a function. Then find the inverse.

2. $f(x) = 2x^4 + 1, x \ge 0$	3. $f(x) = \frac{1}{3}x^2 - 5, x \ge 0$

Homework

7.6 Graphing Square Root and Cube Root Functions

Goal • Graph square root and cube root functions.

Your Notes

VOCABULARY

Radical function

GRAPHS OF SQUARE ROOT/CUBE ROOT FUNCTIONS

Square Root Function

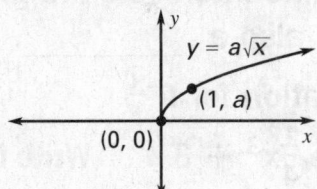

Cube Root Function

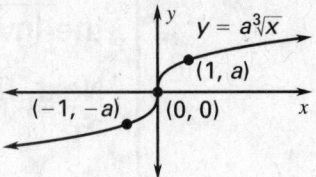

The domain of $y = a\sqrt{x}$ is x ___ 0. The range is y ___ 0 when $a > 0$.

The domain and range of $y = a\sqrt[3]{x}$ are _____.

Example 1 *Graph a Square Root Function*

Graph $y = 2\sqrt{x}$. Then state its domain and range.

Make a table of values. Then plot the points from the table and connect them with a smooth curve.

x	0	1	2	3	4
y	___	___	___	___	___

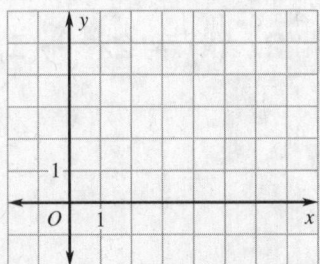

The radicand of a square root is always _____, so the domain is x ___ 0. The range is $y \geq$ ___ .

Example 2 *Graph a Cube Root Function*

Graph $y = -\dfrac{1}{2}\sqrt[3]{x}$. Then state its domain and range.

x	−2	−1	0	1	2
y	___	___	___	___	___

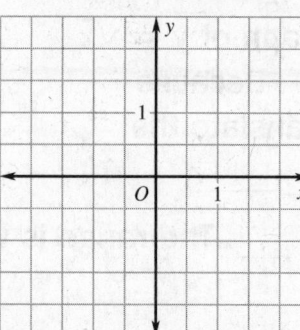

The radicand of a cube root can be _____ real number, so the domain is _____.
You can see from the graph that the range is _____.

✔ *Checkpoint* **Graph the function. Then state its domain and range.**

1. $y = 2\sqrt[3]{x}$

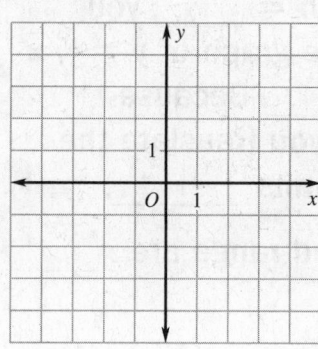

2. $y = -2\sqrt{x}$

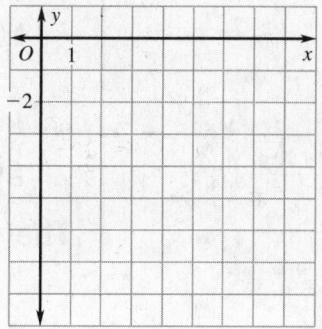

GRAPHS OF RADICAL FUNCTIONS

To graph $y = a\sqrt{x - h} + k$ or $y = a\sqrt[3]{x - h} + k$:

Step 1 Sketch the graph of $y = a\sqrt{x}$ or $y = a\sqrt[3]{x}$.

Step 2 Determine the values of h and k. Translate the graph h units _____ and k units _____. If $h > 0$, translate the graph to the _____; if $h < 0$, translate it to the _____.
If $k > 0$, translate the graph _____; if $k < 0$, translate it _____.

Example 3   *Graph a Square Root Function*

Graph $y = \sqrt{x - 1} + 2$. State its domain and range.

1. **Sketch** the graph of $y = \sqrt{x}$.

2. **Determine** the values of h and k. Because $h =$ ___, you translate the graph of $y = \sqrt{x}$ ___ unit _____. Because $k =$ ___, you translate the graph ___ units ____.

The domain is $x \geq$ ___. The range is $y \geq$ ___.

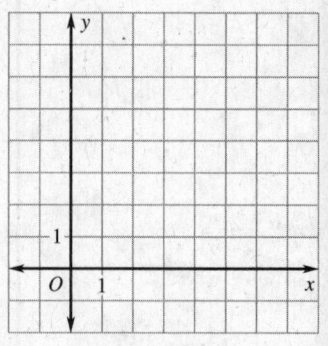

Example 4   *Graph a Cube Root Function*

Graph $y = \sqrt[3]{x + 3} - 2$. State its domain and range.

1. **Sketch** the graph of $y = \sqrt[3]{x}$.

2. **Determine** the values of h and k. Because $h =$ _____, you translate the graph of $y = \sqrt[3]{x}$ ___ units _____. Because $k =$ _____, you translate the graph ___ units _____.

The domain and range are _____.

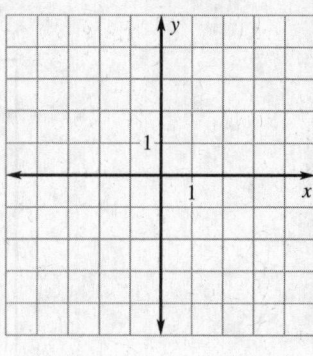

✔ *Checkpoint* **Graph the function. State domain and range.**

3. $y = \sqrt{x + 3} + 2$	4. $y = \sqrt[3]{x} + 1$
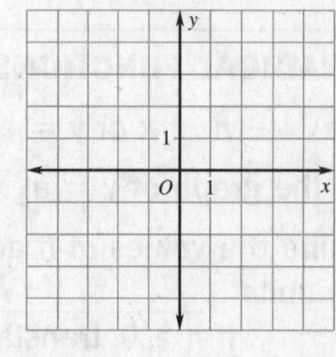	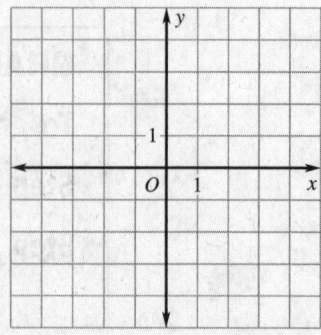

Homework

7.7 Standard Deviation

Goal • Use standard deviation to describe data sets.

VOCABULARY

Standard deviation

STANDARD DEVIATION OF A SET OF DATA

To find the standard deviation of x_1, x_2, x_3, ..., x_n:

Step 1 **Find** the _____ of the data set, $\bar{x}$ (read as "x bar").

Step 2 **Find** the _____ σ (read as "sigma").

$$\sigma = \sqrt{\frac{(x_1 - \bar{x})^2 + (x_2 - \bar{x})^2 + \ldots + (x_n - \bar{x})^2}{n}}$$

Example 1 *Find Standard Deviation*

The height, in inches, of six trees at a nursery are shown. Find the standard deviation of the heights.

| 36 | 48 | 50 | 44 | 53 | 39 |

Solution

1. **Find** the mean.

$$\bar{x} = \frac{36 + 48 + 50 + 44 + 53 + 39}{6} = \underline{\quad}$$

2. **Find** the standard deviation.

$$\sigma =$$

$$\sqrt{\frac{(36-45)^2 + (48-45)^2 + (50-45)^2 + (44-45)^2 + (53-45)^2 + (39-45)^2}{6}}$$

$$= \underline{\quad} = \underline{\quad}$$

The standard deviation is ___.

Example 2   *Compare Data After Adding a Constant*

Suppose that 6 months later, each of the trees in Example 1 had grown 5 inches.

a. Find the standard deviation of the heights after 6 months.

b. Compare this standard deviation with the standard deviation of the trees found in Example 1.

c. Make a box-and-whisker plot of the data used in Example 1 and the new data. What conclusions can you make about the two data sets?

Solution

a. $\bar{x} = \dfrac{41 + 53 + 55 + 49 + 58 + 44}{6} = \underline{\hspace{1cm}}$

$\sigma =$

$$\sqrt{\dfrac{(41-50)^2 + (53-50)^2 + (55-50)^2 + (49-50)^2 + (58-50)^2 + (44-50)^2}{6}}$$

$= \underline{\hspace{1.5cm}} = \underline{\hspace{0.8cm}}$

b. The standard deviation is _____ in Example 1.

c. The two data sets have _____ shape. The graph for the new data is ___ units to the _____ of the graph for the data in Example 1.

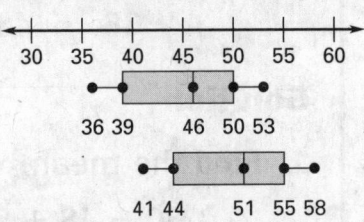

36 39   46 50 53

41 44   51 55 58

✔ *Checkpoint* **Complete the exercise.**

1. The speeds, in miles per hour, of five different cars on a local highway are 69, 62, 64, 60, and 65. (a) Find the standard deviation of the speeds. (b) Find the standard deviation of the speeds if the cars are driven 10 miles per hour slower. (c) Compare the standard deviations.

    Copyright © McDougal Littell/Houghton Mifflin Compar

Example 3   *Compare Data Sets*

The data sets below give the quiz scores for the students in two different biology classes.

Class A: 15, 17, 17, 17, 18, 19, 21, 22, 25

Class B: 16, 18, 19, 21, 22, 22, 22, 24, 25

a. Find the mean and standard deviation for each class.

b. Compare the mean and standard deviation of the two classes.

c. What conclusions can you draw?

Solution

a. Class A: Mean = _____

            Standard deviation $\approx$ _____

     Class B: Mean = _____

            Standard deviation $\approx$ _____

b. The mean for Class A is _____ than the mean for Class B, but its standard deviation is _____ than the standard deviation for Class B.

c. Since the standard deviation for Class A is _____ than the standard deviation for Class B, the scores for Class A are _____ spread out than the scores for Class B.

✔ *Checkpoint* Tell which data set is more spread out.

2. Set A: $\bar{x} = 63$, $\sigma = 6.7$ Set B: $\bar{x} = 58$, $\sigma = 5.98$	**3.** Set A: $\bar{x} = 115$, $\sigma = 1.25$ Set B: $\bar{x} = 95$, $\sigma = 1.25$

Homework

Words to Review

Use your own words and/or an example to explain the vocabulary word.

*n*th root of a real number	Index
Simplest form of a radical	Like radicals
Radical equation	Extraneous solution
Composition of functions	Inverse relation
Inverse functions	Radical function
Standard deviation	

Review your notes and Chapter 7 by using the Chapter Review on pages 401–404 of your textbook.

8.1 Exponential Growth

Goal • Graph exponential growth functions.

Your Notes

VOCABULARY

Exponential function
_____

Exponential growth function
_____

Asymptote

Example 1   *Graph y = ab^x when a = 1 and b > 1*

Graph the function $y = 3^x$.

Solution

Make a table of values for the function.

x	−2	−1	0	1	2
y			__	__	__

Plot the points from the table.

Draw a curve that passes through the plotted points.

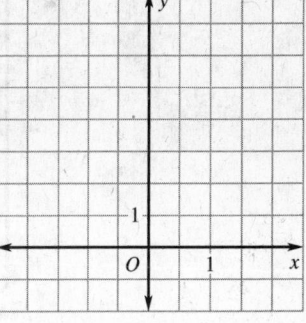

EXPONENTIAL GROWTH GRAPHS

Here are some characteristics of the graph of $y = ab^x$ when $a > 0$ and $b > 1$.

• The graph _____ from left to right.

• The graph passes through (0, ___) and (1, ____).

• The domain is _____.

• The range is _____.

Example 2   *Graph y = ab^x when a ≠ 1 and b > 1*

a. Graph $y = \frac{1}{2} \cdot 4^x$.   **b.** Graph $y = 3 \cdot 3^x$.

Solution

a. Make a table of values. Then plot the points.

x	–2	–1	0	1	2
y	___	___	___	___	___

Draw a curve that passes through the plotted points.

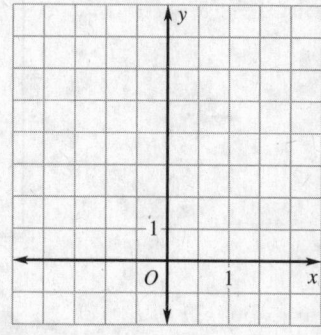

b. Make a table of values. Then plot the points.

x	–3	–2	–1	0	1
y	___	___	___	___	___

Draw a curve that passes through the plotted points.

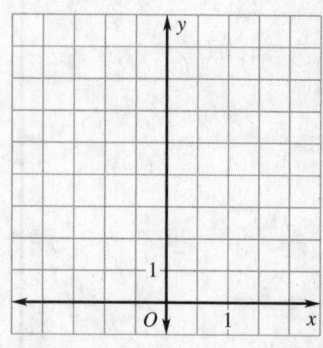

✔ *Checkpoint* **Graph the exponential function.**

1. $y = 6^x$	**2.** $y = 0.2 \cdot 6^x$
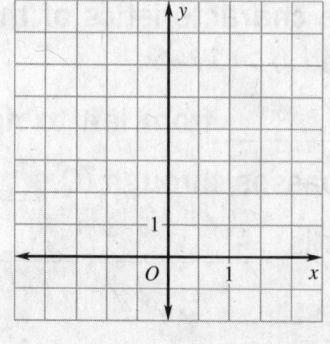	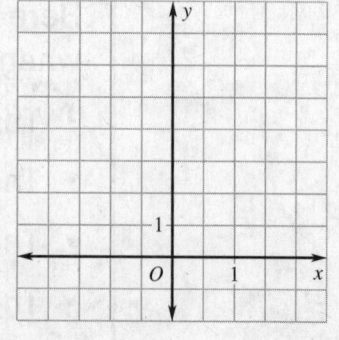

Example 3   *Graph an Exponential Function*

Graph the function. Describe the horizontal asymptote. State the domain and range.

a. $y = 3^{x-1}$ **b.** $y = 3^x + 2$

a. Graph $y = 3^x$, which passes through (0, ___) and (1, ___). Translate the graph ___ unit(s) _____. The graph passes through (1, ___) and (2, ___).

The graph's asymptote is the _____.

The domain is _____, and the range is _____.

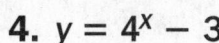

b. Graph $y = 3^x$, which passes through (0, ___) and (1, ___). Translate the graph ___ unit(s) _____. The graph passes through (0, ___) and (1, ___).

The graph's asymptote is the line _____.

The domain is _____, and the range is _____.

✔ *Checkpoint* **Graph the function. Describe the horizontal asymptote. State the domain and range.**

3. $y = 2^x + 2$

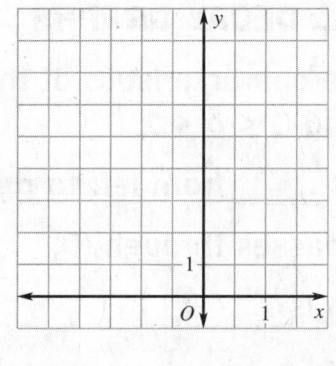

4. $y = 4^x - 3$

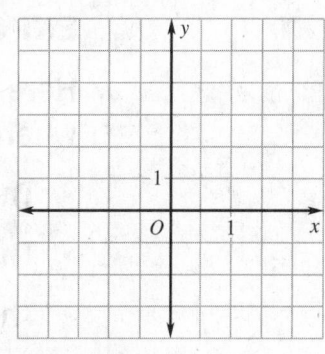

8.2 Exponential Decay

Goal • Graph exponential decay functions.

VOCABULARY

Exponential decay function

Example 1   *Graph y = b^x when 0 < b < 1*

Graph the function $y = \left(\dfrac{1}{3}\right)^x$.

Solution

Make a table of values for the function.

x	–2	–1	0	1	2
y	___	___	___	___	___

Plot the points from the table.

Draw a curve that passes through the plotted points.

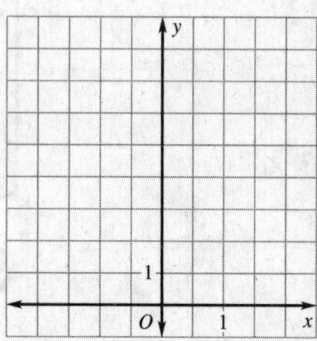

EXPONENTIAL DECAY GRAPHS

Here are some characteristics of the graph of $y = ab^x$ when $a > 0$ and $0 < b < 1$.

• The graph _____ from left to right.

• The graph passes through (0, ___) and (1, _____).

• The domain is _____.

• The range is _____.

Your Notes

Example 2 *Graph $y = ab^x$ when $0 < b < 1$*

a. Graph $y = 2 \cdot \left(\frac{1}{4}\right)^x$. **b.** Graph $y = 3 \cdot \left(\frac{3}{4}\right)^x$.

Solution

a. Make a table of values.

x	–2	–1	0	1	2
y					

Plot the points.

Draw a curve that passes through the plotted points.

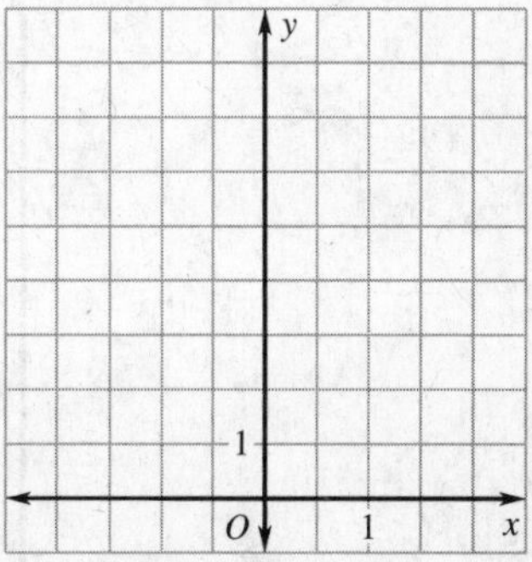

b. Make a table of values.

x	–2	–1	0	1	2
y					

Plot the points.

Draw a curve that passes through the plotted points.

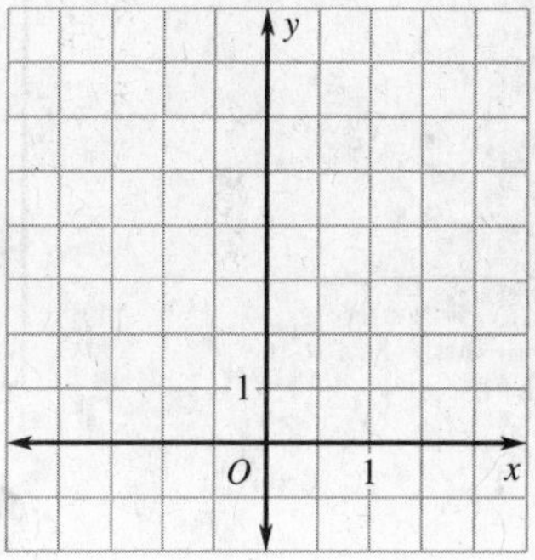

Checkpoint Graph the function.

1. $y = \left(\frac{2}{3}\right)^x$

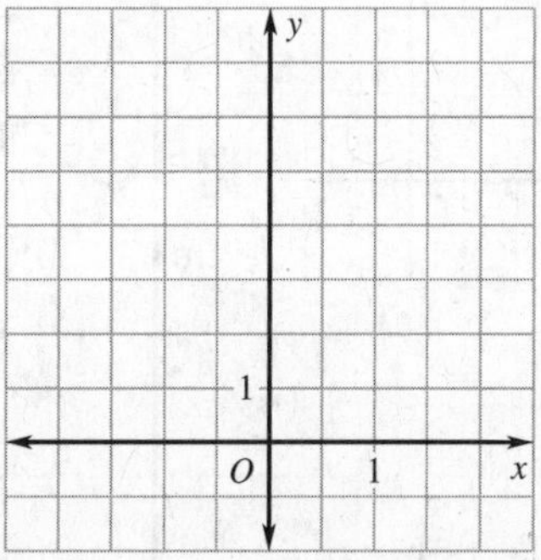

2. $y = 7 \cdot \left(\frac{7}{8}\right)^x$

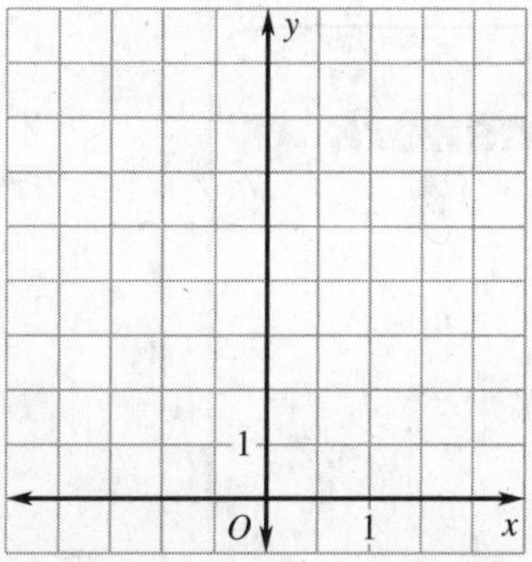

Your Notes

Example 3 — *Graph an Exponential Function*

Graph the function. Describe the horizontal asymptote. State the domain and range.

a. $y = \left(\dfrac{3}{5}\right)^{x+3}$
b. $y = \left(\dfrac{2}{5}\right)^{x} - 2$

a. Graph $y = \left(\dfrac{3}{5}\right)^{x}$. It passes through (0, ___) and $\left(1, \underline{}\right)$.

Translate the graph ____ units _____. The graph passes through (−3, ___) and $\left(-2, \underline{}\right)$.

The graph's asymptote is the _____. The domain is _____, and the range is _____.

b. Graph $y = \left(\dfrac{2}{5}\right)^{x}$. It passes through (0, ___) and $\left(1, \underline{}\right)$.

Translate the graph ____ units _____. The graph passes through (0, ___) and $\left(1, \underline{}\right)$.

The graph's asymptote is _____. The domain is _____, and the range is _____

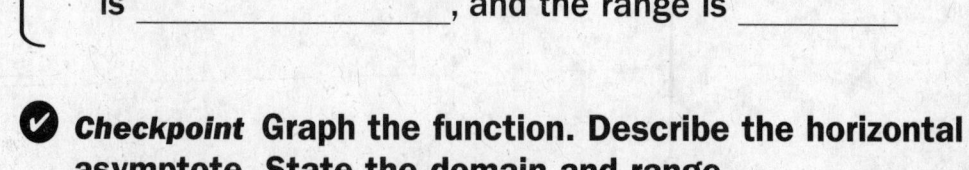

✔ **Checkpoint** **Graph the function. Describe the horizontal asymptote. State the domain and range.**

3. $y = \left(\dfrac{1}{4}\right)^{x+2}$
4. $y = \left(\dfrac{1}{4}\right)^{x} - 4$

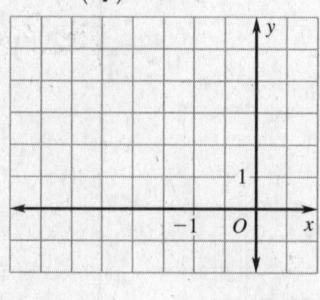 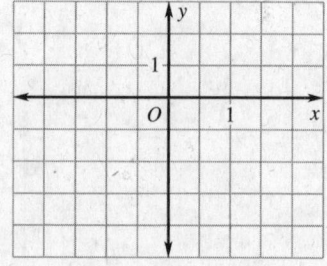

Homework

8.3 Modeling with Exponential Functions

Goal • Write models for exponential growth and decay.

Your Notes

VOCABULARY

Growth factor

Decay factor

Natural base e

Example 1 *Write and Use an Exponential Growth Model*

Buffalo Several years ago, a herd of 38 buffalo was relocated to a state park. Since then, the number of buffalo y in the herd has increased by about 7% per year.

a. Write an exponential growth model that represents the number of buffalo t years after the relocation.

b. Predict the number of buffalo after 7 years.

Solution

a. $y = a(1 + r)^t$ **Exponential growth model**

$y = \underline{\hphantom{aa}}(1 + \underline{\hphantom{aaa}})^t$ **Substitute for a and r.**

$y = \underline{\hphantom{aaaaa}}$ **Simplify.**

b. To predict the number of buffalo after 7 years, substitute ___ for t: $y = \underline{\hphantom{aaaa}} \approx \underline{\hphantom{aa}}$ buffalo.

✔ *Checkpoint* Complete the following exercise.

1. In Example 1, suppose the number of buffalo had increased by 11% per year. Find the number of buffalo after 9 years.

Example 2 **Write and Use an Exponential Decay Model**

Televisions You buy a new television for $1200. The value y (in dollars) of the television decreases by 21% each year.

a. Write an exponential decay model that represents the value of the television after t years.

b. Use the model to estimate the value after 4 years.

Solution

a. $y = a(1 - r)^t$ **Exponential decay model**

    $y = $ _____$(1 - $ _____$)^t$ **Substitute for a and r.**

    $y = $ _____   **Simplify.**

b. To estimate the value of the television after 4 years, substitute ___ for t: $y = $ _____ $\approx$ $ _____.

Example 3 **Write an Exponential Function**

Write a function of the form $y = ab^x$ whose graph passes through (1, 10) and (4, 80).

Solution

Substitute the coordinates of the two given points into $y = ab^x$.

    ____ $= ab$—   **Substitute ____ for y and ___ for x; (1, 10) is on the graph.**

    ____ $= ab$—   **Substitute ____ for y and ___ for x; (4, 80) is on the graph.**

Solve the first equation for a: $a = $ ____. Substitute into the second.

    $80 = $ _____ b^4 **Substitute ____ for a.**

    $80 = $ ____b—   **Quotient of powers property**

    ___ $= $ ____   **Divide each side by ____.**

    ___ $= b$ **Take the positive cube root.**

Because $b = $ ___, it follows that $a = $ ___. So, $y = $ _____.

COMPOUND INTEREST

An initial principal P is deposited in an account that pays _____ at an annual _____ r (expressed as a _____), compounded n times per year.

The amount A in the account after t years can be modeled by this formula:

$$A = \underline{\hspace{3cm}}$$

Example 4   *Find the Balance in an Account*

Finance You deposit $2900 in an account that pays 3.5% annual interest. Find the balance after 3 years if the interest is compounded monthly.

Solution

$A = P\left(1 + \dfrac{r}{n}\right)^{nt}$ Write compound interest formula.

$= \underline{\hspace{5cm}}$ Substitute _____ for P, _____ for r, _____ for n, and ____ for t.

$\approx \underline{\hspace{2cm}}(1.003)^{\underline{\hspace{0.7cm}}}$ Simplify.

$\approx \$\underline{\hspace{3cm}}$ Use a calculator.

The balance after 3 years is about $\$\underline{\hspace{2cm}}$.

✔ **Checkpoint** Complete the following exercises.

2. Write a function of the form $y = ab^x$ whose graph passes through (1, 12) and (3, 192).

_____

3. You deposit $5000 in an account that pays 3.72% annual interest. Find the balance after 3 years if the interest is compounded quarterly.

THE NATURAL BASE e

The natural base e is irrational. It is defined as follows:

As n approaches $+\infty$, $\left(1 + \dfrac{1}{n}\right)^n$ approaches $e \approx$ _____.

Example 5   *Find the Balance in an Account*

Finance You deposit $3500 in an account that pays 5% annual interest compounded continuously. What is the balance after 2 years?

Solution

$A = Pe^{rt}$	Write continuously compound interest formula.
= _____ e_____	Substitute _____ for P, _____ for r, and ___ for t.
= _____ e___	Simplify.
$\approx$ $ _____	Use a calculator.

The balance after 2 years is about $_____.

✔ *Checkpoint* **Complete the following exercise.**

4. You deposit $1000 in an account that pays 4.2% annual interest compounded continuously. Find the balance after 2 years, 4 years, and 6 years.

Goal • Evaluate and graph logarithmic functions.

Your Notes

VOCABULARY

Common logarithm

Logarithm of y with base b

DEFINITION OF LOGARITHM WITH BASE b

Let b and y be _____ numbers such that b ___ 1.

The **logarithm of y with base b** is denoted by $\log_b y$ is defined as follows:

$$\log_b y = \underline{} \text{ if and only if } b^x = \underline{}$$

Example 1 *Rewrite Logarithmic Equations*

LOGARITHMIC FORM	EXPONENTIAL FORM
a. $\log_2 32 = 5$	$2^5 = 32$
b. $\log_9 1 = 0$	$9^0 = \underline{}$
c. $\log_{13} 13 = 1$	$\underline{} = 13$
d. $\log 1000 = 3$	$\underline{} = \underline{}$
e. $\log_{1/3} 9 = -2$	$\underline{} = \underline{}$

✔ **Checkpoint** Rewrite the equation in exponential form.

1. $\log_{18} 1 = 0$	2. $\log_2 64 = 6$
3. $\log 0.0001 = -4$	4. $\log_{1/5} 125 = -3$

SPECIAL LOGARITHM VALUES

Let b be a _____ number with b ___ 1.

LOGARITHM OF 1 $\log_b 1 =$ ___ because b___ $=$ ___

LOGARITHM OF BASE b $\log_b b =$ ___ because b___ $=$ ___

Example 2   *Evaluate Logarithmic Expressions*

Evaluate the expression.

a. $\log_3 81$ **b.** $\log_4 0.25$ **c.** $\log_{1/4} 256$

Solution

To help you find the value of $\log_b y$, ask yourself what _____ of b gives you ___.

a. 3 to what power gives you 81?

     3___ $= 81$, so $\log_3 81 =$ ___

b. 4 to what power gives you 0.25?

     4___ $= 0.25$, so $\log_4 0.25 =$ ___

c. $\frac{1}{4}$ to what power gives you 256?

     $\left(\dfrac{1}{4}\right)$___ $= 256$, so $\log_{1/4} 256 =$ ___

Example 3   *Use Inverse Properties*

a. Evaluate $10^{\log 6.7}$.   **b.** Simplify $\log_3 243^x$.

Solution

a. $10^{\log 6.7} = 10^{\log_{10} 6.7} =$ _____

b. $\log_3 243^x = \log_3 (\text{___})^x = \log_3$ _____ $=$ ___

✔ *Checkpoint* **Complete the following exercises.**

5. Evaluate $\log_{1/5} 25$.	**6.** Simplify $\log_4 64^x$.

GRAPHING LOGARITHMIC FUNCTIONS

The graph of $y = \log_b x$ has the following properties:

- The graph of $y = \log_b x$ is the reflection of the graph of _____ in the line _____.
- The graph of $y = \log_b x$ includes $(1, \underline{\hspace{0.3cm}})$ and $(\underline{\hspace{0.3cm}}, 1)$.
- The _____ is a _____ asymptote.
- The domain is _____, and the range is _____.

Example 4   *Graph Logarithmic Functions*

Graph the function. Describe the vertical asymptote. State the domain and range.

a. $y = \log_2 x$ **b.** $y = \log_2 (x + 1)$

Solution

For both graphs, find the two key points where $y = \underline{\hspace{0.3cm}}$ and $y = \underline{\hspace{0.3cm}}$.

a. Let $x = 1$. Then $y = \log_2 1 = \underline{\hspace{0.3cm}}$, so $(1, \underline{\hspace{0.3cm}})$ is on the graph.

Let $x = 2$. Then $y = \log_2 2 = \underline{\hspace{0.3cm}}$, so $(2, \underline{\hspace{0.3cm}})$ is on the graph.

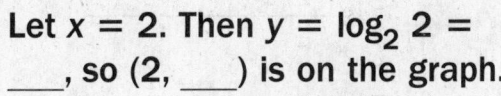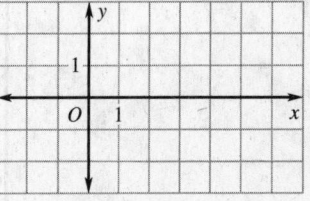

The vertical asymptote is the _____. The domain is _____, and the range is _____.

b. Let $x = 0$. Then $y = \log_2 (0 + 1) = \underline{\hspace{0.3cm}}$, so $(0, \underline{\hspace{0.3cm}})$ is on the graph.

Let $x = 1$. Then $y = \log_2 (1 + 1) = \underline{\hspace{0.3cm}}$, so $(1, \underline{\hspace{0.3cm}})$ is on the graph.

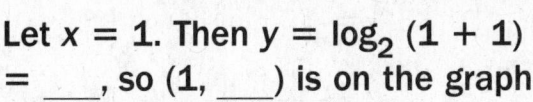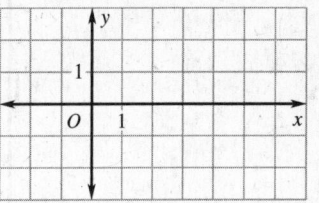

The vertical asymptote is _____. The domain is _____, and the range is _____.

8.5 Properties of Logarithms

Goal • Use the properties of logarithms.

PROPERTIES OF LOGARITHMS

Let b, m, and n be _____ numbers such that b ____ 1.

PRODUCT PROPERTY $\log_b mn = \log_b m$ ____ $\log_b$ ____

QUOTIENT PROPERTY $\log_b \frac{m}{n} = \log_b m$ ____ $\log_b$ ____

POWER PROPERTY $\log_b m^n =$ _____

Example 1   Use Properties of Logarithms

Use $\log_5 4 \approx 0.861$ and $\log_5 9 \approx 1.365$ to find the value of the expression to the nearest thousandth.

a. $\log_5 \frac{4}{9}$ **b.** $\log_5 36$ **c.** $\log_5 81$

Solution

a. $\log_5 \frac{4}{9} = \log_5 4$ ____ $\log_5 9$ Quotient property

$\approx$ _____   Use given values of $\log_5 4$ and $\log_5 9$.

$=$ _____   Simplify.

b. $\log_5 36 = \log_5 (4 \cdot 9)$ Express 36 as a product.

$= \log_5 4$ ____ $\log_5 9$ Product property

$\approx$ _____   Use given values of $\log_5 4$ and $\log_5 9$.

$=$ _____   Simplify.

c. $\log_5 81 = \log_5 9^2$ Express 81 as a power.

$=$ _____   Power property

$\approx$ _____   Use given value of $\log_5 9$.

$=$ _____   Simplify.

178   Lesson 8.5 • **Algebra 2 C&S Notetaking Guide**   Copyright © McDougal Littell/Houghton Mifflin Company

Example 2   *Expand a Logarithmic Expression*

Expand the expression. Assume all variables are positive.

a. $\log_8 4v^5$ **b.** $\log_3 \dfrac{2y}{z^2}$

Solution

a. $\log_8 4v^5 = \log_8 \underline{\quad} + \log_8 \underline{\quad}$ **Product property**

$ = \log_8 \underline{\quad} + \underline{\quad} \log_8 v$ **Power property**

b. $\log_3 \dfrac{2y}{z^2}$

$ = \log_3 \underline{\quad\quad} - \log_3 \underline{\quad\quad}$ **Quotient property**

$ = \log_3 \underline{\quad\quad} - \underline{\quad} \log_3 z$ **Power property**

$ = \log_3 2 + \log_3 \underline{\quad} - \underline{\quad} \log_3 z$ **Product property**

Example 3   *Condense a Logarithmic Expression*

Condense the expression. Assume all variables are positive.

a. $\log_8 4 + \log_8 5$

b. $\log_2 54 - 3 \log_2 3$

c. $4 \log g + 3 \log k$

Solution

a. $\log_8 4 + \log_8 5 = \log_8 (\underline{\quad\quad})$ **Product property**

$ = \log_8 \underline{\quad\quad}$ **Simplify.**

b. $\log_2 54 - 3 \log_2 3$

$ = \log_2 54 - \log_2 \underline{\quad\quad}$ **Power property**

$ = \log_2 \dfrac{}{\underline{\quad}}$ **Quotient property**

$ = \log_2 \underline{\quad}$ **Simplify.**

$ = \underline{\quad}$ **Simplify.**

c. $4 \log g + 3 \log k$

$ = \log \underline{\quad\quad} + \log \underline{\quad\quad}$ **Power property**

$ = \log \underline{\quad\quad\quad}$ **Product property**

✔ **Checkpoint** Use $\log_3 2 \approx 0.631$ and $\log_3 8 \approx 1.893$ to find the value of the expression to the nearest thousandth.

1. $\log_3 4$	**2.** $\log_3 16$

Expand the expression. Assume all variables are positive.

3. $\log_5 21x^3$	**4.** $\log \dfrac{y^3}{4x}$

Condense the expression. Assume all variables are positive.

5. $\log_7 3 + 2\log_7 x - \log_7 y$

6. $\log_2 11 - 3\log_2 x - 2\log_2 z$

8.6 Solve Exponential and Logarithmic Equations

Goal • Solve exponential and logarithmic equations.

Your Notes

EQUAL POWERS PROPERTY

For b ___ 0 and b ___ 1, if $b^x = b^y$, then ___ = ___.

EXAMPLE If $3^x = 3^5$, then $x =$ ___.

Example 1 **Solve Using Equal Powers Property**

Solve $64^x = 16^{x+1}$.

Solution

$64^x = 16^{x+1}$	Write original equation.
$(\underline{})^x = (\underline{})^{x+1}$	Rewrite 64 as 4^3 and 16 as 4^2 so powers have same base.
___ = ___	Power of a power property
___ = ___	Equal powers property
___ = ___	Distributive property
$x =$ ___	Subtract ___ from each side.

✔ **Checkpoint** Solve the equation.

1. $6^{5x+2} = 6^{3x-2}$	2. $7^{3x+2} = 7^{5x}$
3. $25^{x-1} = 5^{3x}$	4. $3^{7x-3} = 9^{2x}$

Your Notes

| Example 2 | *Take a Common Logarithm of Each Side* |

Solve the equation.

a. $6^x = 27$ **b.** $10^{5x-2} = 44$

Solution

a. $6^x = 27$ Write original equation.

_____ $= \log 27$ Take common logarithm of each side.

_____ $= \log 27$ Power property of logarithms

$x =$ _____   Divide each side by log ___.

$x \approx$ _____   Use a calculator.

Solution is about _____. Check in original equation.

b. $10^{5x-2} = 44$ Write original equation.

_____ $= \log 44$ Take common logarithm of each side.

_____ $= \log 44$ $\log 10^x = x$

____ $=$ _____   Add ___ to each side.

$x =$ _____   Divide each side by ___.

$x \approx$ _____   Use a calculator.

Solution is about _____. Check in original equation.

✔ **Checkpoint** **Solve the equation.**

5. $5^x = 72$	**6.** $10^{x-5} = 122$

EQUAL LOGARITHMS PROPERTY

For _____ numbers b, x, and y where b ____ 1:

$\log_b x = \log_b y$ if and only if _____

182 Lesson 8.6 • **Algebra 2 C&S Notetaking Guide**   Copyright © McDougal Littell/Houghton Mifflin Company

Example 3   *Solve a Logarithmic Equation*

Solve $\log_4 (6x - 16) = \log_4 (x - 1)$.

Solution

$\log_4 (6x - 16) = \log_4 (x - 1)$	Write original equation.
_____ $= x - 1$	Equal logarithms property
_____ $=$ _____	Subtract ____ from each side.
____ $=$ ____	Add ____ to each side.
$x =$ ____	Divide each side by ____ .

The solution is ____ . Check this in the original equation.

Example 4   *Exponentiate Each Side*

Solve $\log_5 (3x - 8) = 2$.

Solution

$\log_5 (3x - 8) = 2$	Write original equation.
_____ $= 5^2$	Exponentiate each side using base ____ .
_____ $= 25$	$b^{\log_b x} = x$
____ $=$ ____	Add ____ to each side.
$x =$ ____	Divide each side by ____ .

The solution is ____ . Check this in the original equation.

✔ *Checkpoint* **Solve the equation.**

7. $\log_6 (7x - 13) =$ $\log_6 (2x + 17)$	**8.** $\log_3 (2x + 9) = 3$

Example 5 **Check for Extraneous Solutions**

Solve log $5x$ + log $(x - 1) = 2$. Check for extraneous solutions.

Solution

log $5x$ + log $(x - 1) = 2$	Write original equation.
log [____(_____)] = 2	Product property of logarithms
_____ = ____^{2}	Exponentiate each side using base ____.
____(_____) = _____	$b^{\log_b x} = x$
_____ = ____	Distributive property
_____ = 0	Subtract _____ from each side.
___(_____)(_____) = 0	Factor.
$x = $ ____ or $x = $ ___	Zero product property

The solutions appear to be ____ and ___. Check these in the original equation.

CHECK $x = 5$ log $5($___$)$ + log $($___$- 1) \overset{?}{=} 2$

log ____ + log ___ $\overset{?}{=} 2$

log _____ $\overset{?}{=} 2$

____ $= 2$ ✓

So, ___ is a solution.

CHECK $x = -4$ log $5($____$)$ + log $($____$- 1) \overset{?}{=} 2$

log $($_____$)$ + log $($_____$) \overset{?}{=} 2$

Because log $($_____$)$ and log $($_____$)$ are not defined, _____ is not a solution.

Homework

✓ *Checkpoint* **Complete the following exercise.**

9. Solve $\log_6 (x - 9) + \log_6 x = 2$. Check for extraneous solutions.

Words to Review

Use your own words and/or an example to explain the vocabulary word.

Exponential function	Exponential growth function
Asymptote	Exponential decay function
Growth factor	Decay factor
Natural base e	Common logarithm
Logarithm of *y* with base *b*	

Review your notes and Chapter 8 by using the Chapter Review on pages 455–458 of your textbook.

Goal • Use inverse variation and joint variation models.

Your Notes

VOCABULARY

Inverse variation

Constant of variation

Joint variation

Example 1 *Classify Direct and Inverse Variation*

Tell whether x and y show *direct variation*, *inverse variation*, or *neither*.

a. $\dfrac{y}{9} = x$ b. $xy = 3$

GIVEN EQUATION	REWRITTEN EQUATION	TYPE OF VARIATION
a. $\dfrac{y}{9} = x$	$y = $ ____	_____
b. $xy = 3$	$y = $ ____	_____

✔ **Checkpoint** Tell whether x and y show *direct variation*, *inverse variation*, or *neither*.

1. $y = x + 2$	2. $xy = 5$	3. $\dfrac{y}{2.6} = x$

Example 2   *Write an Inverse Variation Equation*

Write an equation that relates x and y such that x and y vary inversely and $y = 4$ when $x = 2$.

Solution

$$y = \frac{k}{x}$$ Write the inverse variation model.

$$\underline{\quad} = \frac{k}{2}$$ Substitute ____ for y and ____ for x.

$$\underline{\quad} = k$$ Solve for k.

The inverse variation that relates x and y is $y = \underline{\quad}$.

Example 3   *Write an Inverse Variation Model*

Air Pressure The amount of air pressure in a container varies inversely with the volume it takes up. A certain tank of air has a pressure of 100 Pascals with a volume of 10 liters.

a. Write an inverse variation model.

b. Describe the change in pressure as the volume of air in the tank decreases.

Solution

a. Write an inverse variation model relating the pressure P and the volume V.

$$\underline{\quad} = \frac{k}{V}$$ Model for inverse variation

$$\underline{\quad} = \frac{k}{10}$$ Substitute _____ for P and ____ for V.

$$k = \underline{\quad}$$ Solve for k.

The model is $P = \underline{\quad}$.

b. As the volume decreases, the pressure _____.

✔ *Checkpoint* **The variables x and y vary inversely. Use the given values to write an equation relating x and y.**

4. $x = 2, y = 5$	**5.** $x = 3, y = 8$

Example 4 *Check Data for Inverse Variation*

Do the data below show inverse variation? If so, find a model for the relationship between x and y.

x	2	4	6	8	10
y	18	9	6	4.5	3.6

Solution

From the table you can see that xy is equal to ____. For example, 2(____) = ____ and 4(___) = ____. So, the data show _____ variation.

A model for the relationship is $y =$ ____ .

TYPES OF VARIATION

In each equation, k is a constant and $k \neq 0$.

RELATIONSHIP	EQUATION
y varies directly with x.	$y =$ ____
y varies inversely with x.	$y =$ ____
z varies jointly with x and y.	$z =$ ____
y varies directly with the square of x.	$y =$ ____
z varies directly with y and inversely with x.	$z =$ ____

Example 5 *Write a Variation Model*

The variable z varies jointly with x and y. Also, $z = -84$ when $x = -4$ and $y = 3$.

a. Write an equation relating x, y, and z.

b. Find the value of z when $x = 5$ and $y = 2$.

Solution

a. Choose the equation that shows that z varies jointly with x and y.

$z = $ _____   Use the _____ variation model.

_____ $= k($____$)($___$)$ Substitute _____ for z, _____ for x, and ___ for y.

_____ $= k($_____$)$ Multiply.

___ $= k$ Solve for k.

An equation relating x, y, and z is $z = $ _____.

b. Substitute ___ for x and ___ for y, and solve for z.

$z = $ ___$($___$)($___$) = $ ___

✔ *Checkpoint* **Complete the following exercise.**

6. Write an equation for the relationship where x varies jointly with y and z and inversely with the square of t.

Homework

9.2 Graphing Rational Functions

Goal • Graph rational functions.

Your Notes

VOCABULARY

Rational function

_____

Hyperbola

_____

Branches

_____

| **Example 1** | **Graph a Rational Function** |

Graph $y = \dfrac{2}{x}$. State the domain and range.

Solution

Draw the asymptotes. The _____ is the vertical asymptote and the _____ is the horizontal asymptote.

Plot a few points on each side of the _____ asymptote.

$\left(-4, \underline{\quad}\right), (-2, \underline{\quad}), (-1, \underline{\quad}),$

$(1, \underline{\quad}), (2, \underline{\quad}), \left(4, \underline{\quad}\right)$

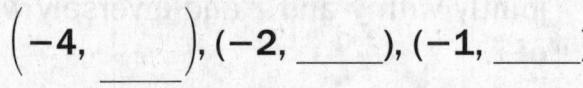

Draw the two _____ of the hyperbola. Each branch _____ the asymptotes and passes through the plotted points.

The domain and the range are the same:

_____.

Copyright © McDougal Littell/Houghton Mifflin Company

GRAPHING RATIONAL FUNCTIONS OF THE FORM

$y = \dfrac{a}{x - h} + k$

The graph of a rational function of the form

$y = \dfrac{a}{x - h} + k$ is a _____ with a _____ asymptote at $x =$ ____ and a _____ asymptote at $y =$ ____.

To graph a rational function, use these steps:

Step 1 **Draw** the asymptotes $x =$ ____ and $y =$ ____.

Step 2 **Plot** points on each side of the _____ asymptote $x =$ ____.

Step 3 **Draw** the two _____ of the _____ that approach the asymptotes and pass through the _____.

Example 2 *Graph a Rational Function*

Graph $y = \dfrac{-6}{x + 3} + 3$. State the domain and range.

Solution

The function is in the form $y = \dfrac{a}{x - h} + k$. So, $a =$ _____, $h =$ _____, and $k =$ ____.

1. **Draw** the asymptotes $x =$ _____ and $y =$ ____.

2. **Plot** a couple of points on each side of the _____.

   $(-9, \_\_\_), (-6, \_\_\_),$
   $(-4, \_\_\_), (-2, \_\_\_\_),$
   $(0, \_\_\_), (3, \_\_\_)$

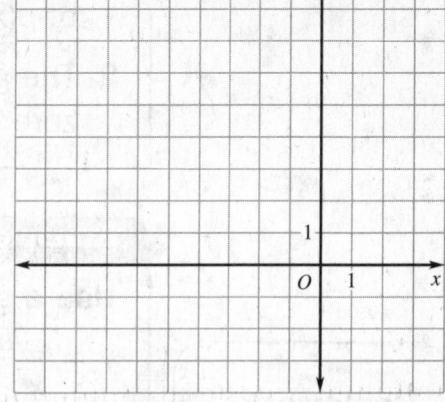

3. **Draw** both _____ of the hyperbola. Each branch _____ the asymptotes and passes through the plotted points.

The domain is _____ except _____.

The range is _____ except ____.

✔ **Checkpoint** Graph the function. State the domain and range.

1. $y = \dfrac{-3}{x}$

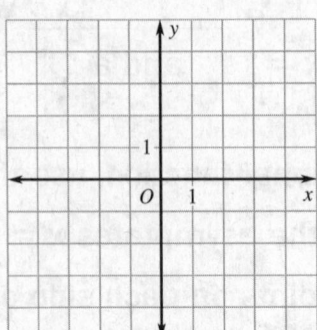

2. $y = \dfrac{-1}{x-2} + 1$

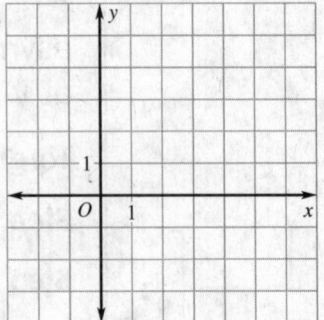

GRAPHS OF GENERAL RATIONAL FUNCTIONS

Let $p(x)$ and $q(x)$ be _____ with no common factors other than $\pm$___. The graph of the rational function $f(x) = \dfrac{p(x)}{q(x)}$ has the following characteristics:

1. The x-intercepts of the graph are the _____ of $p(x)$.

2. The graph has a _____ at each real zero of $q(x)$.

Example 3 **Use a Calculator**

Use a graphing calculator to sketch the graph of $y = \dfrac{4x^2}{x^2 - 4}$.

Solution

Enter the function using parentheses around the _____. The graph at the right shows the calculator screen.

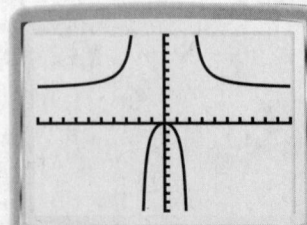

Homework

9.3 Simplifying and Multiplying Rational Expressions

Goal • Simplify and multiply rational expressions.

VOCABULARY

Rational expression

_____

Simplified form

| **Example 1** | **Simplify a Rational Expression** |

Simplify the rational expression, if possible.

a. $\dfrac{12x}{6}$ b. $\dfrac{20x^2}{4x}$ c. $\dfrac{x}{x-1}$

Solution

a. $\dfrac{12x}{6} =$ _____ = _____

b. $\dfrac{20x^2}{4x} =$ _____ = _____

c. $\dfrac{x}{x-1}$ _____

✓ **Checkpoint** Simplify the expression, if possible.

1. $\dfrac{-16x}{6}$	2. $\dfrac{24x^2}{16x^4}$	3. $\dfrac{3x+3}{6x}$

Example 2 *Write in Simplest Form*

Simplify the expression $\dfrac{x^2 + 5x + 4}{2x + 8}$.

Solution

$\dfrac{x^2 + 5x + 4}{2x + 8} =$ _____   Factor numerator and denominator.

$=$ _____   Divide out common factor _____.

✔ *Checkpoint* **Simplify the expression, if possible.**

4. $\dfrac{6x + 12}{2x + 4}$	**5.** $\dfrac{2x^2 - 2}{4x(x + 1)}$

MULTIPLYING RATIONAL EXPRESSIONS

Let a, b, and c be _____ variable expressions.

To multiply, multiply _____ and _____.

$$\dfrac{a}{b} \cdot \dfrac{c}{d} = \underline{\quad\quad}$$

Example 3 *Multiply Rational Expressions*

Multiply $\dfrac{14x^2}{8x^3} \cdot \dfrac{15x}{21x^4}$. Simplify the result.

Solution

$\dfrac{14x^2}{8x^3} \cdot \dfrac{15x}{21x^4} = \dfrac{210x^3}{168x^7}$

$=$ _____

$=$ _____

Example 4   *Multiply Rational Expressions*

Multiply $\dfrac{3x^2 + 15x}{x^2} \cdot \dfrac{2x}{3x - 6}$. Simplify the result.

Solution

$\dfrac{3x^2 + 15x}{x^2} \cdot \dfrac{2x}{3x - 6}$

$= \underline{\hspace{2cm}} \cdot \underline{\hspace{2cm}}$ **Factor the numerators and denominators.**

$= \underline{\hspace{4cm}}$ **Multiply the numerators and denominators.**

$= \underline{\hspace{4cm}}$ **Divide out the common factors.**

$= \underline{\hspace{2cm}}$ **Simplify the expression.**

Example 5   *Multiply by a Polynomial*

Multiply $\dfrac{x^2}{x^2 + 3x - 18} \cdot 5(3 - x)$. Simplify the result.

Solution

$\dfrac{x^2}{x^2 + 3x - 18} \cdot 5(3 - x)$

$= \dfrac{x^2}{x^2 + 3x - 18} \cdot \underline{\hspace{2cm}}$ **Write polynomial as a rational expression.**

$= \underline{\hspace{2cm}} \cdot \underline{\hspace{2cm}}$ **Factor $x^2 + 3x - 18$. Factor -1 out of $(3 - x)$.**

$= \underline{\hspace{3cm}}$ **Multiply. Divide out the common factors.**

$= \underline{\hspace{2cm}}$ **Simplify.**

Homework

✔ *Checkpoint* **Multiply. Simplify the result.**

6. $\dfrac{4x + 10}{5x - 5} \cdot \dfrac{6x^2}{6x + 15}$	7. $\dfrac{4x - 12}{2x^2} \cdot \dfrac{7x}{x - 3}$

9.4 Dividing Rational Expressions

Goal • Divide rational expressions and simplify complex fractions.

VOCABULARY

Complex fraction

DIVIDING RATIONAL EXPRESSIONS

Let a, b, c, and d be nonzero variable expressions. Use these steps to find the quotient $\frac{a}{b} \div \frac{c}{d}$.

Step 1 Rewrite the division as a _____.

$$\frac{a}{b} \div \frac{c}{d} = \frac{a}{b} \cdot \underline{\quad\quad}$$

Step 2 Multiply the _____ and _____.

Step 3 Factor the _____ and _____, if possible.

Step 4 Divide out the _____.

Step 5 Simplify.

Example 1 *Divide Rational Expressions*

Simplify $\frac{8}{x^2} \div \frac{18}{x^3}$.

Solution

$$\frac{8}{x^2} \div \frac{18}{x^3} = \frac{8}{x^2} \cdot \underline{\quad\quad}$$
Rewrite as a product.

$$= \frac{\underline{\quad\quad}}{\underline{\quad\quad}}$$
Multiply the numerators and denominators.

$$= \frac{\underline{\quad\quad}}{\underline{\quad\quad}}$$
Factor the numerators and denominators.

$$= \frac{\underline{\quad\quad}}{\underline{\quad\quad}}$$
Divide common factors x, x, and 2.

$$= \underline{\quad\quad}$$
Simplify the expression.

☑ *Checkpoint* **Write the quotient in simplest form.**

1. $\dfrac{7x}{3} \div \dfrac{2x}{9}$	**2.** $\dfrac{3}{x^2} \div \dfrac{5}{x}$	**3.** $\dfrac{-x^3}{3} \div \dfrac{x^2}{6}$

Example 2 *Divide Rational Expressions*

Simplify $\dfrac{x+4}{5} \div \dfrac{3x+12}{10x}$.

Solution

$\dfrac{x+4}{5} \div \dfrac{3x+12}{10x} = \dfrac{x+4}{5} \cdot \underline{\hspace{2cm}}$ **Rewrite as a product.**

$= \underline{\hspace{2cm}}$ **Multiply.**

$= \underline{\hspace{2cm}}$ **Factor numerators and denominators.**

$= \underline{\hspace{2cm}}$ **Divide out the common factors.**

$= \underline{\hspace{1cm}}$ **Simplify the expression.**

Example 3   *Divide by a Polynomial*

Simplify $\dfrac{2x - 6}{7x} \div (x - 3)$.

Solution

$\dfrac{2x - 6}{7x} \div (x - 3) = \dfrac{2x - 6}{7x} \cdot \underline{}$ Multiply by the reciprocal.

$= \underline{}$ Multiply.

$= \underline{}$ Factor.

$= \underline{}$ Divide out the common factor.

$= \underline{}$ Simplify the expression.

✔ *Checkpoint* **Write the quotient in simplest form.**

4. $\dfrac{x - 3}{3x} \div \dfrac{3 - x}{4}$	**5.** $\dfrac{15x^2}{2 - x} \div \dfrac{3}{4 - 2x}$

Example 4   *Simplify a Complex Fraction*

Simplify $\dfrac{\frac{1}{2x}}{\frac{x - 1}{5}}$.

Solution

$\dfrac{\frac{1}{2x}}{\frac{x - 1}{5}} = \dfrac{1}{2x} \div \dfrac{x - 1}{5}$ Rewrite as a division expression.

$= \dfrac{1}{2x} \cdot \underline{}$ Multiply by the reciprocal.

$= \underline{}$ Simplify.

Example 5 **Simplify a Complex Fraction**

Simplify $\dfrac{\dfrac{3x + 7}{x - 2}}{\dfrac{5x}{x - 2}}$.

Solution

$\dfrac{\dfrac{3x + 7}{x - 2}}{\dfrac{5x}{x - 2}} = \dfrac{3x + 7}{x - 2} \div \dfrac{5x}{x - 2}$ Rewrite as a division expression.

$= \dfrac{3x + 7}{x - 2} \cdot \underline{\hspace{2cm}}$ Multiply by the reciprocal.

$= \underline{\hspace{3cm}}$ Divide out the common factor $(x - 2)$.

$= \underline{\hspace{2cm}}$ Simplify.

✔ **Checkpoint** **Simplify the complex fraction.**

6. $\dfrac{\dfrac{1}{5x}}{\dfrac{x - 3}{5}}$

7. $\dfrac{\dfrac{1}{3x}}{\dfrac{1}{6x - 9}}$

Homework

8. $\dfrac{\dfrac{x(4x + 1)}{x - 3}}{\dfrac{8x + 2}{x + 2}}$

9.5 Adding and Subtracting Rational Expressions

Goal • Add and subtract rational expressions.

Your Notes

> **VOCABULARY**
>
> Least common denominator (LCD)

Example 1 — *Add and Subtract with Like Denominators*

Perform the indicated operation.

a. $\dfrac{1}{x} + \dfrac{6}{x}$ b. $\dfrac{3x}{2x-1} - \dfrac{7}{2x-1}$

c. $\dfrac{2x+5}{5x+15} - \dfrac{2x}{5x+15}$

Solution

a. $\dfrac{1}{x} + \dfrac{6}{x} = \underline{\quad\quad} = \underline{\quad\quad}$ Add numerators and simplify.

b. $\dfrac{3x}{2x-1} - \dfrac{7}{2x-1} = \underline{\quad\quad}$ Subtract numerators.

c. $\dfrac{2x+5}{5x+15} - \dfrac{2x}{5x+15} = \underline{\quad\quad\quad}$ Subtract numerators.

$= \underline{\quad\quad\quad}$ Simplify.

$= \underline{\quad\quad\quad}$ Factor.

$= \underline{\quad\quad\quad}$ Simplify.

✔ **Checkpoint** Perform the indicated operation.

1. $\dfrac{7}{x-7} - \dfrac{x}{x-7}$	2. $\dfrac{2x}{3x+2} + \dfrac{5x+1}{3x+2}$

Example 2   *Find the LCD of Rational Expressions*

Find the least common denominator.

a. $\dfrac{1}{15x}, \dfrac{1}{9x}$ b. $\dfrac{1}{2x + 2}, \dfrac{1}{3x - 3}$

Solution

a. The factors of 15x are ____, ____, and x, and the factors
   of 9x are ____^{2} and ____. Use the _____ power of
   each factor in _____ denominator and _____
   to find the LCD.

$$\text{LCD} = \underline{\quad} \cdot \underline{\quad}^2 \cdot x = \underline{\qquad}$$

b. The factors of 2x + 2 are ____ and _____. The
   factors of 3x − 3 are ____ and _____. Use
   the _____ power of each factor in _____
   denominator and _____ to find the LCD.

$$\text{LCD} = \underline{\quad} \cdot \underline{\quad} \cdot \underline{\qquad} \cdot (x - 1)$$
$$= \underline{\qquad}$$

✔ *Checkpoint* **Find the least common denominator.**

3. $\dfrac{1}{2x}, \dfrac{-3}{14x^2}$

4. $\dfrac{1}{x + 2}, \dfrac{5x}{x + 3}$

5. $\dfrac{2x}{x + 1}, \dfrac{5x + 1}{x^2 + 3x + 2}$

Example 3 **Add with Unlike Denominators**

Perform the indicated operation.

a. $\dfrac{5}{x} + \dfrac{3}{2x^2}$

b. $\dfrac{x}{x-5} + \dfrac{5}{x+1}$

Solution

a. The LCD is _____. Rewrite the expressions so they have _____.

$\dfrac{5}{x} + \dfrac{3}{2x^2} = \dfrac{5}{x} \cdot \underline{\quad} + \dfrac{3}{2x^2} \cdot \underline{\quad}$ Rewrite using the LCD.

$= \dfrac{\underline{\quad}}{\underline{\quad}} + \dfrac{\underline{\quad}}{\underline{\quad}}$ Simplify each term.

$= \dfrac{\underline{\quad}}{\underline{\quad}}$ Add numerators.

$= \dfrac{\underline{\quad}}{\underline{\quad}}$ Factor.

$= \dfrac{\underline{\quad}}{\underline{\quad}}$ Simplify.

b. The LCD is _____.

$\dfrac{x}{x-5} + \dfrac{5}{x+1}$

$= \dfrac{\underline{\quad\quad}}{\underline{\quad\quad}} + \dfrac{\underline{\quad\quad}}{\underline{\quad\quad}}$ Rewrite using the LCD.

$= \dfrac{\underline{\quad\quad}}{\underline{\quad\quad}} + \dfrac{\underline{\quad\quad}}{\underline{\quad\quad}}$ Simplify numerators.

$= \dfrac{\underline{\quad\quad}}{\underline{\quad\quad}}$ Add numerators.

$= \dfrac{\underline{\quad\quad}}{\underline{\quad\quad}}$ Combine like terms.

Example 4 **Subtract with Unlike Denominators**

Subtract $\dfrac{x}{x^2 + 8x + 12} - \dfrac{1}{x^2 - 36}$.

Solution

The factors of $x^2 + 8x + 12$ are _____ and _____, and the factors of $x^2 - 36$ are _____ and _____. So, the LCD is _____.

$$\dfrac{x}{x^2 + 8x + 12} - \dfrac{1}{x^2 - 36}$$

$$= \dfrac{x}{(x + 2)(x + 6)} - \underline{\hspace{2.5cm}}$$ Factor denominators.

$$= \underline{\hspace{3cm}} - \underline{\hspace{3cm}}$$ Rewrite using LCD.

$$= \underline{\hspace{2.5cm}}$$ Subtract numerators.

$$= \underline{\hspace{2.5cm}}$$ Distributive property

$$= \underline{\hspace{2.5cm}}$$ Combine like terms.

✓ **Checkpoint** **Perform the indicated operation.**

6. $\dfrac{7x - 1}{4x^2} - \dfrac{3}{2x}$

7. $\dfrac{5}{x - 2} + \dfrac{4}{x + 2}$

8. $\dfrac{2x - 6}{x^2 - x - 6} - \dfrac{x}{x + 2}$

Homework

Solving Rational Equations

Goal • Solve rational equations.

Your Notes

VOCABULARY

Rational equation

Cross multiply

| Example 1 | *Solve an Equation by Cross Multiplying* |

Solve $\dfrac{7}{x} = \dfrac{5}{x - 1}$.

Solution

$\dfrac{7}{x} = \dfrac{5}{x - 1}$ Write the original equation.

$7(\underline{\hspace{2cm}}) = \underline{\hspace{1cm}}$ Cross multiply.

$\underline{\hspace{2cm}} = 5x$ Use distributive property.

$\underline{\hspace{1cm}} = 5x + \underline{\hspace{1cm}}$ Add $\underline{\hspace{0.7cm}}$ to each side.

$\underline{\hspace{1cm}} = \underline{\hspace{1cm}}$ Subtract $\underline{\hspace{1cm}}$ from each side.

$x = \underline{\hspace{1cm}}$ Divide each side by $\underline{\hspace{0.7cm}}$.

✓ *Checkpoint* **Solve the equation. Check your solution.**

1. $\dfrac{2y + 1}{9} = \dfrac{y}{6}$	2. $\dfrac{1}{2x - 1} = \dfrac{-3}{x + 1}$
3. $\dfrac{2}{7} = \dfrac{x}{2x + 6}$	4. $\dfrac{5k}{k - 1} = \dfrac{25}{6}$

Example 2   *Multiply by the LCD*

Solve $\dfrac{2}{5} + \dfrac{1}{x} = \dfrac{3}{x}$.

Solution

The least common denominator is ____.

$$\dfrac{2}{5} + \dfrac{1}{x} = \dfrac{3}{x}$$ Write original equation.

$$\dfrac{2}{5} \cdot \underline{\quad} + \dfrac{1}{x} \cdot \underline{\quad} = \dfrac{3}{x} \cdot \underline{\quad}$$ Multiply each term by the LCD ____.

$$\underline{\quad} + \underline{\quad} = \underline{\quad}$$ Simplify each side.

$$\underline{\quad} = \underline{\quad}$$ Subtract ____ from each side.

$$x = \underline{\quad}$$ Divide each side by ____.

The solution is ____.

CHECK $\dfrac{2}{5} + \underline{\quad} = \underline{\quad}$ ✓

Example 3   *Solve Equations with Extraneous Solutions*

Solve $6 + \dfrac{6}{x-2} = \dfrac{3x}{x-2}$.

Solution

$$6 + \dfrac{6}{x-2} = \dfrac{3x}{x-2}$$

$$6 \cdot \underline{\hspace{3cm}} + \dfrac{6}{x-2} \cdot \underline{\hspace{2cm}} = \dfrac{3x}{x-2} \cdot \underline{\hspace{2cm}}$$

$$6\underline{\hspace{2cm}} + \underline{\quad} = \underline{\quad}$$

$$\underline{\hspace{2cm}} + 6 = \underline{\quad}$$

$$\underline{\hspace{2cm}} = \underline{\quad}$$

$$\underline{\hspace{2cm}} = 0$$

$$\underline{\quad} = \underline{\quad}$$

$$x = \underline{\quad}$$

The solution ____ is _____ because it leads to division by ____ in the _____ equation. So, the original equation has _____.

✓ Checkpoint Solve the equation. Check your solutions.

5. $\dfrac{11}{4} - \dfrac{3}{x} = \dfrac{5}{2x}$	6. $1 + \dfrac{4}{x+2} = \dfrac{2x}{x+2}$

Example 4 **Solve an Equation with Two Solutions**

Solve $\dfrac{3}{x-1} + \dfrac{2}{x+3} = 1$.

Solution

The least common denominator is (_____)(_____).

$$\dfrac{3}{x-1} + \dfrac{2}{x+3} = 1$$

$$\dfrac{3}{x-1} \cdot \underline{\hspace{3cm}} + \dfrac{2}{x+3} \cdot \underline{\hspace{3cm}}$$

$$= 1 \cdot \underline{\hspace{3cm}}$$

$$3\underline{\hspace{2cm}} + 2\underline{\hspace{2cm}} = \underline{\hspace{3cm}}$$

$$3x + \underline{\hspace{1cm}} + 2x - \underline{\hspace{1cm}} = \underline{\hspace{3cm}}$$

$$5x + \underline{\hspace{1cm}} = \underline{\hspace{3cm}}$$

$$0 = \underline{\hspace{3cm}}$$

$$0 = (\underline{\hspace{1.5cm}})(\underline{\hspace{1.5cm}})$$

$$x = \underline{\hspace{1cm}} \quad \text{or} \quad x = \underline{\hspace{1.5cm}}$$

The solutions are ___ and ____ . Check these in the original equation.

✓ Checkpoint Solve the equation. Check your solutions.

7. $\dfrac{3}{x-2} - \dfrac{x+1}{x-1} = 1$	8. $\dfrac{4}{x^2 - 5x - 4} + \dfrac{3}{x-1} = 1$

Words to Review

Use your own words and/or an example to explain the vocabulary word.

Inverse variation	Constant of variation
Joint variation	Rational function
Hyperbola	Branch
Rational expression	Simplified form
Complex fraction	Least common denominator
Rational equation	Cross multiply

Review your notes and Chapter 9 by using the Chapter Review on pages 507–510 of your textbook.

10.1 Populations and Surveys

Goal • Use unbiased samples and surveys to make predictions.

Your Notes

VOCABULARY

Population

Sample

Unbiased sample

Biased sample

Example 1 *Identify a Population and Sample*

Politics A mayoral candidate surveys 200 potential voters in the city to obtain their opinions on the issues that the mayor will face once the election is over. Identify the population and the sample for this situation.

Solution

The _____ consists of the residents of the city who are potential voters. The _____ is the _____ people from this population who are _____.

✔ *Checkpoint* Complete the following exercise.

---

1. A sports reporter surveys every fifth person leaving one exit from a soccer stadium to determine the most popular player on the soccer team. Identify the population and the sample for this situation.

Copyright © McDougal Littell/Houghton Mifflin Compan

| **Example 2** | *Identify Potentially Biased Samples* |

School News The editor of the school newspaper conducts a survey to determine which class students like best. Tell whether the sample chosen is likely to be biased. Explain.

a. Survey all of the students enrolled in band.

b. Survey every tenth student from an alphabetized list of the student body.

c. Survey all of the girls enrolled in the school.

Solution

a. This sample is _____ to be biased because students who are enrolled in band are _____ to choose band as their favorite class.

b. This sample is _____ to be biased since it samples every tenth student in the student body.

c. This sample is _____ to be biased because the boys may have a different opinion than the _____.

✔ *Checkpoint* **Tell whether the sample chosen is likely to be biased. Explain.**

2. To study support for placing a stop sign at an intersection, the people living within one block of the proposed new sign are surveyed.

3. To study support for moving the city festival from June to July, festival organizers survey every fourth household throughout the city.

Example 3 **Identify Potentially Biased Survey Questions**

Explain why the survey question may be biased. Then rewrite the question to remove the bias.

a. Do you prefer vanilla ice cream or the chocolate ice cream we had for dessert the last three evenings?

b. Did you prefer the first entertainer or the exciting closing act?

Solution

a. This question is _____ because it implies that there is something wrong with having chocolate ice cream three evenings in a row. A more neutral wording might be _____

_____

b. This question is _____ since it suggests that the closing act was better than the first entertainer. A more neutral wording might be _____

✔ *Checkpoint* **Explain why the survey question may be biased. Then rewrite the question to remove the bias.**

4. A teacher asked her students if they preferred to organize their math homework the way she likes or the way their previous math teacher had them organize it.

Example 4 *Make a Prediction from a Sample*

School Dance You want to find out if students at your school favor holding the school dance on Friday or Saturday. Of the 840 students in your school, you survey 70 students who were chosen in an unbiased way. You find that 50 of the 70 students favor Saturday. Predict how many students at your school prefer Saturday.

Solution

You can predict that the _____ of students in the population who are in favor of Saturday will be _____ as the ratio in the _____ that favor Saturday.

$$\frac{\text{Population size in favor}}{\text{Population size}} = \underline{\hspace{3cm}}$$

$$\frac{x}{840} = \underline{\hspace{1cm}}$$ **Substitute known values.**

$$70x = \underline{\hspace{2cm}}$$ **Cross product property**

$$x = \underline{\hspace{1cm}}$$ **Simplify.**

You can predict that about _____ students favor Saturday.

✔ *Checkpoint* **Complete the following exercise.**

5. In Example 4, suppose that 21 out of 45 students surveyed preferred Saturday. Predict how many of the 840 students favor Saturday.

10.2 Samples and Margin of Error

Goal • Classify sampling methods and find sampling error.

VOCABULARY

Convenience sample

Self-selected sample

Systematic sample

Random sample

Margin of error

Example 1 *Classify a Sample*

Retail In order to determine a community's desire for further retail growth in the city, the city planners have decided to survey everyone who works at a local supermarket.

a. Classify the sample as *convenience*, *self-selected*, *systematic*, or *random*. Explain your reasoning.

b. Tell whether this method is likely to result in a biased sample. Explain.

Solution

a. This is a _____ sample since city planners surveyed easy-to-reach members of the _____.

b. The survey is _____ to be _____. People who work at the local supermarket _____ necessarily represent the views of the entire city population.

✓ Checkpoint Complete the following exercise.

1. Suppose in Example 1 that the city planners decided to survey every fifth person listed in the city phone directory. Classify the sample. Then tell whether this method is likely to result in a biased sample.

Example 2 *Choose a Random Sample*

Vacation You are planning to conduct a survey to see which state will be visited by the most students in your school during your next summer vacation. You have a list of the names of all 400 students at your school. Describe two ways you can choose a random sample of 50 students to survey.

Solution

Method 1 Write the _____ of each student on a piece of paper and place all _____ pieces in a box. Draw out _____ pieces of paper and record the names.

Method 2 Assign each student a number from 1 through _____. Using a calculator, generate _____ _____ numbers in the sequence from ____ through _____. Survey the students corresponding to those numbers.

MARGIN OF ERROR FORMULA

If you take a _____ sample of size *n* from a large _____, you can use the following formula to approximate the _____ of _____ S.

$$\text{Margin of error} = \underline{}$$

This means that if ____% of the _____ responds a certain way, then it's likely that the _____ from _____ to _____ contains the actual percent of the population that would respond the _____.

Example 3 *Find and Interpret a Margin of Error*

Running In a random survey of 900 runners, 52.5% said they preferred to run in the morning.

a. What is the margin of error for the survey?

b. Give an interval that is likely to contain the actual percent of runners who prefer to run in the morning.

Solution

a. Margin of error = _____   Margin of error formula

$$= \underline{\hspace{2cm}}$$ Substitute _____ for *n*.

$$= \underline{\hspace{1.5cm}}, \text{ or } \underline{\hspace{1cm}}\%$$

The margin of error is _____%.

b. To find an interval that is likely to contain the actual population percent, _____ and ____ ____% to the sample result _____%.

_____% − _____% = _____%   **Lower bound of interval**

_____% + _____% = _____%   **Upper bound of interval**

It is likely that from _____% to _____% of the runners surveyed prefer to run in the morning.

☑ *Checkpoint* **Complete the following exercise.**

2. In a survey of 4900 airline passengers, 79% favor nonstop flights. What is the margin of error for the survey? Give an interval that is likely to contain the percent of all the passengers who prefer nonstop flights.

Homework

10.3 Transformations of Data

Goal • Find how statistical measures are affected by changes to data sets.

| **Example 1** | *Compare Data After Adding a Constant* |

Bowling You and five of your friends go bowling. Your "1st game" scores are shown below. Suppose that each of you bowl one more game and each of you increase your score by 12 pins, shown as "2nd game."

1st game: 100, 110, 160, 170, 180, 180

2nd game: 112, 122, 172, 182, 192, 192

a. Compare the mean, median, and mode of the first game to the second game. What do you observe?

b. Compare the ranges and the differences between the upper and lower quartiles for the first game to those for the second game. What do you observe?

Solution

a.

	First game	**Second game**
Mean	$\dfrac{900}{6} =$ ___	___ = ___
Median	$\dfrac{160 + 170}{2} =$ ___	___ = ___
Mode	___	___

The mean, median, and mode each _____ by ___.

b. **1st game:** Range = ___ − ___ = ___

Upper quartile − lower quartile

= ___ − ___ = ___

2nd game: Range = ___ − ___ = ___

Upper quartile − lower quartile

= ___ − ___ = ___

The range and the difference between the upper and lower quartiles _____.

Example 2 **Compare Data After Multiplying by a Constant**

Suppose the friends in Example 1 bowl a third game and increase their pin totals by 20% from their original scores, giving the scores shown as "3rd game."

1st game: 100, 110, 160, 170, 180, 180

3rd game: 120, 132, 192, 204, 216, 216

a. Compare the mean, median, and mode of the first game to the third game. What do you observe?

b. Compare the ranges and the differences between the upper and lower quartiles for the first game to those for the third game. What do you observe?

Solution

a.

	First game	Third game
Mean	$\dfrac{900}{6} = $ _____	_____ $= $ _____
Median	$\dfrac{160 + 170}{2} = $ _____	_____ $= $ _____
Mode	_____	_____

Find the percent increase in each measure:

Mean: _____ $= $ _____%

Median: _____ $= $ _____%

Similarly, you can show that the mode _____ by _____%.

The mean, median, and mode each _____ by _____%.

b. 1st game: Range = _____ − _____ = _____

Upper quartile − lower quartile

= _____ − _____ = _____

3rd game: Range = _____ − _____ = _____

Upper quartile − lower quartile

= _____ − _____ = _____

Find the percent increase in each measure:

Range: _____ = _____%

Difference: _____ = _____%

The range and the difference between the upper and lower quartiles each _____ by _____%.

✔ *Checkpoint* **Use the information below.**

Regular prices of 6 hats: $12, $24, $18, $10, $20, $24
Prices after 50% discount: $6, $12, $9, $5, $10, $12

---

1. Compare the mean, median, and mode of the set of original prices and the set of discounted prices. What do you observe?

---

2. Compare the ranges and the differences between the upper and lower quartiles for the original prices and the discount prices. What do you observe?

Example 3   *Graph Data After Adding a Constant*

Make a box-and-whisker plot of the first game data and the second game data from Example 1. How do the two graphs compare?

Solution

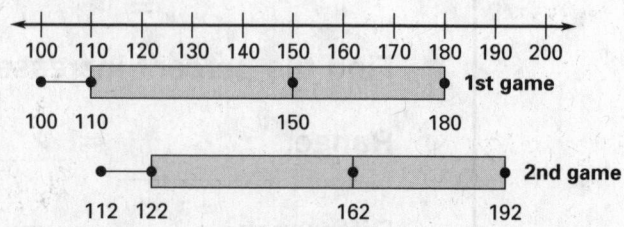

The two box-and-whisker plots are _____, but the plot for the second game data is shifted _____ units to the _____ compared to the plot for the first game data.

✔ *Checkpoint* Complete the following exercise.

3. Make a box-and-whisker plot of the two data sets found in Checkpoint 1. How do the graphs compare?

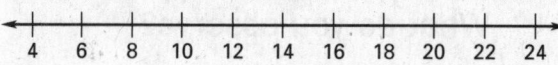

Homework

The Fundamental Counting Principle and Permutations

Goal • Use the fundamental counting principle and permutations.

Your Notes

VOCABULARY

Permutation _____

Factorial _____

FUNDAMENTAL COUNTING PRINCIPLE

Two Events If one event can occur in m ways and another event can occur in n ways, then the number of ways that _____ events can occur is _____.

Three Events If one event can occur in m ways, a second event in n ways, and a third event in p ways, then the number of ways _____ events can occur is _____.

The counting principle also extends to four or more events.

Example 1 *Use the Fundamental Counting Principle*

Ice Cream You stop to buy a single-dip ice cream cone. You have 3 choices for the cone, 15 choices of ice cream, and 5 choices for a topping. How many different ice cream cones could you order?

Solution

Number of ice cream cones = ____ • ____ • ____ = _____

There are _____ different single-dip ice cream cones.

Example 2   *Use the Fundamental Counting Principle*

License Plates The license plates in one state have 3 letters followed by 3 digits on them.

a. How many license plates are possible if letters and digits can be repeated?

b. How many license plates are possible if letters and digits cannot be repeated?

Solution

a. There are ____ choices for each letter and ____ choices for each digit. Use the fundamental counting principle.

Number of license plates

= ____ • ____ • ____ • ____ • ____ • ____

= _____

The number of different license plates is _____.

b. If you cannot repeat the letters and digits, there are ____ choices for the first letter but only ____ choices for the second letter, and ____ choices for the third letter. There are ____ choices for the first digit, ___ choices for the second digit, and ___ choices for the third digit.

Number of license plates

= ____ • ____ • ____ • ____ • ____ • ___

= _____

The number of different license plates is _____.

✔ *Checkpoint* **Complete the following exercise.**

1. Customers of an online banking service must create a personal identification number (PIN) when opening their account. The PIN, which consists of 6 digits followed by 2 letters, must be entered in order to access their online account. How many PINs are possible if the digits and letters can be repeated? if they cannot be repeated?

PERMUTATION OF *n* OBJECTS

The number of permutations of *n* distinct objects is ____!.

$n! =$ ____ $\cdot$ (_____) $\cdot$ (_____) $\cdot \cdots \cdot$ ____ $\cdot$ ____

Example 3   *Find the Number of Permutations*

Automobile Racing At a local speedway, 10 drivers have entered the novice race.

a. In how many different orders can the drivers finish the race?

b. In how many different ways can 4 of the drivers finish first through fourth?

Solution

a. This is a permutation of ____ drivers. So, there are ____! different orders.

$$10! = \underline{\quad} \cdot \underline{\quad} \cdot \cdots \cdot \underline{\quad} \cdot \underline{\quad} = \underline{\qquad\qquad}$$

The drivers can finish in _____ different ways.

b. Any of the 10 drivers can finish first. Then one of ____ drivers can finish second. Then one of ____ drivers can finish third. And then one of ____ drivers can finish fourth. The number of different orders is:

$$10 \cdot \underline{\quad} \cdot \underline{\quad} \cdot \underline{\quad} = \underline{\qquad}$$

The drivers can finish first through fourth in _____ different ways.

PERMUTATIONS OF *n* OBJECTS TAKEN *r* AT A TIME

The number of _____ of ____ objects taken ____ at a time is denoted by $_nP_r$ and is given by the following formula:

$$_nP_r = \underline{\qquad\qquad}$$

Example 4   *Permutations of n Objects Taken r at a Time*

How many three-letter permutations can you form from the letters in the word *EQUATION*? How many eight-letter permutations can be formed?

Solution

Find the number of _____ of 8 objects taken ___ at a time.

$$_8P\_\_ = \frac{\quad}{\quad} = \frac{8!}{5!} = \underline{\hspace{2cm}}$$

$$= \_\_ \cdot \_\_ \cdot \_\_ = \underline{\hspace{1.5cm}}$$

Find the number of _____ of 8 objects taken ___ at a time.

$$_8P\_\_ = \frac{\quad}{\quad} = \underline{\hspace{1.5cm}}$$

$$= \underline{\hspace{1.5cm}}$$

✔ *Checkpoint* **Complete the following exercises.**

2. In how many ways can 6 horses finish a race?

3. In how many different ways can you draw 5 cards from a standard deck of 52 cards?

Homework

10.5 Combinations and Pascal's Triangle

Goal • Use combinations and relate them to Pascal's triangle.

VOCABULARY

Combination

_____

Pascal's triangle

COMBINATIONS OF *n* OBJECTIVES TAKEN *r* AT A TIME

The number of _____ of ____ _____
objects taken ____ at a time is indicated by $_nC_r$ and is
given by the formula:

$$_nC_r = \frac{_nP_r}{r!} = \underline{\quad\quad\quad}$$

Example 1   *Find Combinations*

Books You are selecting 7 books from a stack of
32 books. If the order of the books you choose is not
important, how many different groups of 7 books are
possible?

Solution

Use the combinations formula with *n* = ____ and *r* = ____.

$$_{32}C_{\underline{\;}} = \underline{\qquad\qquad} = \underline{\qquad} = \underline{\qquad\qquad}$$

There are _____ different ways to select ____ books
from a stack of ____ books.

✔ **Checkpoint** **Complete the following exercise.**

1. In Example 1, suppose that 20 books are to be chosen from the stack of 32 books. How many different groups of 20 books are possible?

Example 2 *Distinguish Permutations and Combinations*

Tell whether the question can be answered using a *permutation* or a *combination*. Then find the answer.

a. At a family-reunion dinner, your mother tells you that you must try at least 2 of the 5 different vegetables being offered. How many different pairs of vegetables can you choose to try?

b. There are 9 finalists in a gymnastics ring event. Medals are awarded to the gymnasts who finish first, second, and third in the event. In how many ways can the gymnasts finish first through third?

Solution

a. The order in which you choose the vegetables _____ important. Use a _____ to answer the question.

$$_5C\_\_ = \frac{}{} = \frac{}{}$$

$$= \_\_\_ \text{ pairs of vegetables}$$

b. The order in which the medals are given ____ important. Use a _____ to answer the question.

$$_9P\_\_ = \frac{}{} = \frac{}{} = \_\_\_ \text{ ways}$$

Your Notes

✓ *Checkpoint* **Tell whether the question can be answered using a *permutation* or a *combination*. Find the answer.**

---

2. In how many ways can you chose 3 different pizza toppings from a list of 7 toppings?

_____

3. In how many ways can 4 shoppers line up at the checkout counter?

Example 3 *Find Combinations of Multiple Events*

A video store is having a special on new releases. There are 41 new releases: 12 comedies, 8 action, 7 drama, 5 suspense, and 9 family movies.

a. In how many ways can you chose 3 movies?

b. Suppose you want to rent exactly 2 comedies and 3 family movies. In how many different ways can you do this?

Solution

a. This is a simple _____ with $n =$ ____ and $r =$ ___. The number of 3-movie choices is:

$$\frac{}{}C\frac{}{} = \frac{}{\rule{1cm}{0.4pt}} = \frac{}{\rule{1cm}{0.4pt}}$$

$$= \underline{\hspace{1cm}} \text{ choices}$$

b. This is a multiple event: You must choose the comedies *and* the family movies. You can choose 2 of the 12 comedies in $\underline{\ }C\underline{\ }$ ways. You can choose 3 of the 9 family movies in $\underline{\ }C\underline{\ }$ ways. Multiply to find the total number of possibilities.

$$_{12}C\underline{\ } \cdot {_9}C\underline{\ } = \frac{}{\rule{1cm}{0.4pt}} \cdot \frac{}{\rule{1cm}{0.4pt}}$$

$$= \frac{\rule{1.5cm}{0.4pt} \cdot \rule{1cm}{0.4pt}}{}$$

$$= \underline{\hspace{1cm}} \text{ ways}$$

✓ *Checkpoint* **Refer to the movie choices in Example 4 to complete the following exercises.**

4. In how many ways can you chose 4 of the newly released suspense movies?

_____

5. Suppose you want to rent exactly 2 action movies and 2 dramas. In how many different ways can you do this?

Example 4   *Use Pascal's Triangle*

Class Representatives Out of 7 finalists, your class must choose 3 class representatives. Use Pascal's triangle to find the number of combinations of 3 students who can be chosen as representatives.

Solution

The _____ row of Pascal's triangle represents _____ of 7 objects taken r at a time where r is from 0 to 7. You need to find $_7C$___.

$n =$ ___ (7th row)

___   ___   ___   ___   ___   ___   ___   ___

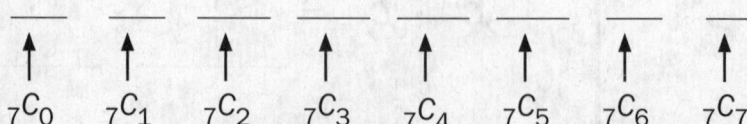

$_7C_0$ $_7C_1$ $_7C_2$ $_7C_3$ $_7C_4$ $_7C_5$ $_7C_6$ $_7C_7$

There are ____ combinations of 3 students who can be chosen as class representatives.

Homework

10.6 Introduction to Probability

Goal • Find theoretical and experimental probabilities.

VOCABULARY

Probability

_____

Theoretical probability

_____

_____

Experimental probability

_____

_____

Geometric probability

THEORETICAL PROBABILITY OF AN EVENT

When all outcomes are _____, the _____ probability that an event A will occur is:

$$P(A) = \underline{\hspace{6cm}}$$

The theoretical probability of an event is often simply called its probability.

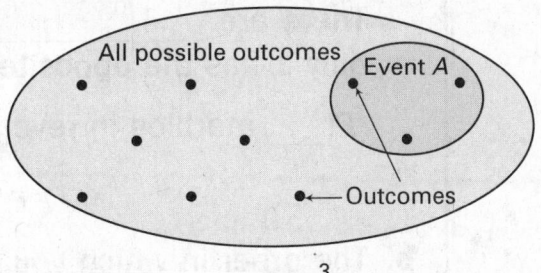

$$P(A) = \frac{3}{10}$$

Example 1   *Find the Probability of an Event*

A cube with 3 red faces, 2 blue faces, and 1 green face is rolled. What is the probability that the green face lands up?

Solution

The _____ sides represent the ___ possible outcomes. _____ corresponds to the event "green face lands up."

$P(\text{green}) = \dfrac{}{}$

Example 2   *Use Permutations or Combinations*

A jar contains 7 marbles numbered 1 through 7.

a. You draw a marble out of the jar and record the number on the marble. Without replacing the first marble, you draw a second marble and record the number on it. You continue the process until all of the marbles have been drawn. If you repeat the experiment, what is the probability that you will draw the marbles in exactly the opposite order from the first drawings?

b. Suppose you draw 2 marbles one after the other without replacing the first one. What is the probability that both of the numbers are odd?

Solution

a. Any ordering of the marbles is a possible _____. There are ___! _____ of the marbles, but only 1 has the opposite order of the first drawings.

$P(\underline{} \text{ marbles in reverse order}) = \dfrac{}{} = \dfrac{}{}$

$\approx \dfrac{}{}$

b. The order in which you draw the two marbles _____ important. There are $\underline{}C\underline{}$ ways to draw two marbles and $\underline{}C\underline{}$ ways to draw two marbles with an odd number.

$P(\underline{} \text{ odd numbers}) = \dfrac{{}_4C_2}{{}_7C_2} = \dfrac{}{}$

$\approx \underline{}$, or about ___%

✓ *Checkpoint* **Use a standard deck of 52 playing cards to find the given probability. One card is drawn at random.**

1. drawing a red queen	**2.** drawing a club

EXPERIMENTAL PROBABILITY OF AN EVENT

For a given number of trials of an experiment, the
_____ probability that an event *A* will occur is:

$$P(A) = \underline{\hspace{7cm}}$$

Example 3 *Find Experimental Probabilities*

Exam Grades The exam grades for the students in a history class are shown in the bar graph below. What is the experimental probability that a randomly chosen student in this history class received a grade of *C* or better.

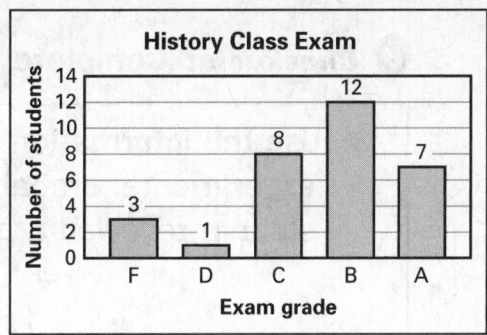

History Class Exam

Solution

Find the total number of students in the class.

$3 + 1 + \underline{\hspace{1cm}} + \underline{\hspace{1cm}} + \underline{\hspace{1cm}} = \underline{\hspace{1cm}}$

There are $\underline{\hspace{1cm}} + \underline{\hspace{1cm}} + \underline{\hspace{1cm}} = \underline{\hspace{1cm}}$ students who received a grade of *C* or better.

$P(\text{at least a } C) = \dfrac{}{} \approx \underline{\hspace{1.5cm}}$

Example 4	*Find a Geometric Probability*

Darts You are throwing darts at the target shown. If a dart is equally likely to hit anywhere on the target, what is the probability that it lands inside the square measuring 8 inches by 8 inches but outside of the square measuring 4 inches by 4 inches?

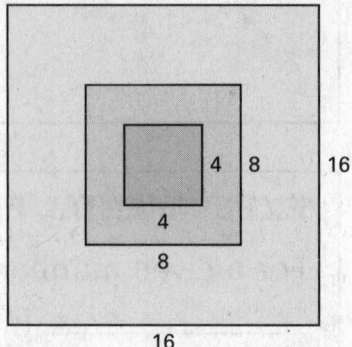

Solution

The area of the 8-inch by 8-inch square _____ the area of the 4-inch by 4-inch square is (___ • ___) − (___ • ___)
= ____ square inches. The area of the entire target is
(___ • ___) = _____ square inches.

P(dart inside 8 by 8 square but *not* inside 4 by 4 square)

= ____ = _____ , or _____%

☑ *Checkpoint* **Complete the following exercises.**

3. Use the information in Example 3 to find the experimental probability that a randomly selected student received a grade of B or better.

4. Using Example 4, what is the probability that the dart lands in the 4-inch by 4-inch square?

10.7 Probability of Compound Events

Goal • Find probabilities of unions and intersections.

VOCABULARY

Compound event

_____

Overlapping events

_____

Disjoint or mutually exclusive events

_____

Complement of an event

PROBABILITY OF COMPOUND EVENTS

Overlapping Events If A and B are overlapping events, then $P(A$ and $B)$ ____ 0, and the probability of A or B is:

$$P(\underline{\hspace{2cm}}) = P(A) \underline{\hspace{1cm}} P(B) \underline{\hspace{1cm}} P(\underline{\hspace{2cm}})$$

Disjoint Events If A and B are disjoint events, then $P(A$ and $B)$ ____ 0, and the probability of A or B is:

$$P(\underline{\hspace{2cm}}) = P(A) \underline{\hspace{1cm}} P(B)$$

Example 1   *Find P(A or B) for Disjoint Events*

Dice You roll a six-sided die. What is the probability of rolling a 2 *or* a 5?

Solution

Let event A be rolling a 2 and let event B be rolling a 5.
Event A has ____ outcome and event B has ____ outcome.
Events A and B are _____ events.

$$P(A \text{ or } B) = P(A) \underline{\hspace{1cm}} P(B) = \underline{\hspace{0.6cm}} + \underline{\hspace{0.6cm}} = \underline{\hspace{0.6cm}} \approx \underline{\hspace{1.5cm}}$$

The probability is about _____, or about ____%.

Example 2 *Find P(A or B) for Overlapping Events*

Dice You roll a six-sided die. What is the probability of rolling an odd number *or* a number less than 3?

Solution

Let event *A* be rolling an odd number. Let event *B* be rolling a number less than 3. Event *A* has ___ outcomes and event *B* has ___ outcomes. _____ of the outcomes is common to both *A* and *B*.

$P(A \text{ or } B) = P(A) \text{___} P(B) \text{___} P(A \text{ and } B)$

$$= \frac{\quad}{\quad} + \frac{\quad}{\quad} - \frac{\quad}{\quad} = \frac{\quad}{\quad} , \text{ or about } \text{_____}$$

The probability is about _____, or about ____%.

Example 3 *Find P(A and B) for Overlapping Events*

Music In a survey of 300 students, 150 like pop music or country music. There are 97 students who like pop music and there are 83 students who like country music. What is the probability that a student selected at random likes both pop music *and* country music?

Solution

Let *A* represent the event "likes pop music." Let *B* represent the event "likes country music." You need to find $P(\text{_____})$.

You are given:

$P(A) = \dfrac{\quad}{\quad} \qquad P(B) = \dfrac{\quad}{\quad} \qquad P(A \text{ or } B) = \dfrac{\quad}{\quad}$

$P(A \text{ or } B) = P(A) + P(B) - P(A \text{ and } B)$ **Write formula.**

$$= \frac{\quad}{\quad} + \frac{\quad}{\quad} - P(A \text{ and } B) \qquad \textbf{Substitute.}$$

$$P(A \text{ and } B) = \frac{\quad}{\quad} + \frac{\quad}{\quad} - \frac{\quad}{\quad} \qquad \textbf{Solve for } P(A \text{ and } B).$$

$$= \frac{\quad}{\quad} = \frac{\quad}{\quad} , \text{ or } \text{____}$$

The probability is _____, or ____%.

✔ *Checkpoint* **Complete the following exercises.**

1. You roll a six-sided die. What is the probability of rolling a number less than 4 *or* an even number?

---

2. In a survey of 125 people, 90 of them like orange juice or grape juice. There are 62 people who like orange juice and 43 people who like grape juice. What is the probability that a randomly selected person likes both orange juice and grape juice?

PROBABILITY OF THE COMPLEMENT OF AN EVENT

The sum of the probabilities of an event and its _____ is ___.

$P(A) + P($_____$) = $___ , so $P($_____$) = $___ $- P(A)$

Example 4 *Find the Probabilities of Compliments*

When two six-sided dice are rolled, there are 36 possible outcomes. Find the probability of the given event.

a. The sum is not 7.

b. The sum is greater than or equal to 5.

Solution

a. $P(\text{sum is not 7}) = 1 - P(\underline{\hspace{2cm}})$

$$= 1 - \frac{}{\underline{\hspace{1cm}}}$$

$$= \frac{}{\underline{\hspace{1cm}}}$$

$$\approx \underline{\hspace{2cm}}$$

b. $P(\text{sum} \geq 5) = 1 - P(\underline{\hspace{2cm}})$

$$= 1 - \frac{}{\underline{\hspace{1cm}}}$$

$$= \frac{}{\underline{\hspace{1cm}}}$$

$$\approx \underline{\hspace{2cm}}$$

✔ *Checkpoint* Complete the following exercise.

3. Use the information in Example 4 to find the probability that the sum is not 8.

Homework

10.8 Probability of Independent and Dependent Events

Goal • Find the probability of independent and dependent events.

Your Notes

VOCABULARY

Independent events

_____

Dependent events

_____

Conditional probability

Example 1 *Identify Events*

Tell whether the events are *independent* or *dependent*. Explain.

a. You get to choose a book to read from your friend's library. After you make your choice, your friend chooses a book.

b. You roll a number cube and it shows a 2. You roll the number cube again and it shows a 5.

Solution

a. _____; after you have chosen a book, there are _____ books for your friend to choose from.

b. _____; what happens on the first roll has no _____ on the _____ roll.

Your Notes

✓ *Checkpoint* **Tell whether the events are *independent* or *dependent*. Explain.**

> **1.** You draw a card from a deck of playing cards and then replace it. You then draw a second card.

Example 2   *Find Conditional Probabilities*

Eye Color The results of a survey about eye color are shown in the table below.

a. What is the probability that a person who was surveyed has blue eyes?

b. What is the probability that a person who was surveyed was a male with blue eyes?

	Green eyes	Blue eyes	Brown eyes	Hazel eyes	Totals
Male	27	35	15	23	100
Female	12	9	38	41	100

Solution

a. $P(\text{blue eyes}) = \dfrac{\text{Number of people with blue eyes}}{\text{Total number of people}}$

$$= \underline{\quad} = \underline{\quad}$$

b. $P(\text{blue eyes} \mid \text{male})$

$$= \dfrac{\text{Number of males with blue eyes}}{\text{Total number of males}}$$

$$= \underline{\quad} = \underline{\quad}$$

✓ *Checkpoint* **Complete the following exercise.**

> **2.** Use the table in Example 2 to find the probability that a person who was surveyed has hazel eyes given that the person is a female.

Notice that if events *A* and *B* are independent, then $P(B|A)$ is just $P(B)$. So the first formula given here is a special case of the second formula.

PROBABILITY OF INDEPENDENT AND DEPENDENT EVENTS

Independent Events If *A* and *B* are _____ events, then the probability that both *A* and *B* occur is

$$P(\underline{\hspace{2cm}}) = P(\underline{\hspace{1cm}}) \underline{\hspace{1cm}} P(\underline{\hspace{1cm}}).$$

Dependent Events If *A* and *B* are _____ events, then the probability that both *A* and *B* occur is

$$P(\underline{\hspace{2cm}}) = P(\underline{\hspace{1cm}}) \underline{\hspace{1cm}} P(\underline{\hspace{2cm}}).$$

Example 3   *Independent and Dependent Events*

Marbles A bag contains 15 yellow, 10 red, and 12 blue marbles. Suppose you randomly select two marbles. Find the probability that the first marble is yellow and the second is *not* yellow in the situation described.

a. You replace the first marble before selecting the second one.

b. You do *not* replace the first marble before selecting the second one.

Solution

a. If you _____ the first marble before selecting the second one, the events are _____. Let *A* represent the first marble being yellow and *B* represent the second marble *not* being yellow.

$$P(A \text{ and } B) = P(A) \cdot P(\underline{\hspace{1cm}})$$

$$= \frac{15}{37} \cdot \underline{\hspace{1cm}}$$

$$\approx 0.41 \cdot \underline{\hspace{1cm}}$$

$$\approx \underline{\hspace{1cm}}$$

b. If you do not _____ the first marble before selecting the second one, the events are _____.

$$P(A \text{ and } B) = P(A) \cdot P(\underline{\hspace{1cm}})$$

$$= \underline{\hspace{1cm}} \cdot \underline{\hspace{1cm}}$$

$$\approx \underline{\hspace{1cm}} \cdot \underline{\hspace{1cm}}$$

$$\approx \underline{\hspace{1cm}}$$

Example 4   *Probability of Three Dependent Events*

Pencils Your teacher passes around a box with 10 red pencils, 8 pink pencils, and 13 green pencils. If you and the two people in your group are the first three students to randomly select a pencil, what is the probability that all three of you select a pink pencil?

Solution

Let event *A* be that you choose a pink pencil, event *B* be that the second group member chooses a pink pencil, and event *C* be that the third group member chooses a pink pencil. Since the pencils are not replaced, these events are _____.

$$P(A \text{ and } B \text{ and } C) = \frac{8}{31} \cdot \underline{\quad} \cdot \underline{\quad}$$

$$\approx \underline{\quad} \cdot \underline{\quad} \cdot \underline{\quad}$$

$$\approx \underline{\quad}$$

The probability that all three of you select a pick pencil is about _____.

✔ **Checkpoint** **Complete the following exercise.**

3. From Example 4, what is the probability that all three of you choose a red pencil?

Homework

Words to Review

Use your own words and/or an example to explain the vocabulary word.

Population	Sample
Unbiased sample	Biased sample
Convenience sample	Self-selected sample
Systematic sample	Random sample
Margin of error	Permutation
Factorial	Combination

Pascal's triangle	Probability
Theoretical probability	Experimental probability
Geometric probability	Compound event
Overlapping events	Disjoint or mutually exclusive events
Complement of an event	Independent events
Dependent events	Conditional probability

Review your notes and Chapter 10 by using the Chapter Review on pages 575–578 of your textbook.

11.1 Matrix Operations

Goal • Perform matrix addition, subtraction, and scalar multiplication.

VOCABULARY

Matrix

Element

Dimensions of a matrix

Equal matrices

Scalar

Scalar multiplication

Example 1 *Compare Matrices*

Tell whether matrix *A* is equal to matrix *B*. Explain.

$$A = \begin{bmatrix} 2 & -4 \\ 0 & 12 \end{bmatrix} \qquad B = \begin{bmatrix} (1+1) & -1(4) \\ 0 & (14-2) \end{bmatrix}$$

Solution

The dimension of both matrices is _____. Each element shown in matrix *A* ____ equal to the _____ element found in matrix *B*. So, matrix *A* and matrix *B* are _____.

Your Notes

✓ *Checkpoint* **Tell whether the matrices are equal. Explain.**

1. $\begin{bmatrix} 5 & -4 \\ 8 & 24 \\ -2 & 0 \end{bmatrix}, \begin{bmatrix} 5 & 2(-2) \\ 8 & (-8-16) \\ -2 & 0(-7) \end{bmatrix}$

Example 2 *Add and Subtract Matrices*

Add or subtract, if possible. If not possible, state the reason.

a. $\begin{bmatrix} 6 & -2 \\ 1 & 3 \end{bmatrix} - \begin{bmatrix} 3 \\ 2 \end{bmatrix}$

b. $\begin{bmatrix} -2 & 1 \\ 0 & 3 \\ 7 & 6 \end{bmatrix} + \begin{bmatrix} 1 & -4 \\ -2 & 9 \\ 1 & 5 \end{bmatrix}$

c. $\begin{bmatrix} 3 & 0 & -4 \end{bmatrix} - \begin{bmatrix} -5 & 4 & 0 \end{bmatrix}$

Solution

a. The dimensions of $\begin{bmatrix} 6 & -2 \\ 1 & 3 \end{bmatrix}$ are _____ and the dimensions of $\begin{bmatrix} 3 \\ 2 \end{bmatrix}$ are _____. So, you _____ subtract the matrices.

b. The dimensions of both matrices are _____. So, add the matrices.

$\begin{bmatrix} -2 & 1 \\ 0 & 3 \\ 7 & 6 \end{bmatrix} + \begin{bmatrix} 1 & -4 \\ -2 & 9 \\ 1 & 5 \end{bmatrix} =$

_____

$=$

_____

c. The dimensions of both matrices are _____. So, subtract the matrices.

$\begin{bmatrix} 3 & 0 & -4 \end{bmatrix} - \begin{bmatrix} -5 & 4 & 0 \end{bmatrix}$

$=$ _____

$=$ _____

Copyright © McDougal Littell/Houghton Mifflin Compan

✓ *Checkpoint* Add or subtract, if possible. If not possible, state the reason.

2. $\begin{bmatrix} 8 & -3 \\ 2 & 0 \end{bmatrix} + \begin{bmatrix} -1 & 0 \\ 4 & 7 \end{bmatrix}$	3. $\begin{bmatrix} -1 \\ 3 \end{bmatrix} - \begin{bmatrix} 9 \\ 0 \end{bmatrix}$

Example 3 *Multiply a Matrix by a Scalar*

Perform the indicated operation.

a. $-2\begin{bmatrix} -3 & 0 \\ 1 & -2 \end{bmatrix}$

b. $6\begin{bmatrix} -1 & -1 \end{bmatrix}$

Solution

a. $-2\begin{bmatrix} -3 & 0 \\ 1 & -2 \end{bmatrix} =$ _____ $=$ _____

b. $6\begin{bmatrix} -1 & -1 \end{bmatrix} =$ _____ $=$ _____

Example 4 *Perform Multiple Operations*

Perform the indicated operations:

$$-3\left(\begin{bmatrix} 2 & -1 \\ 4 & 5 \end{bmatrix} - \begin{bmatrix} 2 & -3 \\ -2 & 8 \end{bmatrix}\right).$$

Solution

$$-3\left(\begin{bmatrix} 2 & -1 \\ 4 & 5 \end{bmatrix} - \begin{bmatrix} 2 & -3 \\ -2 & 8 \end{bmatrix}\right)$$

$$= -3\begin{bmatrix} 2 - 2 & -1 - (-3) \\ 4 - (-2) & 5 - 8 \end{bmatrix}$$

$$= \underline{\hspace{4cm}}$$

$$= \underline{\hspace{4cm}}$$

Example 5 *Solve a Matrix Equation*

Solve the matrix equation for *x* and *y*.

$$\begin{bmatrix} 3x & 1 \\ 0 & 6 \end{bmatrix} + \begin{bmatrix} 1 & -3 \\ 2 & -2y \end{bmatrix} = \begin{bmatrix} -2 & -2 \\ 2 & 0 \end{bmatrix}$$

Solution

To solve the matrix equation, _____ the matrices on the left side of the equation, _____ the element involving *x* with its corresponding element, _____ the element involving *y* with its corresponding element, and then solve for *x* and *y*.

$$\begin{bmatrix} 3x & 1 \\ 0 & 6 \end{bmatrix} + \begin{bmatrix} 1 & -3 \\ 2 & -2y \end{bmatrix} = \begin{bmatrix} -2 & -2 \\ 2 & 0 \end{bmatrix}$$ **Original equation**

$$= \begin{bmatrix} -2 & -2 \\ 2 & 0 \end{bmatrix}$$ **Add corresponding matrix elements.**

Equate corresponding elements for *x* and solve the resulting equation.

_____ = _____   **Equate corresponding elements**
                    _____ **and** _____.

3*x* = _____   **Subtract ____ from each side.**

x = _____   **Divide each side by ___.**

Equate corresponding elements for *y* and solve the resulting equation.

_____ = ___   **Equate corresponding elements**
                    _____ **and** ___.

−2*y* = _____   **Subtract ____ from each side.**

y = ___   **Divide each side by _____.**

✓ *Checkpoint* **Perform the indicated operation(s).**

4. $\begin{bmatrix} 2 & 0 \\ -1 & 4 \end{bmatrix} - 2\begin{bmatrix} 0 & -3 \\ 7 & 0 \end{bmatrix}$

5. $-3\begin{bmatrix} -1 & 3 & -2 \\ 2 & 9 & -6 \end{bmatrix}$

Solve the matrix equations for *x* and *y*.

6. $\begin{bmatrix} x & 4 \\ 3 & 2y \end{bmatrix} = \begin{bmatrix} -5 & 4 \\ 3 & -8 \end{bmatrix}$

7. $\begin{bmatrix} 3 & -2x \\ 1 & 7 \end{bmatrix} - \begin{bmatrix} 1 & -6 \\ -5y & 4 \end{bmatrix}$

$= \begin{bmatrix} -2 & 3 \\ -4 & -3 \end{bmatrix}$

PROPERTIES OF MATRIX ADDITION AND SUBTRACTION

Let *A*, *B*, and *C* be matrices with the same dimensions, and let *k* be a scalar.

**Associative Property
of Addition** $\quad (A + B) + C =$ _____

**Commutative Property
of Addition** $\quad A + B =$ _____

**Distributive Property
of Addition** $\quad k(A + B) =$ _____

**Distributive Property
of Subtraction** $\quad k(A - B) =$ _____

11.2 Multiplying Matrices

Goal • Multiply matrices.

| **Example 1** | *Describe Matrix Products* |

Given the dimensions of matrices *A* and *B*, tell whether the product *AB* is defined. If so, give the dimensions of *AB*.

a. *A*: 3 × 4, *B*: 2 × 3   **b.** *A*: 2 × 3, *B*: 3 × 3

Solution

a. Because the number of columns in *A* (_____) _____ equal the number of _____ in *B* (_____), the product *AB* _____ defined.

b. Because *A* is a _____ matrix and *B* is a _____ matrix, the product *AB* ____ defined. The _____ of *AB* are _____ .

MATRIX MULTIPLICATION

To find the product of two matrices, multiply the elements of each _____ of the first matrix by the elements of each _____ of the second matrix, and then _____ the products, as shown below.

ALGEBRA

$$\begin{bmatrix} a & b \\ c & d \end{bmatrix} \cdot \begin{bmatrix} e & f \\ g & h \end{bmatrix} = \begin{bmatrix} ae + bg & af + bh \\ ce + dg & cf + dh \end{bmatrix}$$

EXAMPLE

$$\begin{bmatrix} 3 & -4 \\ 1 & -2 \end{bmatrix} \begin{bmatrix} 2 & -1 \\ 5 & 3 \end{bmatrix} =$$

$$= \begin{bmatrix} -14 & -15 \\ -8 & -7 \end{bmatrix}$$

Example 2 *Multiply Matrices*

Find the product AB when $A = \begin{bmatrix} 2 & -2 \\ 3 & 1 \end{bmatrix}$ and $B = \begin{bmatrix} 1 & 3 \\ 2 & 5 \end{bmatrix}$.

Solution

Multiply the numbers in the first _____ of A by the numbers in the first _____ of B, _____ the products, and put the result in the _____ row, _____ column of AB.

$$\begin{bmatrix} 2 & -2 \\ 3 & 1 \end{bmatrix} \begin{bmatrix} 1 & 3 \\ 2 & 5 \end{bmatrix} = \begin{bmatrix} 2(1) + (-2)(2) & \\ & \end{bmatrix}$$

Multiply the numbers in the first _____ of A by the numbers in the second _____ of B, _____ the products, and put the result in the _____ row, _____ column of AB.

$$\begin{bmatrix} 2 & -2 \\ 3 & 1 \end{bmatrix} \begin{bmatrix} 1 & 3 \\ 2 & 5 \end{bmatrix} = \underline{\hspace{6cm}}$$

Multiply the numbers in the _____ row of A by the numbers in the _____ column of B, _____ the products, and put the result in the _____ row, _____ column of AB.

$$\begin{bmatrix} 2 & -2 \\ 3 & 1 \end{bmatrix} \begin{bmatrix} 1 & 3 \\ 2 & 5 \end{bmatrix} = \underline{\hspace{6cm}}$$

Multiply the numbers in the second row of A by the numbers in the _____ column of B, _____ the products, and put the result in the _____ row, _____ column of AB.

$$\begin{bmatrix} 2 & -2 \\ 3 & 1 \end{bmatrix} \begin{bmatrix} 1 & 3 \\ 2 & 5 \end{bmatrix} = \underline{\hspace{6cm}}$$

Simplify the product matrix.

$$\begin{bmatrix} 2 & -2 \\ 3 & 1 \end{bmatrix} \begin{bmatrix} 1 & 3 \\ 2 & 5 \end{bmatrix} = \underline{\hspace{4cm}}$$

✔ *Checkpoint* **Given the dimensions of the matrices *A* and *B*, tell whether the product *AB* is defined. If so, give the dimensions of *AB*.**

1. *A*: 3 × 4, *B*: 4 × 2	**2.** *A*: 2 × 2, *B*: 3 × 5

Find the product. If it is not defined, state the reason.

3. $\begin{bmatrix} 3 & 2 \\ 1 & 0 \end{bmatrix}\begin{bmatrix} 4 & 0 \\ 3 & 2 \end{bmatrix}$	**4.** $\begin{bmatrix} 3 \\ -4 \end{bmatrix}\begin{bmatrix} -2 & 5 \end{bmatrix}$

PROPERTIES OF MATRIX MULTIPLICATION

Let *A*, *B*, and *C* be matrices.

Associative Property of Matrix Multiplication $\qquad A(BC) = (\underline{\quad\quad})\underline{\quad}$

Left Distributive Property $\qquad A(B + C) = \underline{\quad\quad} + \underline{\quad\quad}$

Right Distributive Property $\qquad (A + B)C = \underline{\quad\quad} + \underline{\quad\quad}$

Example 3 *Use a Property of Matrix Multiplication*

Let $A = \begin{bmatrix} 2 & -1 \\ 4 & 1 \end{bmatrix}$, $B = \begin{bmatrix} 0 & -3 \\ 5 & 1 \end{bmatrix}$, and $C = \begin{bmatrix} 0 & 4 \\ 2 & 3 \end{bmatrix}$.

Simplify $AC + BC$.

Solution

$AC + BC$

= (_____)____   **Right Distributive Property**

= _____   **Substitute for A, B, and C.**

= _____   **Add A and ____.**

= $\begin{bmatrix} \\ \end{bmatrix}$ **Multiply.**

= _____   **Simplify.**

✓ *Checkpoint* **Complete the following exercise.**

5. Use the matrices in Example 3 to find $AC + BC$ without using the distributive property. Compare your answer to the solution in Example 3.

Homework

11.3 Solving Linear Systems Using Inverse Matrices

Goal • Find inverse matrices and use them to solve linear systems.

VOCABULARY

Identity matrix

Inverse matrices

Coefficient matrix

Matrix of variables

Matrix of constants

Example 1 *Verify Inverse Matrices*

Are $A = \begin{bmatrix} 2 & -3 \\ -5 & 8 \end{bmatrix}$ and $B = \begin{bmatrix} 8 & 3 \\ 5 & 2 \end{bmatrix}$ inverses?

Solution

You can show that A and B are inverses by showing $AB = \underline{\quad}$ and $\underline{\quad} = \underline{\quad}$.

$$AB = \begin{bmatrix} 2 & -3 \\ -5 & 8 \end{bmatrix}\begin{bmatrix} 8 & 3 \\ 5 & 2 \end{bmatrix}$$

$$= \underline{\hspace{5cm}} \qquad = \underline{\hspace{2cm}}$$

$$BA = \begin{bmatrix} 8 & 3 \\ 5 & 2 \end{bmatrix}\begin{bmatrix} 2 & -3 \\ -5 & 8 \end{bmatrix}$$

$$= \underline{\hspace{5cm}} \qquad = \underline{\hspace{2cm}}$$

✔ *Checkpoint* Tell whether the matrices are inverses.

1. $\begin{bmatrix} -2 & -3 \\ 3 & 4 \end{bmatrix}, \begin{bmatrix} 4 & 3 \\ -3 & -2 \end{bmatrix}$

2. $\begin{bmatrix} 1 & 3 \\ 2 & 7 \end{bmatrix}, \begin{bmatrix} 7 & -3 \\ -2 & -1 \end{bmatrix}$

Example 2 *Find the Inverse of a Matrix*

Use a graphing calculator to find the inverse of matrix A. Then use the calculator to verify that $AA^{-1} = I$ and $A^{-1}A = I$.

$$A = \begin{bmatrix} 3 & 2 & -1 \\ 7 & 5 & 0 \\ 5 & 3 & -2 \end{bmatrix}$$

Solution

Enter matrix A into the graphing calculator and calculate _____. Then find the products _____ and _____ to verify that you obtain the 3 × 3 _____ matrix.

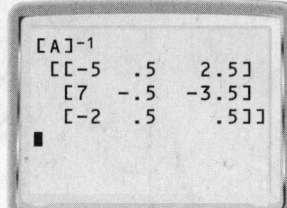
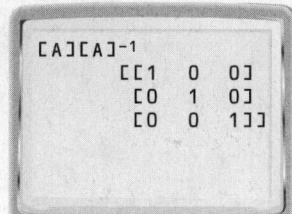
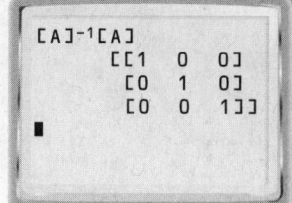

Find the inverse of A.   Verify $AA^{-1} = I$.   Verify $A^{-1}A = I$.

✔ *Checkpoint* Use a graphing calculator to find the inverse of matrix A.

3. $\begin{bmatrix} 1 & 1 \\ 7 & 8 \end{bmatrix}$

4. $\begin{bmatrix} 2 & 5 & 2 \\ 5 & 2 & 0 \\ 5 & 4 & 1 \end{bmatrix}$

5. $\begin{bmatrix} -3 & 1 & -8 \\ 1 & -2 & 1 \\ 2 & -2 & 5 \end{bmatrix}$

Example 3   *Write a Matrix Equation*

Write the system of equations as a matrix equation.

$-4x + y = -10$ **Equation 1**

$7x + 2y = 25$ **Equation 2**

Solution

You can write a matrix equation by finding the

_____ matrix A, the matrix of _____ X, and

the matrix of _____ B. Then write the equation

____ = ___.

coefficient	matrix of	matrix of
matrix (___)	variables (___)	constants (___)

_____ $\cdot \begin{bmatrix} x \\ y \end{bmatrix} =$ _____

✔ *Checkpoint* **Write the system of linear equations as a matrix equation.**

6. $-4x - 7y = 16$	**7.** $3x - 4y = 5$
$-2x - 3y = -4$	$2x - 3y = 3$

USING AN INVERSE MATRIX TO SOLVE A LINEAR SYSTEM

To find the _____ of a linear system, use a graphing calculator:

Step 1 Write the system as a matrix equation $AX = B$.

Step 2 Enter matrix A into the graphing calculator.

Step 3 Enter matrix B into the graphing calculator.

Step 4 Multiply the _____ of matrix ___ by matrix ___.

The solution of $AX = B$ is $X =$ _____.

Example 4 **Solve a Linear System**

Use an inverse matrix to solve the linear system.

$2x + 3y = 15$ **Equation 1**

$x - 2y = -17$ **Equation 2**

Solution

Write the system as a matrix equation:

$$ \underline{\hspace{2cm}} \cdot \begin{bmatrix} x \\ y \end{bmatrix} = \underline{\hspace{2cm}} $$

Then use a graphing calculator to solve the system.

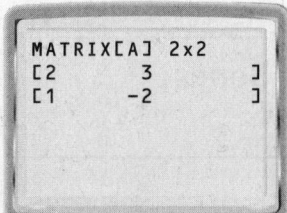

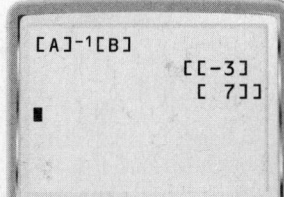

Enter matrix *B*.   Enter matrix *A*.   Multiply A^{-1} by *B*.

So, $X = \underline{\hspace{1.5cm}} = \underline{\hspace{1.5cm}}$, or $\begin{bmatrix} x \\ y \end{bmatrix} = \underline{\hspace{1.5cm}}$.

The solution is (____, ____).

✓ *Checkpoint* Use an inverse matrix to solve the system.

8. $x + y = 5$ $4x + 3y = 1$	9. $x - y = 0$ $x + y = 10$	10. $2x - y = -2$ $4x + y = 20$

Homework

11.4 An Introduction to Sequences and Series

Goal • Use and write sequence and series.

VOCABULARY

Sequence

Terms of a sequence

Series

Example 1 *Write the Terms of a Sequence*

Write the first six terms of the sequence.

a. $a_n = 2^n$ **b.** $a_n = 3n - 1$

Solution

To find a _____ of a sequence given the _____ for the sequence, substitute the term's _____ into the rule.

a. $a_1 = 2^1 = $ ____   1st term

$a_2 = 2\text{_} = $ ____   2nd term

$a_3 = 2\text{_} = $ ____   3rd term

$a_4 = 2\text{_} = $ ____   4th term

$a_5 = 2\text{_} = $ ____   5th term

$a_6 = 2\text{_} = $ ____   6th term

b. $a_1 = 3(1) - 1 = $ ____   1st term

$a_2 = 3(\text{__}) - 1 = $ ____   2nd term

$a_3 = 3(\text{__}) - 1 = $ ____   3rd term

$a_4 = 3(\text{__}) - 1 = $ ____   4th term

$a_5 = 3(\text{__}) - 1 = $ ____   5th term

$a_6 = 3(\text{__}) - 1 = $ ____   6th term

Checkpoint Write the first five terms of the sequence.

1. $a_n = n - 2$	**2.** $a_n = 3 - n$	**3.** $a_n = n^2$

Example 2   *Write a Rule for a Sequence*

For the given sequence, describe the pattern, write the next term, and write a rule for the *n*th term.

a. 4, 8, 12, 16, . . .   b. 2, 4, 8, 16, . . .

Solution

First, find the _____ in the sequence. Then use the _____ to write the next _____.

a. You can write the terms as $a_1 = 4(\_\_\_)$, $a_{\_\_} = 4(\_\_\_)$, $a_{\_\_} = 4(\_\_\_)$, $a_{\_\_} = 4(\_\_\_)$, and so on. So, each term is being multiplying by ___. The next term is $a_5 = 4(\_\_) = \_\_\_\_$. A rule for the *n*th term is $a_n = \_\_\_\_$.

b. You can write the terms as $a_1 = 2\_$, $a_2 = \_\_\_\_$, $a_3 = \_\_\_\_$, $a_4 = \_\_\_\_$, and so on. So, 2 is being raised to _____ integer _____. The next term is $a_5 = 2\_ = \_\_\_\_$. A rule for the *n*th term is $a_n = \_\_\_\_$.

Checkpoint For the given sequence, describe the pattern, write the next term, and write a rule for the *n*th term.

4. 4, 5, 6, 7, 8, . . .
5. −2, −4, −6, −8, −10, . . .

Your Notes

Example 3 **Graph a Sequence**

Graph the sequence 2, 5, 8, 11, 14.

Solution

Make a table of values.

n	1	2	3	4	5
a_n	___	___	___	___	___

Plot the points. Do not _____
the points with a _____. The
sequence is defined only for
_____ values of n.

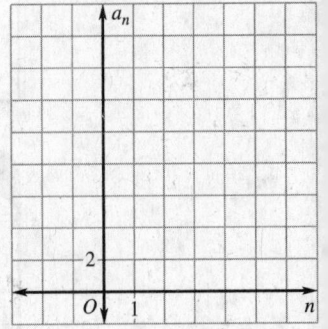

✔ **Checkpoint** **Graph the sequence.**

6. 3, 6, 9, 12, 15

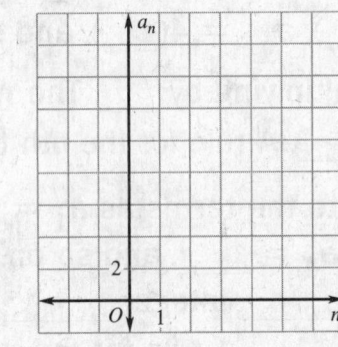

7. −2, −4, −6, −8, −10

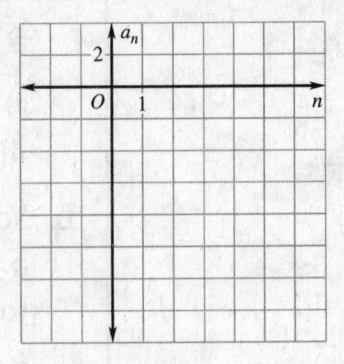

Example 4 **Find the Sum of the Series**

Find the sum of the series.

a. 2 + 4 + 6 + 8   b. 5 + 9 + 13 + 17

Solution

a. 2 + 4 + 6 + 8 = ____

b. 5 + 9 + 13 + 17 = ____

Copyright © McDougal Littell/Houghton Mifflin Company

FORMULAS FOR SPECIAL SERIES

Sum of n 1's

$$\underbrace{1 + 1 + 1 + 1 + \cdots + 1}_{n \text{ terms}} = \underline{\quad}$$

Sum of the first n positive integers

$$1 + 2 + 3 + 4 + \cdots + \underline{\quad} = \underline{\qquad\qquad}$$

Sum of the squares of the first n positive integers

$$1^2 + 2^2 + 3^2 + 4^2 + \cdots + \underline{\quad}^2 = \underline{\qquad\qquad}$$

✔ **Checkpoint** **Find the sum of the series.**

8. $2 + 6 + 10 + 14 + 18$

9. $5 + 10 + 15 + 20 + 25$

10. sum of twelve 1's

11. sum of the first 9 positive integers

11.5 Arithmetic Sequences and Series

Goal • Write rules for arithmetic sequences and find sums of arithmetic series.

VOCABULARY

Arithmetic sequence _____

_____

Common difference _____

_____

Arithmetic series _____

Example 1   *Identify Arithmetic Sequences*

Tell whether the sequence is arithmetic.

a. $-4, -8, -12, -16, -20$ b. $2, 4, 7, 11, 16$

Solution

To tell whether a sequence is arithmetic, find the _____ of _____ terms.

a. $a_2 - a_1 = $ _____ $- (-4) = $ _____
   $a_3 - a_2 = $ _____ $- ($ _____ $) = $ _____
   $a_4 - a_3 = $ _____ $- ($ _____ $) = $ _____
   $a_5 - a_4 = $ _____ $- ($ _____ $) = $ _____

   Each difference is _____, so the sequence ____ arithmetic.

b. $a_2 - a_1 = $ ___ $- 2 = $ ___
   $a_3 - a_2 = $ ___ $-$ ___ $= $ ___
   $a_4 - a_3 = $ ___ $-$ ___ $= $ ___
   $a_5 - a_4 = $ ___ $-$ ___ $= $ ___

   The differences _____, so the sequence _____ arithmetic.

✔ *Checkpoint* **Tell whether the sequence is arithmetic.**

1. 3, 6, 9, 12, 15	**2.** 2, 5, 9, 14, 20	**3.** 1, 3, 5, 7, 9

RULE FOR AN ARITHMETIC SEQUENCE

The *n*th term of an arithmetic sequence with
_____ a_1 and _____ *d* can be
found using the following rule.

$$a_n = \underline{\quad} + (\underline{\quad} - \underline{\quad})\underline{\quad}$$

Example 2   *Write a Rule for a Sequence*

Write a rule for the *n*th term of the arithmetic sequence
2, 9, 16, 23, … . Then find a_{11}.

Solution

The sequence is _____ with first term $a_1 = \underline{\quad}$.
The common difference is $d = \underline{\quad} - \underline{\quad} = \underline{\quad}$. A rule
for the *n*th term is as follows.

$a_n = a_1 + (n - 1)d$ Write general rule.

$\quad = \underline{\quad} + (\underline{\quad} - \underline{\quad})\underline{\quad}$ Substitute ___ for a_1
                                             and ___ for *d*.

$\quad = \underline{\qquad\qquad}$ Use distributive property.

$\quad = \underline{\qquad}$ Simplify.

You can find the 11th term by substituting 11 for ___ in
the rule $a_n = \underline{\qquad}$.

$$a_{11} = \underline{\quad}(11) - \underline{\quad} = \underline{\quad} - \underline{\quad} = \underline{\quad}$$

Example 3 **Graph a Sequence**

One term of an arithmetic sequence is $a_{10} = 30$. The common difference is $d = 3$.

a. Write a rule for the nth term.

b. Graph the sequence.

Solution

a. Find the _____ term.

$$a_n = a_1 + (n - 1)d$$ Write general rule.

$$a_{\underline{}} = a_1 + (\underline{} - 1)d$$ Substitute ____ for n.

$$\underline{} = a_1 + \underline{}(\underline{})$$ Substitute ____ for a_{10} and ___ for d.

$$\underline{} = a_1 + \underline{}$$ Multiply.

$$\underline{} = a_1$$ Subtract ____ from each side.

Write a rule for the nth term.

$$a_n = a_1 + (n - 1)d$$ Write general rule.

$$= \underline{} + (n - 1)\underline{}$$ Substitute.

$$= \underline{} + \underline{}$$ Distributive property

$$= \underline{}$$ Simplify.

b. Make a table of values and plot the points.

n	1	2	3	4	5	6
a_n	___	___	___	___	___	___

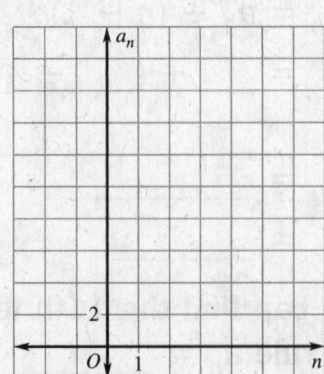

Copyright © McDougal Littell/Houghton Mifflin Company

4. Write a rule for the nth term of the sequence
4, 6, 8, 10, 12, ... Then find a_{13}.

5. Write a rule for the nth term of
the sequence where $a_4 = -5$
and $d = -2$. Then graph the
sequence.

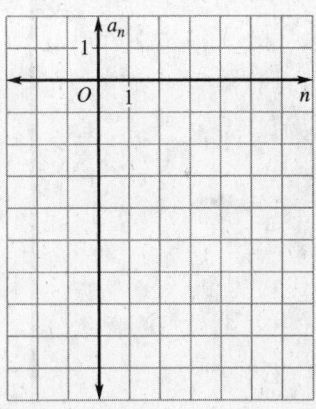

THE SUM OF A FINITE ARITHMETIC SERIES

The sum of the first n terms of an arithmetic series is
given by the following formula.

$$S_n = \underline{\hspace{3cm}}$$

In words, the _____ of the first ____ terms of an
arithmetic series, _____, is the _____ of the first and
nth terms, _____ by the _____ of terms.

Example 4   *Find the Sum of an Arithmetic Series*

Shopping A display of canned tomatoes has 2 cans in the top row, 5 cans in the second row from the top, 8 cans in the third row from the top, 11 cans in the fourth row from the top, and so on. If there are 15 rows, how many cans are in the display?

Solution

Notice that the first term is $a_1 = 2$. The common difference is $d =$ ___ $-$ ___ $=$ ___. You need to write a rule for the nth term so that you can find the 15th term.

$a_n = a_1 + (n-1)d$	Write general rule.
$=$ ___ $+ (n-1)$___	Substitute ___ for a_1 and ___ for d.
$=$ ___ $+$ _____	Use distributive property.
$=$ _____	Simplify.

Find the 15th term.

$$a_{15} = \underline{\hspace{3cm}} = \underline{\hspace{1cm}}$$

Find the sum of the first 15 terms.

$S_n = n\left(\dfrac{a_1 + a_n}{2}\right)$	Write formula for S_n.
$S_{\underline{\ }} = \underline{\hspace{3cm}}$	Substitute _____ for n.
$= \underline{\hspace{3cm}}$	Substitute ___ for a_1 and ____ for a_{15}.
$= \underline{\hspace{1.5cm}}$	Simplify.

There are _____ cans in the display.

✅ *Checkpoint* **Complete the following exercise.**

Homework

6. Find the sum of the first 10 terms of the arithmetic series $1 + 4 + 7 + 10 + 13 + \cdots$.

11.6 Geometric Sequences and Series

Goal • Write rules for geometric sequences and find sums of geometric series.

Your Notes

VOCABULARY

Geometric sequence

Common ratio

Geometric series

| **Example 1** | *Identify Geometric Sequences* |

Tell whether the sequence is geometric.

a. $-2, 4, -8, 16, \ldots$ b. $3, 6, 18, 72, \ldots$

Solution

To tell whether a sequence is geometric, find the _____ of _____ terms. If the ratios are _____, the sequence is geometric.

a. $\dfrac{a_2}{a_1} =$ _____ $=$ _____ $\dfrac{a_3}{a_2} =$ _____ $=$ _____

$\dfrac{a_4}{a_3} =$ _____ $=$ _____

The _____ are _____, so the sequence _____ geometric.

b. $\dfrac{a_2}{a_1} =$ _____ $=$ _____ $\dfrac{a_3}{a_2} =$ _____ $=$ _____

$\dfrac{a_4}{a_3} =$ _____ $=$ _____

The _____ are _____, so the sequence _____ geometric.

Checkpoint Tell whether the sequence is geometric.

1. $-3, 3, -3, 3, \ldots$	**2.** $-4, -2, 0, 2, \ldots$

RULE FOR A GEOMETRIC SEQUENCE

The nth term of a geometric sequence with first term ____ and common ratio ___ can be found using the following rule.

$$a_n = \underline{\hspace{2cm}}$$

Example 2 *Write a Rule for the nth Term*

Write a rule for the nth term of the geometric sequence 972, −324, 108, –36, ... Then find a_{10}.

Solution

The sequence is geometric with first term $a_1 = \underline{\hspace{1.5cm}}$.

The common ratio is $r = \dfrac{\underline{\hspace{1.5cm}}}{\underline{\hspace{1cm}}} = \underline{\hspace{1cm}}$. Substitute these values in the general rule.

$a_n = a_1 r^{n-1}$ **Write general term.**

$a_n = \underline{\hspace{1cm}} \left(\underline{\hspace{1cm}} \right)^{n-1}$ **Substitute for a_1 and for r.**

A rule for the nth term is $a_n = \underline{\hspace{2.5cm}}$. To find the 10th term of the sequence, substitute ____ for n.

$a_{10} = 972 \underline{\hspace{2cm}} = 972 \underline{\hspace{1.5cm}}$

$= 972 \underline{\hspace{2cm}} = \underline{\hspace{1.5cm}} = \underline{\hspace{1.5cm}}$

✓ *Checkpoint* Write a rule for the *n*th term of the geometric sequence.

3. 7, 14, 28, 56, . . .	4. 3, 12, 48, 192, . . .

Example 3 *Write a Rule for the nth Term*

One term of a geometric sequence is $a_3 = -18$. The common ratio is $r = 3$.

a. Write a rule for the *n*th term.   b. Graph the sequence.

Solution

a. Find the first term.

$$a_n = a_1 r^{n-1}$$ Write general rule.

$$a_{\underline{}} = a_1 r^{\underline{} - 1}$$ Substitute ___ for *n*.

$$\underline{} = a_1(\underline{})^{\underline{}}$$ Substitute for a_3 and *r*.

$$\underline{} = a_1(\underline{})$$ Evaluate power.

$$\underline{} = a_1$$ Divide each side by ___.

Write a rule for the *n*th term; $a_1 = $ _____ and $r = $ ___.

$$a_n = a_1 r^{n-1}$$ Write general rule.

$$a_n = \underline{}$$ Substitute for a_1 and *r*.

b. Make a table of values and plot the points.

n	a_n
1	_____
2	_____
3	_____
4	_____
5	_____

THE SUM OF A FINITE GEOMETRIC SERIES

The sum of the first n terms of a geometric series with _____ r ($r \neq$ ___) is given by the following formula.

$$S_n = a_1 \underline{\hspace{3cm}}$$

Example 4 *Find the Sum of a Geometric Series*

Find the sum of the first 8 terms of the geometric series 3, 12, 48, 192, 768, ...

Solution

The first term is $a_1 =$ ___. The common ratio is $r =$ ___.

$$S_n = a_1\left(\frac{1 - r^n}{1 - r}\right)$$ **Write general rule.**

$S_{\underline{\ }} = a_1 \underline{\hspace{2cm}}$ **Substitute ___ for n.**

$= \underline{\hspace{2cm}}$ **Substitute ___ for a_1 and ___ for r.**

$= \underline{\hspace{2cm}}$ **Evaluate power.**

$= \underline{\hspace{2cm}}$ **Subtract.**

$= \underline{\hspace{1.5cm}}$ **Multiply.**

✔ *Checkpoint* **Find the sum of the first 7 terms of the geometric series.**

Homework

5. $-3 + (-6) + (-12) + \cdots$

6. $7 + 21 + 63 + 189 + \cdots$

11.7 Infinite Geometric Series

Goal • Find sums of infinite geometric series.

Your Notes

| Example 1 | *Find Partial Sums* |

Consider the geometric series $1 + \frac{1}{3} + \frac{1}{9} + \frac{1}{27} + \frac{1}{81} + \cdots$. Find and graph the partial sums S_n for $n = 1, 2, 3, 4, 5$. Describe what happens to S_n as n increases.

Solution

Compute the _____ of the first n terms for the given _____ of n. Then graph the sums.

$S_1 = 1$

$S_{\underline{\ }} = 1 + \frac{1}{3} = \underline{\ \ \ } \approx \underline{\ \ \ }$

$S_{\underline{\ }} = 1 + \frac{1}{3} + \frac{1}{9} = \underline{\ \ \ } \approx \underline{\ \ \ }$

$S_{\underline{\ }} = 1 + \frac{1}{3} + \frac{1}{9} + \frac{1}{27} = \underline{\ \ \ } \approx \underline{\ \ \ }$

$S_{\underline{\ }} = 1 + \frac{1}{3} + \frac{1}{9} + \frac{1}{27} + \frac{1}{81} = \underline{\ \ \ } \approx \underline{\ \ \ }$

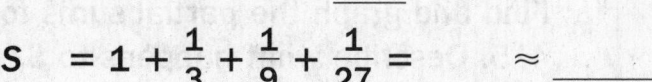

You can see from the graph and from the _____ that the sum appears to be approaching _____ as n increases.

THE SUM OF AN INFINITE GEOMETRIC SERIES

The sum of an _____ geometric series with first term _____ and common ratio ____ is given by

$$S = \underline{\ \ \ \ \ }$$

where $|r|$ ____ 1. If $|r|$ ____ 1, the series has _____.

Copyright © McDougal Littell/Houghton Mifflin Company   Lesson 11.7 • **Algebra 2 C&S Notetaking Guide**   **267**

Example 2 — *Find Sums of Infinite Geometric Series*

Find the sum of the infinite geometric series, if it exists.

a. $a_1 = 2, r = 0.1$

b. $-3 + (-6) + (-12) + (-36) + \cdots$

Solution

Identify the _____ and _____. Then substitute the values into the formula for the sum of an infinite geometric series, if the sum exists.

a. Here, $a_1 = 2$ and $r = 0.1$.

$$S = \frac{a_1}{1 - r} = \underline{\hspace{2cm}} = \underline{\hspace{1.5cm}} \quad \text{or} \quad \underline{\hspace{1.5cm}}$$

b. Here, $a_1 = \underline{\hspace{1cm}}$ and $r = \underline{\hspace{0.6cm}}$.

Since $r \underline{\hspace{0.6cm}} 1$, there is _____.

✔ *Checkpoint* **Complete the following exercise.**

1. Consider the series $\dfrac{3}{4} + \dfrac{9}{16} + \dfrac{27}{64} + \dfrac{81}{256} + \dfrac{243}{1024} + \cdots$.
Find and graph the partial sums for S_n for $n = 1, 2, 3, 4, 5$. Describe what happens to S_n as n increases.

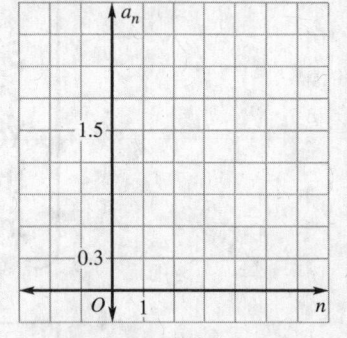

Find the sum of the infinite geometric series, if it exists.

2. $a_1 = 5, r = 0.5$	**3.** $\dfrac{1}{2} + \dfrac{1}{6} + \dfrac{1}{18} + \cdots$

Example 3   *Find the Common Ratio*

What is the common ratio of the infinite geometric series with sum S = 2 and first term $a_1 = \frac{12}{7}$?

Solution

$S = \dfrac{a_1}{1 - r}$ Write rule for sum.

$2 = \dfrac{\frac{12}{7}}{1 - r}$ Substitute 2 for S and $\frac{12}{7}$ for a_1.

$2(\underline{\hspace{1cm}}) = \underline{\hspace{1cm}}$ Multiply each side by _____.

$1 - r = \underline{\hspace{1cm}}$ Divide each side by ___.

$-r = \underline{\hspace{1cm}} - \underline{\hspace{0.5cm}}$ Subtract ___ from each side.

$r = \underline{\hspace{1cm}}$ Solve for *r*.

The common ratio is ___ .

Example 4   *Write a Repeating Decimal as a Fraction*

Write 0.090909. . . as a fraction.

Solution

Rewrite the repeating decimal as a _____.

0.090909. . .

$= 0.09 + \underline{\hspace{1.5cm}} + \underline{\hspace{1.5cm}} + \cdots$

$= 9(\underline{\hspace{1cm}}) + 9(\underline{\hspace{1cm}}) + 9(\underline{\hspace{1cm}}) + \cdots$

$= \dfrac{a_1}{1 - r}$ Write rule for sum.

$= \dfrac{}{}$ Substitute 9(_____) for a_1 and _____ for *r*.

$= \underline{\hspace{1cm}}$ or $\underline{\hspace{0.5cm}}\underline{\hspace{0.5cm}}$ Write as a quotient of integers.

✓ *Checkpoint* **Find the common ratio of the infinite geometric series with the given sum and first term.**

4. $S = \frac{1}{2}, a_1 = \frac{1}{4}$	5. $S = 9, a_1 = 3$	6. $S = \frac{25}{2}, a_1 = 5$

Write the repeating decimal as a fraction.

7. $0.1111\ldots$	8. $0.7777\ldots$	9. $0.080808\ldots$

Example 5 *Use an Infinite Series as a Model*

Swings A person is given a push on a swing. On the first swing, the person travels a distance of 4 feet. On each successive swing, the person travels 75% of the distance of the previous swing. What is the total distance the person swings?

Solution

The total distance d that the person swings is given by an infinite geometric series with $a_1 = \underline{\quad}$ and $r = \underline{\quad}$.

$d = \underline{\quad} + \underline{\quad}(\underline{\quad}) + \underline{\quad}(\underline{\quad})^2 + \underline{\quad}(\underline{\quad})^3 + \cdots$

Homework

$d = \dfrac{a_1}{1 - r}$ Write rule for sum of an infinite geometric series.

$= \underline{\qquad}$ Substitute $\underline{\quad}$ for a_1 and $\underline{\quad}$ for r.

$= \underline{\quad}$ Simplify.

The total distance the person swings is $\underline{\quad}$ feet.

Words to Review

Use your own words and/or an example to explain the vocabulary word.

Matrix	Element
Dimensions of a matrix	Equal matrices
Scalar	Scalar multiplication
Identity matrix	Inverse matrices
Coefficient matrix	Matrix of variables

Matrix of constants	Sequence
Terms of a sequence	Series
Arithmetic sequence	Common difference
Arithmetic series	Geometric sequence
Common ratio	Geometric series

Review your notes and Chapter 11 by using the Chapter Review on pages 635–638 of your textbook.

12.1 Right Triangle Trigonometry

Goal • Evaluate trigonometric functions of acute angles.

Your Notes

VOCABULARY

Sine (sin)

Cosine (cos)

Tangent (tan)

Cosecant (csc)

Secant (sec)

Cotangent (cot)

RIGHT TRIANGLE DEFINITION OF TRIGONOMETRIC FUNCTIONS

Let θ be an _____ angle of a _____ triangle. The six trigonometric functions of θ are defined as follows:

$\sin \theta =$ _____ $\csc \theta =$ _____

$\cos \theta =$ _____ $\sec \theta =$ _____

$\tan \theta =$ _____ $\cot \theta =$ _____

Notice that the _____ in the second column are the _____ of the ratios in the _____ column.

$\csc \theta =$ _____   _____ $= \dfrac{1}{\cos \theta}$ $\cot \theta =$ _____

Example 1   *Evaluate Trigonometric Functions*

Evaluate the six trigonometric functions of the angle θ shown in the triangle.

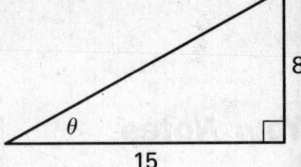

Solution

From the _____ theorem, the length of

the _____ is $\sqrt{8^2 + 15^2}$ = _____ = _____.

$\sin \theta = \dfrac{\text{opp}}{\text{hyp}} = $ _____ $\csc \theta = $ _____ $=$ _____

$\cos \theta = \dfrac{\text{adj}}{\text{hyp}} = $ _____ $\sec \theta = $ _____ $=$ _____

$\tan \theta = \dfrac{\text{opp}}{\text{adj}} = $ _____ $\cot \theta = $ _____ $=$ _____

☑ *Checkpoint* **Complete the following exercise.**

1. Evaluate the six trigonometric functions of the angle θ shown in the triangle.

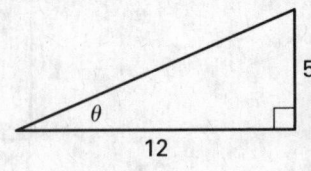

Example 2 **Find a Missing Side Length**

Find the value of *x* for the right triangle shown.

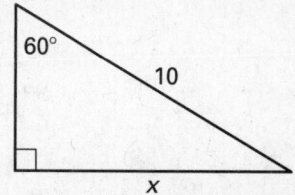

Solution

Write an equation using a trigonometric function that involves the ratio of *x* and 10. Then solve the equation for *x*.

$$\underline{\quad} \ 60° = \frac{\text{opp}}{\text{hyp}} \qquad \text{Write trigonometric equation.}$$

$$\underline{\quad} \ 60° = \underline{\quad} \qquad \text{Substitute.}$$

$$\underline{\quad} = \underline{\quad} \ \underline{\quad} \qquad \text{Use table to find } \underline{\quad\quad}.$$

$$\underline{\quad} = x \qquad \text{Multiply each side by } \underline{\quad}.$$

The length of the longer leg is $\underline{\quad} \approx \underline{\quad}$.

Example 3 **Use a Calculator**

Find the value of *x* for the right triangle.

a.
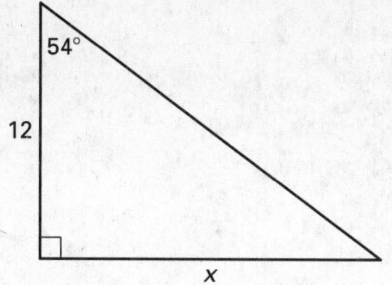

b.
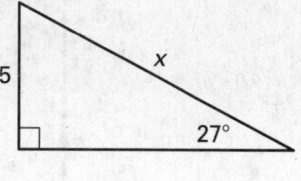

Solution

a. $\qquad \tan \theta = \dfrac{}{\underline{\quad}}$

$\qquad \tan \underline{\quad} = \dfrac{}{\underline{\quad}}$

$\qquad \underline{\quad}(\underline{\quad\quad}) = x$

$\qquad \underline{\quad} \approx x$

b. $\underline{\quad} \ \theta = \dfrac{\text{opp}}{\text{hyp}}$

$\qquad \underline{\quad\quad} = \dfrac{}{\underline{\quad}}$

$\qquad x(\underline{\quad\quad}) = \underline{\quad}$

$\qquad x \approx \dfrac{}{\underline{\quad\quad}}$

$\qquad x \approx \underline{\quad}$

> Be sure your calculator is set to DEGREE mode when you evaluate the trigonometric functions of the angles.

Checkpoint Find the value of *x* for the right triangle.

2.

x

5

45°

3.

8

x

15°

Example 4 *Use Trigonometry in Real-life*

Construction How tall is the building?

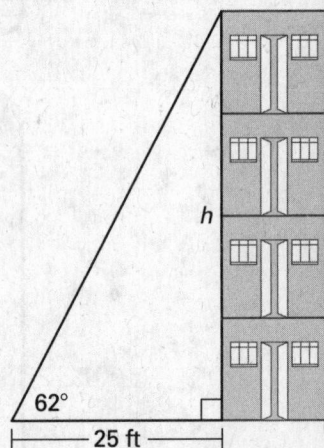

h

62°

25 ft

Solution

Write an equation using a trigonometric function that involves the _____ of *h* and____. Then _____ the equation for *h*.

tan *θ* = ____	**Write trigonometric equation.**
tan ____ = ____	**Substitute.**
____(tan ____) = *h*	**Multiply each side by ____.**
_____ ≈ *h*	**Simplify.**

The height of the building is about _____ feet.

Homework

12.2 Functions of Any Angle

Goal • Evaluate the trigonometric functions of any angle.

VOCABULARY

Initial side

Terminal side

Standard position

Coterminal

Quadrantal angle

Example 1 *Draw Angles in Standard Position*

Draw an angle with the given measure in standard position.

a. 160°   b. −115°

Solution

a. Because 160° is _____ more than 90°, the terminal side is _____ counterclockwise past the positive ___-axis.

b. Because −115° is negative and _____ more than −90°, the terminal side is _____ clockwise past the negative ___-axis.

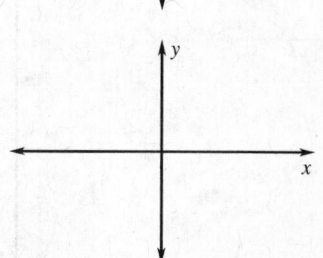

✅ **Checkpoint** Draw an angle with the given measure in standard position.

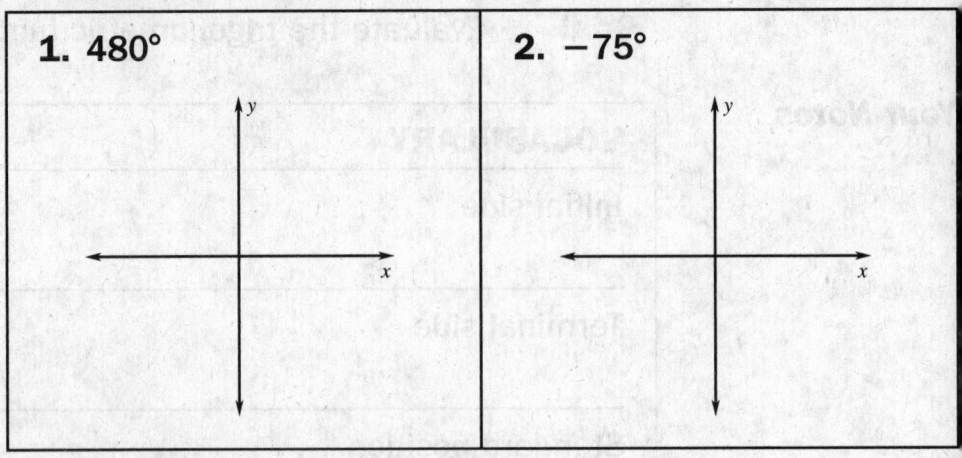

1. 480°	**2.** −75°

Example 2 **Find Coterminal Angles**

Find one positive angle and one negative angle that are coterminal with the given angle.

a. −55°   **b.** 425°

Solution

There are many correct answers. Choose a multiple of _____ and add or subtract.

a. −55° + 360° = _____   Add 360°.

   −55° − 360° = _____   Subtract 360°.

b. 425° + _____ = _____   Add _____.

   425° − _____ = _____   Subtract ____ times 360°.

✅ **Checkpoint** Find one positive angle and one negative angle that are coterminal with the given angle.

3. 70°	**4.** −40°

GENERAL DEFINITION OF TRIGONOMETRIC FUNCTIONS

Let θ be an angle in _____ position and (x, y) be any point (except the _____) on the _____ side of θ. The six trigonometric functions of θ are defined as follows.

$\sin \theta = \dfrac{}{}$ $\csc \theta = \dfrac{}{}$ ($\_\_ \neq 0$)

$\cos \theta = \dfrac{}{}$ $\sec \theta = \dfrac{}{}$ ($\_\_ \neq 0$)

$\tan \theta = \dfrac{}{}$ ($\_\_ \neq 0$) $\cot \theta = \dfrac{}{}$ ($\_\_ \neq 0$)

Example 3 *Evaluate Trigonometric Functions Given a Point*

Let $(-12, 5)$ be a point on the terminal side of angle θ in standard position. Evaluate the sine, cosine, and tangent functions of θ.

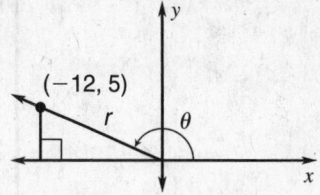

Solution

Use the _____ theorem to find the _____ of r.

$$r = \sqrt{x^2 + y^2} = \sqrt{(-12)^2 + 5^2} = \underline{} = \underline{}$$

Find the _____ of each function using $x =$ _____, $y =$ ___, and $r =$ ____.

$\sin \theta = \dfrac{y}{r} = \underline{}$ $\cos \theta = \dfrac{x}{r} = \underline{}$

$\tan \theta = \dfrac{y}{x} = \underline{}$

✔ *Checkpoint* Evaluate the sine, cosine, and tangent functions of θ for each point on the terminal side of angle θ.

5. $(-4, -3)$	**6.** $(15, -8)$	**7.** $(-24, 7)$

Example 4   *Trigonometric Functions of a Quadrantal Angle*

Evaluate sine, cosine, and tangent of $\theta = 270°$.

Solution

When $\theta = 270°$, you know that $x =$ ___ and $y =$ ___.

$\sin \theta = \dfrac{y}{r} =$ ___ $=$ ___ $\cos \theta = \dfrac{x}{r} =$ ___ $=$ ___

_____ $= \dfrac{y}{x} =$ ___ , so tan θ is _____.

Example 5   *Positive and Negative Trigonometric Functions*

Determine whether the sine, cosine, and tangent functions of the given angle are positive or negative.

a.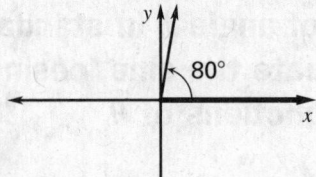

b.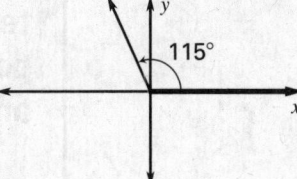

c.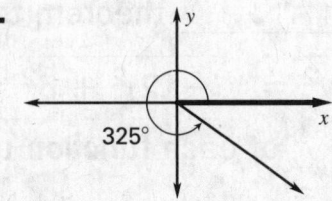

d.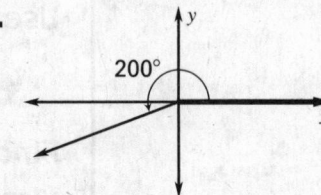

Solution

a. Because the _____ side lies in Quadrant ___,
sin 80° is _____, cos 80° is _____, and
tan 80° is _____.

b. Because the _____ side lies in Quadrant ___,
sin 115° is _____, cos 115° is _____, and
tan 115° is _____.

c. Because the _____ side lies in Quadrant ___,
sin 325° is _____, cos 325° is _____, and
tan 325° is _____.

Homework

d. Because the _____ side lies in Quadrant ___,
sin 200° is _____, cos 200° is _____, and
tan 200° is _____.

12.3 Graphing the Trigonometric Functions

Goal • Graph the sine, cosine, and tangent functions.

VOCABULARY

Periodic

Cycle

Period

GRAPHING THE SINE AND COSINE FUNCTIONS

To graph $y = a \sin bx$ and $y = a \cos bx$ when $a > $ ____
and $b > $ ____, you can use these characteristics. The

period is _____ .

Characteristic	$y = a \sin bx$	$y = a \cos bx$
Intercepts	$(0°, 0)$, $\left(\dfrac{180°}{b}, 0\right)$, _____	_____ , _____
Maximum(s)	_____	$(0°, 0)$, _____
Minimum	_____	_____

Example 1 **Graph a Sine Function**

Graph $y = 2 \sin 180x$.

Solution

Find the characteristics of the graph using $a =$ ___ and $b =$ _____. There is one intercept at $(0°, 0)$ and the period is _____ $=$ ___.

Find two other intercepts.

$$\left(\frac{180°}{b}, 0\right) = \left(\underline{\quad}, 0\right) = (\underline{\quad}°, 0)$$

$$\left(\frac{360°}{b}, 0\right) = \left(\underline{\quad}, 0\right) = (\underline{\quad}°, 0)$$

Find the maximum and minimum.

$$\left(\frac{90°}{b}, a\right) = \left(\underline{\quad}, \underline{\quad}\right)$$

$$= (\underline{\quad}°, \underline{\quad})$$

$$\left(\frac{270°}{b}, -a\right) = \underline{\qquad\qquad}$$

$$= \underline{\qquad\qquad}$$

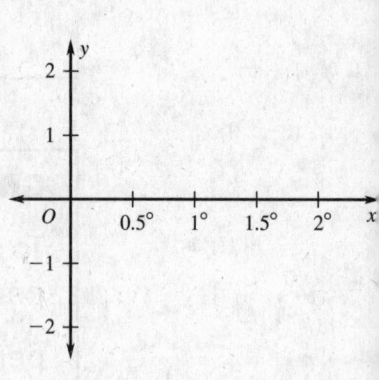

✔ Checkpoint Complete the following exercise.

1. Graph $y = 3 \sin x$.

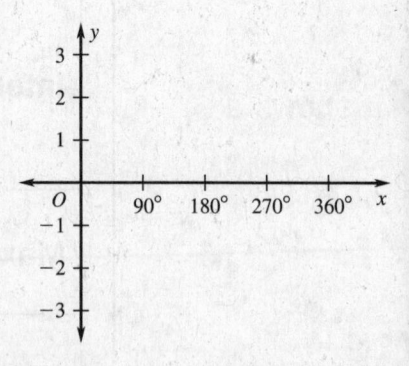

Example 2 | *Graph a Cosine Function*

Graph $y = 4 \cos 2x$.

Solution

Find the characteristics of the graph using $a =$ ____ and $b =$ ____. The period is $\dfrac{}{} =$ _____.

Find two intercepts.

$\left(\dfrac{90°}{b}, 0\right) = \left(\underline{}, 0\right) = (\underline{}°, 0)$

$\left(\dfrac{270°}{b}, 0\right) = \left(\underline{}, 0\right) = (\underline{}°, 0)$

The maximums are at $(0°, \underline{})$ and

$\left(\dfrac{360°}{b}, a\right) = \left(\underline{}, \underline{}\right)$

$= (\underline{}°, \underline{}).$

The minimum is at

$\left(\dfrac{180°}{b}, -a\right) = \underline{}$

$= \underline{}.$

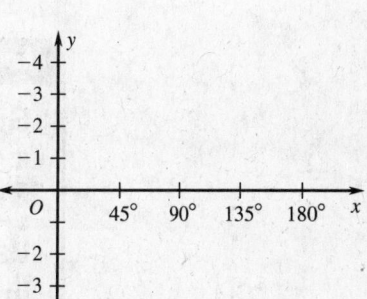

✔ *Checkpoint* **Complete the following exercise.**

2. Graph $y = \cos 180x$.

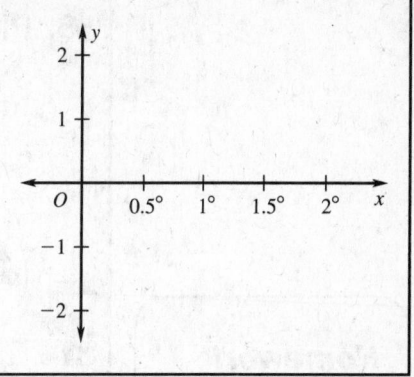

GRAPHING THE TANGENT FUNCTION

To graph $y = a \tan bx$ on the interval $-\dfrac{90°}{b} < x < \dfrac{90°}{b}$:

Step 1 Plot the ____-intercept at (0°, ____).

Step 2 Draw the vertical _____ at

$x = -\dfrac{90°}{b}$ and $x = $ _____ .

Step 3 Plot the points halfway between the x-intercept at (_____) and the asymptotes,

_____ and _____ .

Example 3 *Graph a Tangent Function*

Graph $y = 2 \tan x$.

Solution

Use $a = $ ____ and $b = $ ____ to find the key points on the interval _____° $< x <$ ____°.

1. Plot the x-intercept at (0°, ____).

2. Draw the vertical asymptotes.

$x = -\dfrac{90°}{b} = $ _____ $= $ _____ and

$x = $ ____ $= $ ____ $= $ ____

3. Plot the halfway points.

$\left(-\dfrac{45°}{b}, -a\right) = \left(\underline{\hspace{1cm}}, \underline{\hspace{0.5cm}}\right)$

$= (\underline{\hspace{1cm}}°, \underline{\hspace{1cm}})$

$\left(\dfrac{45°}{b}, a\right) = $ _____

$= $ _____

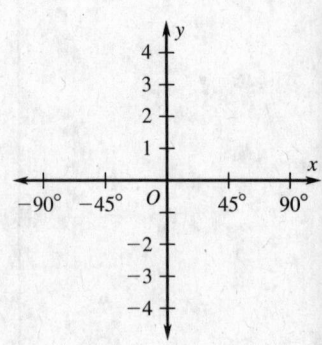

The Law of Sines

Goal • Use the law of sines to find the sides and angles of a triangle.

Your Notes

VOCABULARY

Law of sines

LAW OF SINES

If △ABC has sides of length a, b, and c, then:

$$\frac{\sin A}{a} = \underline{\hspace{1.5cm}} = \underline{\hspace{1.5cm}}.$$

Also, $\frac{a}{\sin A} = \underline{\hspace{1.5cm}} = \underline{\hspace{1.5cm}}.$

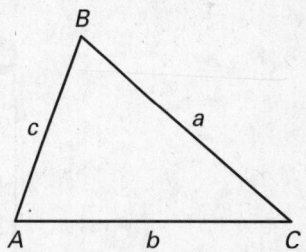

Example 1 *Solve for a Side (AAS)*

Find the length c given that A = 28°, a = 8, and C = 50°.

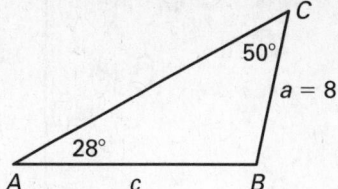

Solution

$$\frac{a}{\sin A} = \frac{c}{\sin C}$$ Write the law of sines.

$$\underline{\hspace{2cm}} = \frac{c}{\sin 50°}$$ Substitute for A, a, and C.

$$\underline{\hspace{2cm}} = c$$ Solve for the variable.

$$\underline{\hspace{2cm}} \approx c$$ Simplify using a calculator.

Example 2 *Find Two Angle Measures*

Find two values of θ between $0°$ and $180°$ that satisfy $\sin\theta = 0.9063$.

Solution

Use the _____ sine function on your calculator to find the angle between $0°$ and _____$°$.

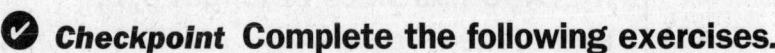

$$\theta = \sin^{-1}(\underline{\hspace{1.5cm}}) \approx \underline{\hspace{1cm}}°$$

To find the second angle, subtract _____$°$ from $180°$.

$$180° - \underline{\hspace{1cm}}° = \underline{\hspace{1.5cm}}°$$

So, $\sin\theta = 0.9063$ when $\theta = \underline{\hspace{1cm}}°$ and when $\theta = \underline{\hspace{1cm}}°$.

✔ *Checkpoint* **Complete the following exercises.**

1. In $\triangle ABC$, $C = 14°$, $B = 117°$, and $b = 21$. Find the value of c.

2. Find two values of θ between $0°$ and $180°$ that satisfy $\sin\theta = 0.7660$.

Your Notes

POSSIBLE TRIANGLES IN SSA CASE

Consider a triangle in which you are given *a*, *b* and *A*. By fixing side *b* and angle *A*, you can sketch the possible positions of side *a* to figure out how many triangles can be formed. In the diagrams below, *h* = ____ sin ____.

A is obtuse.

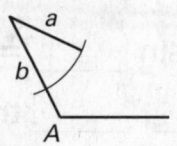

$a \leq b$

_____

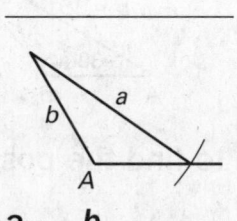

a ___ b

_____

A is acute.

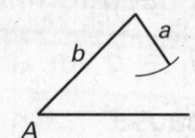

h ___ a

_____

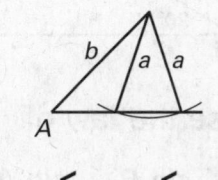

___ < ___ < ___

_____

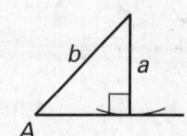

h ___ a

_____

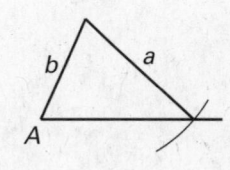

a ___ b

_____

Example 3   *Solve for an Angle (SSA)*

Find the measure of angle *C* given that *A* = 94°, *a* = 18, and *c* = 13.

First make a sketch. Because *A* is _____ and *a* > ___ , you know that only _____ triangle can be formed.

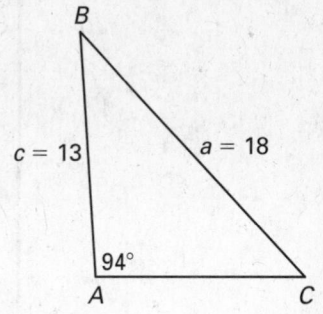

$\dfrac{\sin C}{c} = \dfrac{\sin A}{a}$ **Write law of sines.**

$\dfrac{\sin C}{13} = $ _____   **Substitute for *c*, *A*, and *a*.**

$\sin C = $ _____   **Multiply each side by ____.**

$\sin C \approx $ _____   **Simplify using a calculator.**

$C \approx \sin^{-1}($ _____ $)$ **Use _____ sine function.**

$C \approx $ _____   **Simplify.**

The measure of angle *C* is about _____.

Example 4 **Solve for an Angle (SSA)**

Find the measure of angle *B* given that *A* = 30°,
a = 10, and *b* = 15.

Solution

First make a sketch. Because *A* is _____, and *a* ___ *b*,
you need to find ___.

$$h = b \sin A = \underline{\quad} \sin \underline{\quad} = \underline{\quad}$$

Because ___ < ___ < ___, _____ triangles can be formed.

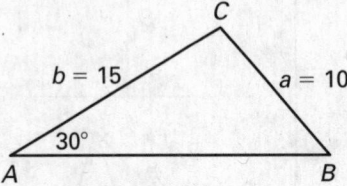 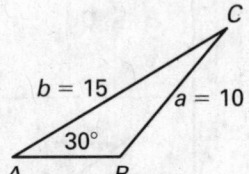

Use the law of _____ to find the possible measures of *B*.

$$\frac{\sin B}{b} = \frac{\sin A}{a} \qquad \text{Write law of sines.}$$

$$\frac{\sin B}{15} = \underline{\qquad} \qquad \text{Substitute for } b, A, \text{ and } a.$$

$$\sin B = \underline{\qquad} \qquad \text{Multiply each side by } \underline{\quad}.$$

$$\sin B = \underline{\qquad} \qquad \text{Simplify using a calculator.}$$

There are two angles between 0° and 180° for which
sin *B* = _____. One angle is acute and the other
is _____. Use a calculator to find the acute angle:

$$B = \sin^{-1}(\underline{\qquad}) \approx \underline{\qquad}$$

The second angle is *B* = 180° − _____ = _____.
So, there are two possible triangles with the following
angle measures:

30°, _____, _____ and 30°, _____, _____.

✔ *Checkpoint* **Complete the following exercise.**

3. Find the measure of angle B given that A = 50°,
a = 8, and b = 10.

Example 5   *Recognize an Impossible Triangle*

**Find the measure of angle A given that a = 12, b = 5,
and B = 60°.**

Solution

$$\frac{\sin A}{a} = \frac{\sin B}{b}$$ **Write law of sines.**

$$\frac{\sin A}{12} = \underline{\hspace{2cm}}$$ **Substitute for a, B, and b.**

$$\sin A = \underline{\hspace{2cm}}$$ **Multiply each side by ____.**

$$\sin A \approx \underline{\hspace{2cm}}$$ **Simplify using a calculator.**

Because the value of sin θ is always between _____
and ____ , there is _____ angle that _____ this
equation. So it is _____ to draw the indicated
triangle.

✔ *Checkpoint* **Complete the following exercise.**

4. Find the measure of angle A given that a = 10,
b = 7, and B = 60°.

Homework

12.5 The Law of Cosines

Goal • Use the law of cosines to find the sides and angles of a triangle.

Your Notes

VOCABULARY

Law of cosines

Example 1 *Solve for a Side (SAS)*

Find the length *b* given that *a* = 12, *c* = 16, and *B* = 54°.

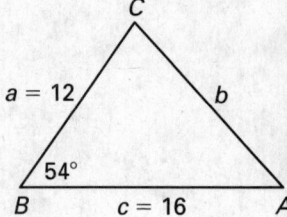

Solution

$b^2 = a^2 + c^2 - 2ac \cos B$

$b^2 = \underline{}^2 + 16^2 - 2(12)(\underline{}) \cos \underline{}$

$b^2 = 144 + \underline{} - \underline{} \cos \underline{}$

$b^2 \approx \underline{}$

$b \approx \underline{} \approx \underline{}$

✔ *Checkpoint* **Find the unknown side length of the triangle to the nearest tenth.**

1.

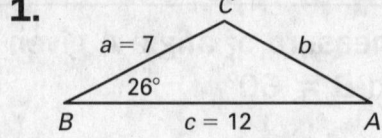

2.

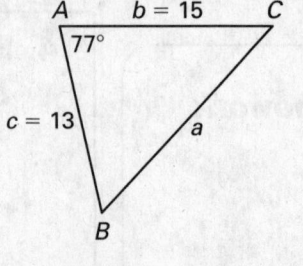

Copyright © McDougal Littell/Houghton Mifflin Company

Example 2 *Solve for an Angle (SSS)*

Find the measure of angle *B*.

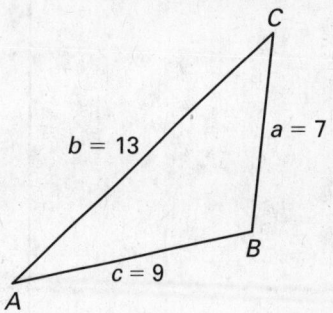

Solution

$$b^2 = a^2 + c^2 - 2ac \cos B$$ Write law of cosines.

$\cos B =$ _____   Rewrite formula by solving for cos *B*.

$\cos B =$ _____   Substitute for *a*, *b*, and *c*.

$\cos B \approx$ _____   Simplify using a calculator.

Use the _____ _____ function to find the angle measure.

$B \approx \cos^{-1}($_____$) \approx$ _____

✔ *Checkpoint* Complete the following exercises.

3. Find the measure of angle *C* if *a* = 4, *b* = 8, and *c* = 11.	**4.** Find the measure of angle *A* if *a* = 3, *b* = 5, and *c* = 7.

Your Notes

CHOOSING A METHOD

Method	Given Information
Law of sines	2 angles and 1 _____ (AAS or _____)
	2 sides and the _____ opposite one of them (SSA)
Law of cosines	3 sides (_____)
	2 sides and their _____ angle (SAS)

Example 3   *Choose a Method*

Find length a given that $b = 4$, $B = 32°$, and $C = 120°$.

Solution

You know two angles and one side. Use law of _____.
Use the fact that the _____ of the angle measures
is _____ to find A.

$A = 180° - $ _____ $- 32° = $ _____

$$\frac{a}{\sin A} = \frac{b}{\sin B}$$ **Write law of sines.**

$$\underline{} = \underline{}$$ **Substitute for A, B, and b.**

$$a = \underline{}$$ **Solve for the variable.**

$$a \approx \underline{}$$ **Simplify using a calculator.**

✔ **Checkpoint** Complete the following exercises.

Homework

5. Find c to the nearest tenth.

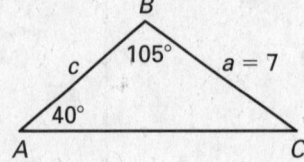

6. Find t to the nearest tenth.

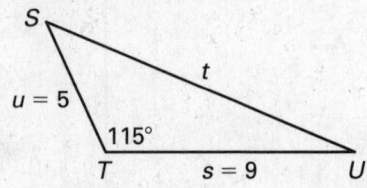

    Copyright © McDougal Littell/Houghton Mifflin Company

Words to Review

Use your own words and/or an example to explain the vocabulary word.

Sine	Cosine
Tangent	Cosecant
Secant	Cotangent
Initial side	Terminal side
Standard position	Coterminal
Quadrantal angle	Periodic

Cycle	Period

Law of sines	Law of cosines

Review your notes and Chapter 12 by using the Chapter Review on pages 682–684 of your textbook.

13.1 Distance and Midpoint Formulas

Goal • Find the distance between and midpoint of two points.

Your Notes

VOCABULARY

Distance formula

_____

Midpoint formula

THE DISTANCE FORMULA

The distance d between two points $(x_1, \underline{\quad})$ and $(\underline{\quad}, y_2)$ is

$$d = \underline{\hspace{4cm}}.$$

Example 1   Find the Distance Between Two Points

Find the distance between $(-5, -3)$ and $(3, 6)$.

Solution

Let $(x_1, y_1) = (-5, -3)$ and $(x_2, y_2) = \underline{\hspace{2cm}}$.

> It does not matter which ordered pair is (x_1, y_1) and which is (x_2, y_2).

$d = \sqrt{(x_2 - x_1)^2 + (y_2 - y_1)^2}$ **Write the distance formula.**

$\quad = \sqrt{(3 - (-5))^2 + (6 - (-3))^2}$ **Substitute values.**

$\quad = \underline{\hspace{2.5cm}}$ **Subtract in parentheses.**

$\quad = \underline{\hspace{2.5cm}}$ **Evaluate powers.**

$\quad = \underline{\hspace{1.5cm}}$ **Simplify.**

$\quad \approx \underline{\hspace{1.5cm}}$ **Use a calculator.**

Example 2 **Classify a Triangle Using the Distance Formula**

Classify △*ABC* as scalene, isosceles, or equilateral.

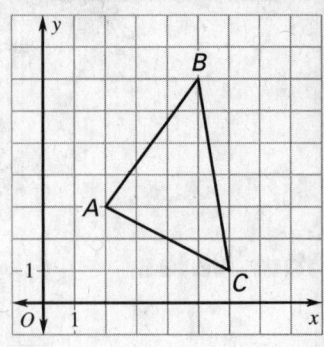

Solution

Find the distances between the _____.

AB = _____ = _____ = ____

BC = _____ = _____

AC = _____ = _____

Because _____ of the sides have the same length, △*ABC* is _____.

✔ *Checkpoint* **Complete the following exercises.**

1. Find the distance between $(-7, 3)$ and $(5, -2)$.

2. The vertices of a triangle are $(2, 1)$, $(4, 6)$, and $(7, 3)$. Classify △*TUV* as *scalene*, *isosceles*, or *equilateral*.

THE MIDPOINT FORMULA

The midpoint M of the line segment joining $A(\underline{})$ and $B(x_2, y_2)$ is

$$M = \underline{}.$$

Example 3   *Find the Midpoint of a Line Segment*

Find the midpoint of the line segment joining $(-6, 5)$ and $(2, -3)$.

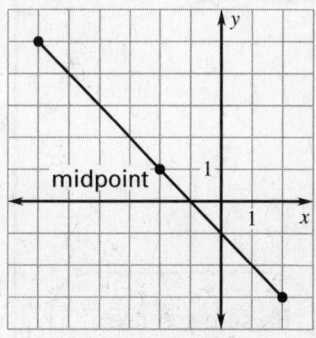

midpoint

Solution

Let $(x_1, y_1) = (-6, 5)$ and $(x_2, y_2) = (\underline{})$.

$\left(\dfrac{x_1 + x_2}{2}, \dfrac{y_1 + y_2}{2} \right) = \underline{}$ **Substitute values into the formula.**

$= \underline{}$ **Simplify numerators.**

$= (\underline{})$ **Simplify.**

✔ *Checkpoint* **Find the midpoint of the line segment joining the two points.**

3. $(-6, 5)$ and $(1, 1)$	4. $(8, -3)$ and $(-4, 6)$

Example 4   *Find a Perpendicular Bisector*

Write an equation for the perpendicular bisector of the line segment joining $A(-4, 1)$ and $B(2, 3)$. Let A be (x_1, y_1) and B be (x_2, y_2).

Solution

1. Find the midpoint of the line segment.

$$\left(\frac{x_1 + x_2}{2}, \frac{y_1 + y_2}{2}\right) = \left(\underline{\hspace{1cm}}, \underline{\hspace{1cm}}\right) = (\underline{\hspace{0.5cm}}, \underline{\hspace{0.5cm}})$$

2. Calculate the slope of the line segment.

$$m = \frac{y_2 - y_1}{x_2 - x_1} = \underline{\hspace{1.5cm}} = \underline{\hspace{0.5cm}} = \underline{\hspace{0.5cm}}$$

3. Find the slope of the perpendicular bisector.

Its slope is the _____ of ___, or ____.

4. Write the equation. Use point-slope form.

$y - y_1 = m(x - x_1)$ **Point-slope form**

$y - \underline{\ } = (\underline{\ })(x - \underline{\ })$ **Substitute ___ for y_1, ___ for m, and ___ for x_1.**

$y - 2 = -3(\underline{\hspace{1cm}})$ **Simplify inside the parentheses.**

$y - 2 = \underline{\ }x - \underline{\ }$ **Distributive property**

$y = \underline{\hspace{1cm}}$ **Simplify.**

> Be sure you use the midpoint found in Step 1 and the slope found in Step 3 in the point-slope equation.

✔ *Checkpoint* **Complete the following exercise.**

5. Write an equation for the perpendicular bisector of the line segment joining $A(-5, 6)$ and $B(3, -2)$.

Homework

13.2 Parabolas

Goal • Graph and write equations of parabolas.

VOCABULARY

Focus

_____

Directrix

STANDARD EQUATION OF A PARABOLA WITH VERTEX AT (0, 0)

The standard form of the equation of a parabola with vertex at (0, 0) is as follows:

EQUATION	FOCUS	DIRECTRIX	AXIS OF SYMMETRY
$x^2 = 4p$___	(0, ___)	$y = -$___	Vertical ($x = $ ___)
$y^2 = $ ___ x	(p, ___)	___ $= -p$	_____
			($y = $ ___)

Example 1   *Graph Equations of Parabolas*

Graph the equation $y = -4x^2$. Identify the focus, directrix, and axis of symmetry.

Solution

1. **Write** the equation in standard form.

   $y = -4x^2$ **Write original equation.**

   _____ $= x^2$ **Multiply each side by** _____ .

2. **Identify** the focus, directrix, and axis of symmetry. The equation has the form $x^2 = 4py$ where $4p = $ _____ , so

   $p = $ _____ . The focus is $(0, p) = \left(0, \underline{\quad}\right)$. The

   directrix is $y = -p = $ _____ . The axis of symmetry is __ $= 0$.

---

3. Draw the parabola. Make a table of values by choosing values for *x*. Plot the points.

x	−2	−1	0	1	2
y	−16	_____	0	−4	_____

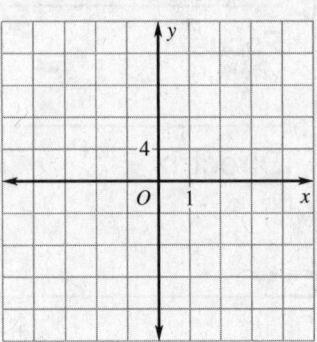

✔ *Checkpoint* **Complete the following exercise.**

1. Graph $y = -\frac{1}{4}x^2$. Identify the focus, directrix, and axis of symmetry.

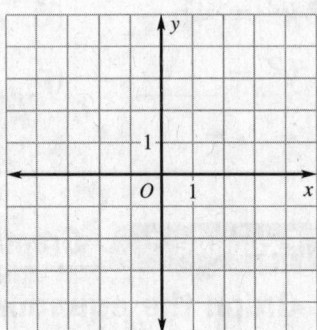

Example 2 *Write an Equation of a Parabola*

Write an equation of the parabola.

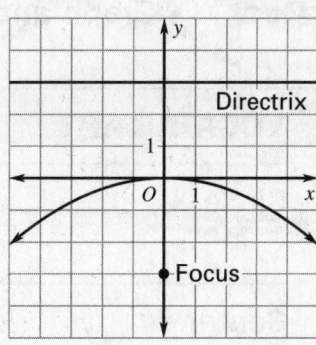

Solution

The directrix is $y = -p =$ ___. Use the equation for a parabola with a _____ axis of symmetry, so $p =$ ____.

$x^2 =$ _____	**Standard equation**
$x^2 = 4($____$)y$	**Substitute** _____ **for** p.
$x^2 =$ _____	**Simplify.**

✔ *Checkpoint* **Complete the following exercise.**

2. Write the standard form of the equation of the parabola with vertex at $(0, 0)$ and directrix at $x = -\frac{3}{4}$.

Homework

13.3 Circles

Goal • Graph and write equations of circles.

VOCABULARY

Circle

Center

Radius

STANDARD EQUATION OF A CIRCLE WITH CENTER AT (0, 0) AND RADIUS *r*

$$\underline{} + \underline{} = \underline{}$$

Example 1 *Graph an Equation of a Circle*

Graph $y^2 = -x^2 + 16$.

Solution

1. **Write** the equation in standard form.

   $y^2 = -x^2 + 16$ **Write original equation.**

   $\underline{} + y^2 = 16$ **Add** ____ **to each side.**

2. **Identify** the center and the radius. In this form you can see that the graph is a _____ with center at

   the _____ and with radius $r =$ _____ $=$ ___ .

3. **Plot** several points that are ___ units from the origin. The points (0, ___), (___, 0), (0, _____), and (_____, 0) are most convenient.

4. **Draw** a circle that passes through the four _____ .

Example 2   *Write an Equation of a Circle*

The point $(-3, 4)$ lies on a circle with center at the origin. Write the standard form of the equation of the circle.

Solution

Because the point $(-3, 4)$ is on the circle, the _____ of the circle must be the distance between the _____ $(0, 0)$ and that point.

$r = \sqrt{(x_2 - x_1)^2 + (y_2 - y_1)^2}$ Use the _____ formula.

$= $ _____   Substitute values.

$= $ _____ $= $ _____   Simplify.

Use the standard form with $r = $ ____ to write an equation of the circle.

$x^2 + y^2 = r^2$ **Standard form**

$x^2 + y^2 = (\_\_\_)^2$ **Substitute ____ for r.**

$x^2 + y^2 = $ ____   **Simplify.**

✔ *Checkpoint* **Complete the following exercises.**

1. Graph the equation $x^2 = 4 - y^2$. Identify the radius of the circle.

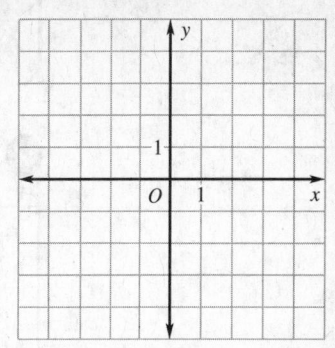

2. Write the standard form of the equation of the circle that passes through the point $(6, -3)$ with center at the origin.

Example 3 **Write an Equation of a Tangent Line**

Write an equation of the line that is tangent to the circle $x^2 + y^2 = 17$ at $(4, -1)$.

Solution

A line is tangent to the circle at $(4, -1)$ if it is _____ to the radius of the circle at (____, ____).

1. **Calculate** the _____ of the radius through (____, ____) and center (____, ____).

    $$m = \text{_____} = \text{\_\_\_\_}$$

2. **Find** the slope of the tangent line at $(4, -1)$. Because the tangent line at $(4, -1)$ is _____ to the radius, its slope is the _____ of _____, or ____.

3. **Write** an equation. Use point-slope form.

    $$y - y_1 = \text{\_\_\_\_}(x - x_1)$$ **Point-slope form**

    $$y - \text{\_\_\_\_\_} = \text{\_\_\_}(\text{\_\_\_} - \text{\_\_\_})$$ **Substitute ____ for m and $(4, -1)$ for (x_1, y_1).**

    $$y + \text{\_\_\_} = \text{\_\_\_\_} - \text{\_\_\_\_}$$ **Simplify; use the distributive property.**

    $$y = \text{_____}$$ **Solve for y.**

✔ *Checkpoint* **Complete the following exercise.**

3. Write an equation of the line that is tangent to the circle $x^2 + y^2 = 34$ at $(-3, -5)$.

Example 4   *Use a Circle as a Model*

Lighthouse The beam from Oak Island Lighthouse in North Carolina can be seen for up to 24 miles.

a. Write an inequality to describe the region in which the lighthouse beam is visible. Assume that the lighthouse is at the origin.

b. You are on a ship that is 18 miles east and 9 miles north of the lighthouse. Can you see the lighthouse beam from your ship?

Solution

a. Write an inequality for the region lit by the beam. This region is all the points that satisfy the inequality $x^2 + y^2 <$ _____ ^{2}.

b. Substitute the coordinates of your ship, (____, ____), into the inequality from part (a).

$$x^2 + y^2 < \underline{\qquad}^2 \qquad \text{Inequality from part (a)}$$

$$\underline{\qquad}^2 + \underline{\qquad}^2 \overset{?}{<} 576 \qquad \text{Substitute} \underline{\qquad} \text{ for } x \text{ and}$$
$$\underline{\qquad} \text{ for } y.$$

$$\underline{\qquad} + \underline{\qquad} \overset{?}{<} 576 \qquad \text{Simplify.}$$

$$\underline{\qquad} < 576 \qquad \text{The inequality is } \underline{\qquad}.$$

Because the inequality is _____ for the coordinates of your ship, you _____ see the lighthouse beam.

✔ *Checkpoint* **Complete the following exercise.**

4. In Example 4, suppose your ship is located 19 miles south and 16 miles east of the lighthouse. Can you see the lighthouse beam? Justify your answer.

13.4 Ellipses

Goal • Graph and write equations of ellipses.

VOCABULARY

Ellipse

_____

Foci

_____

Vertices

_____

Major axis

_____

Center

_____

Co-vertices

_____

Minor axis

STANDARD EQUATION OF AN ELLIPSE WITH CENTER AT (0, 0)

The standard form of the equation of an ellipse with center at (0, 0) is as follows:

EQUATION	MAJOR AXIS	VERTICES	CO-VERTICES
$\dfrac{x^2}{a^2} + \dfrac{y^2}{b^2} = 1$	_____	$(\pm\underline{\ \ }, 0)$	$(0, \pm\underline{\ \ })$
	_____	$(0, \pm\underline{\ \ })$	$(\pm\underline{\ \ }, 0)$

The major and _____ axes are of lengths _____ and _____, respectively, where _____ > b > 0.

The _____ of the ellipse lie on the _____ axis, c units from the _____ where $c^2 = \underline{\ \ }^2 - \underline{\ \ }^2$.

Example 1   *Graph an Equation of an Ellipse*

Graph $9x^2 + 36y^2 = 324$. Identify the vertices, co-vertices, and foci of the ellipse.

Solution

1. **Write** the equation in standard form.

$$9x^2 + 36y^2 = 324 \qquad \text{Write original equation.}$$

$$\frac{}{} + \frac{}{} = 1 \qquad \text{Divide each side by } \underline{}.$$

$$\frac{}{} + \frac{}{} = 1 \qquad \text{Simplify.}$$

2. **Identify** the vertices, co-vertices, and foci. Note that $a^2 = 36$, so $a = \underline{}$. Also $b^2 = 9$, so $b = \underline{}$. Because the denominator of the x^2-term is _____ than the denominator of the y^2-term, the major axis is _____.

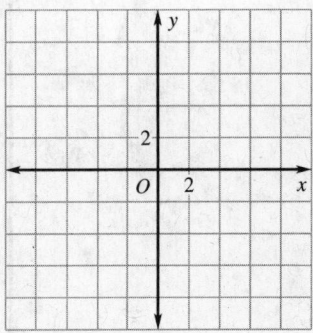

So, the vertices are at $(\pm a, 0) = (\pm\underline{}, 0)$ and the co-vertices are at $(0, \pm b) = (0, \pm\underline{})$.

Next, find the foci.

$c^2 = a^2 - b^2 = \underline{} - \underline{} = \underline{}$, so $c = \pm\underline{}$.

3. **Draw** the _____ that passes through each _____ and co-vertex.

✔ *Checkpoint* **Complete the following exercise.**

Think of x^2 as $\frac{x^2}{1}$ so $b^2 = 1$.

1. **Graph** the equation $x^2 + \dfrac{y^2}{25} = 1$. Identify the vertices, co-vertices, and foci of the ellipse.

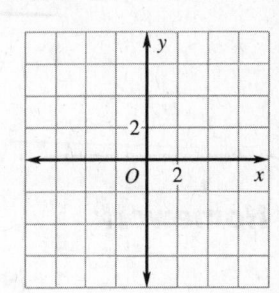

Example 2 **Write an Equation of an Ellipse**

Write an equation of the ellipse that has a vertex at (0, 7), a co-vertex at (−4, 0), and center at (0, 0).

Solution

1. **Sketch** the ellipse. By symmetry you know the ellipse has another vertex at (0, _____) and another _____ at (___, 0).

2. **Identify** the values of a and b. Because the given vertex is on the ___-axis, the major axis is _____ with $a = $ ___. The minor axis is _____ with $b = $ ___.

3. **Write** an equation.

$$\frac{x^2}{b^2} + \frac{y^2}{a^2} = 1$$ Equation for an ellipse with a _____ major axis

$$\frac{}{} + \frac{}{} = 1$$ Substitute ___ for a and ___ for b.

$$\frac{}{} + \frac{}{} = 1$$ Simplify.

✔ *Checkpoint* Write an equation of the ellipse with the given characteristics and center at (0, 0).

2. Vertex: (−9, 0) Co-vertex: (0, 4)	3. Vertex: (0, 7) Focus: (0, −3)

Homework

13.5 Hyperbolas

Goal • Graph and write equations of hyperbolas.

Your Notes

VOCABULARY

Hyperbola
_____

Foci
_____

Vertices
_____

Transverse axis
_____

Center

STANDARD EQUATION OF A HYPERBOLA WITH CENTER AT (0, 0)

The standard form of the equation of an ellipse with center at (0, 0) is as follows:

EQUATION	TRANSVERSE AXIS	ASYMPTOTES	VERTICES
$\dfrac{x^2}{a^2} - \dfrac{y^2}{b^2} = 1$	_____	$y = \pm \underline{\;\;} x$	$(\pm \underline{\;\;}, 0)$
_____	_____	$y = \pm \underline{\;\;} x$	$(0, \pm \underline{\;\;})$

The major and _____ axes are of lengths _____ and _____, respectively, where ___ > b > 0.

The _____ of the hyperbola lie on the _____ axis, c units from the _____ where $c^2 = \underline{\;\;}^2 + \underline{\;\;}^2$.

Example 1   *Graph an Equation of a Hyperbola*

Graph $36y^2 - 9x^2 = 324$. Identify the vertices, foci, and asymptotes of the hyperbola.

Solution

1. **Write** the equation in standard form.

$36y^2 - 9x^2 = 324$ **Write original equation.**

$\dfrac{}{} - \dfrac{}{} = 1$ **Divide each side by** _____ **and simplify.**

2. **Identify** the vertices, foci, and asymptotes. Note that $a^2 = 9$, so $a =$ ____. Also $b^2 = 36$, so $b =$ ____. The y^2-term is _____, so the transverse axis is _____ and the vertices are at $(0, \pm$____$)$.

$c^2 = a^2 + b^2$

$ = \underline{}^2 + \underline{}^2$

$ = \underline{}$, so $c = \pm\underline{}$

The foci are $(0, \pm\underline{})$, and the asymptotes are

$y = \pm \dfrac{}{} x$, or $y = \pm \dfrac{}{} x$.

3. **Draw** the hyperbola. Draw a _____ centered at the origin that is $2a =$ ____ units high and $2b =$ ____ units wide. The asymptotes are the _____ of the rectangle.

Draw the _____ of the hyperbola passing through the _____ and approaching the _____.

     Copyright © McDougal Littell/Houghton Mifflin Company

Example 2 *Write an Equation of a Hyperbola*

Write an equation of the hyperbola with foci at (−5, 0) and (5, 0) and vertices at (−4, 0) and (4, 0).

Solution

The foci and vertices lie on the ___-axis, so the transverse axis is _____. The foci are each ___ units from the center, so ___ = 5. The _____ are each ___ units from the center, so $a =$ ___. Find the value of b^2.

$$c^2 = a^2 + b^2$$

$$\underline{}^2 = \underline{}^2 + b^2$$

$$b^2 = \underline{}$$

Write an equation of the hyperbola.

$$\frac{x^2}{a^2} - \frac{y^2}{b^2} = 1$$ Standard equation for hyperbola with _____ axis

$$\frac{}{} - \frac{}{} = 1$$ Substitute $\underline{}^2 = $ ____ for a^2 and ___ for b^2.

⊘ *Checkpoint* **Complete the following exercises.**

1. Graph the equation $\dfrac{x^2}{49} - \dfrac{y^2}{9} = 1$. Identify the vertices, foci, and asymptotes of the hyperbola.

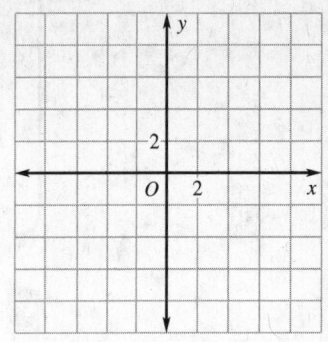

2. Write an equation of the hyperbola with foci at (0, −8) and (0, 8) and vertices at (0, −5) and (0, 5).

Example 3 *Write a Hyperbolic Model*

Lamp The diagram shows the hyperbolic cross section of a lamp.

a. Write an equation for the cross section of the lamp.

b. The lamp is 10 inches high. How wide is the base?

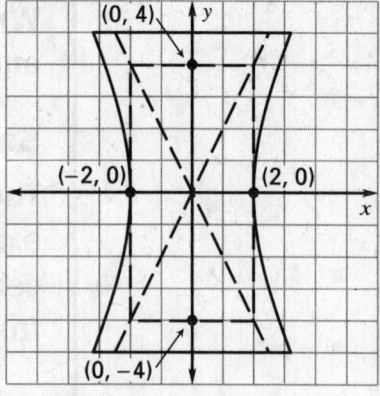

Solution

a. From the diagram, $a =$ ____ and ____ $= 4$. Because the transverse axis is _____, an equation for the cross section of the lamp is

$$\frac{}{} - \frac{}{} = 1, \text{ or } \frac{}{} - \frac{}{} = 1.$$

b. Find the positive ___-coordinate at the lamp's bottom edge. Because the lamp is 10 inches tall, substitute ___ for y in the equation from part (a) and solve for x.

$$\frac{x^2}{4} - \frac{}{} = 1 \qquad \text{Substitute \_\_\_ for y.}$$

$$x^2 = \frac{}{} \qquad \text{Solve for } x^2.$$

$$x \approx \underline{} \qquad \text{Solve for x; x must be positive.}$$

So the lamp has a width of 2x, or about 2(____) = ____ inches.

✔ *Checkpoint* **Complete the following exercise.**

3. Write an equation for the hyperbolic cross section of the lamp in Example 3 if the vertices are at (±3, 0) and the foci are at (±5, 0). If the lamp is 15 inches high, how wide is the base?

Homework

13.6 Graphing and Classifying Conics

Goal • Translate and graph conic sections.

Your Notes

VOCABULARY

Conic sections (conics)

_____

General second-degree equation

_____

Discriminant

STANDARD EQUATIONS OF TRANSLATED CONICS

In the following equations the point (h, k) is the _____ of the parabola and the _____ of the other conics.

Circle $(x - h)^2 +$ _____ $=$ ___^{2}

Parabola   HORIZONTAL AXIS: $(y - \underline{\ \ })^2 = 4\underline{\ \ }(x - \underline{\ \ })$

VERTICAL AXIS: $(x - \underline{\ \ })^2 = 4\underline{\ \ }(y - \underline{\ \ })$

Ellipse   HORIZONTAL AXIS: $\dfrac{(x - h)^2}{a^2} + \underline{\hspace{1cm}} = 1$

VERTICAL AXIS: $\dfrac{(x - h)^2}{b^2} + \underline{\hspace{1cm}} = 1$

Hyperbola HORIZONTAL AXIS: $\underline{\hspace{1cm}} - \dfrac{(y - k)^2}{b^2} = 1$

VERTICAL AXIS: $\dfrac{(y - k)^2}{a^2} - \underline{\hspace{1cm}} = 1$

Example 1 *Graph a Translated Circle*

Graph $(x + 3)^2 + (y - 2)^2 = 4$.

1. **Compare** the given equation to the _____ _____ of a _____. The graph is a circle with center at $(-3, \_\_\_)$ and radius ____ = ___. Plot the center.

2. **Plot** several points that are each ___ units from the center.

   First plot two points ___ units to the left and right of the center, $(\_\_\_, 2)$ and $(\_\_\_, \_\_\_)$. Then plot two points ___ units above and below the center, $(-3, \_\_\_)$, and $(\_\_\_, \_\_\_)$.

3. **Draw** a _____ that passes through the four points.

Example 2 *Graph a Translated Hyperbola*

Graph $\dfrac{(y + 2)^2}{16} - \dfrac{(x - 1)^2}{4} = 1$.

1. **Compare** the equation to the standard equations of translated conics. The form tells you that its graph is a _____. The y-term is positive, so the transverse axis is _____ with center at $(h, k) = (\_\_\_, \_\_\_)$. You know $a^2 = 16$ so $a = \_\_\_$, and $b^2 = \_\_\_$ so $b = \_\_\_$.

2. **Plot** the vertices $a = \_\_\_$ units above and below the center, at $(\_\_\_, \_\_\_)$ and $(\_\_\_, \_\_\_)$.

3. **Identify** the foci using $c^2 = a^2 + b^2$. Substitute values and solve for c. The foci are $c = \_\_\_\_\_ \approx 4.5$ units above and below the center at $(1, \_\_\_\_\_)$ and $(1, \_\_\_\_\_)$.

4. **Draw** a rectangle centered at $(\_\_\_, \_\_\_\_\_)$ that is $2a = \_\_\_$ units high and $2b = \_\_\_$ units wide. The hyperbola's asymptotes are the _____ of the rectangle. Draw the hyperbola so it passes through the _____ and approaches the _____.

✔ **Checkpoint** **Graph the equation.**

1. $(x - 2)^2 + (y + 3)^2 = 9$

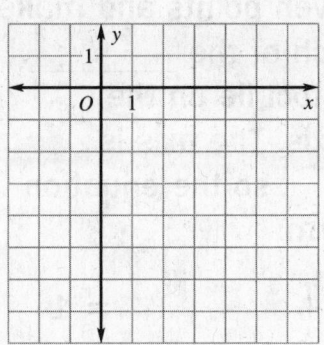

2. $\dfrac{(x + 3)^2}{9} - \dfrac{(y - 1)^2}{25} = 1$

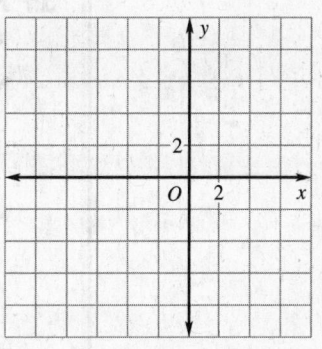

Example 3 **Write an Equation of a Translated Parabola**

Write an equation of the parabola with vertex at (2, 1) and focus at (5, 1).

Solution

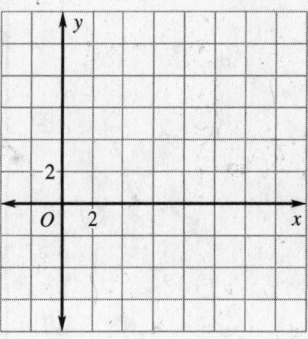

1. Plot the given points. Sketch the _____. The parabola opens _____, so its equation has the form $(y - k)^2 = $ _____ where p ___ 0.

2. Find the values of h and k. The _____ is at $(h, k) = (2, 1)$ so $h = $ ___ and $k = $ ___.

3. Find the value of p. The vertex $(2, 1)$ and focus $(5, 1)$ both lie on the line $y = $ ___. The distance between them is $|p| = |5 - $ ___$| = $ ___. Because p ___ 0, $p = $ ___, and $4p = $ ___.

4. Write the equation.

$(y - k)^2 = 4p(x - h)$ **Standard form**

$(y - $ ___$)^2 = $ ___$(x - $ ___$)$ **Substitute** ___ **for** k, ___ **for** $4p$, **and** ___ **for** h.

Example 4 | *Write an Equation of a Translated Ellipse*

Write an equation of the ellipse with foci at (−2, 3) and (4, 3) and co-vertices at (1, 4) and (1, 2).

1. **Plot** the given points and make a rough sketch of the _____. Notice the foci lie on the _____ axis. The axis is _____, so the equation has this form:

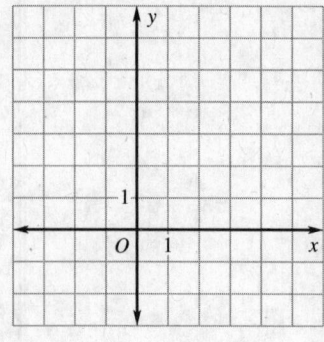

$$\frac{\qquad}{\rule{1.5cm}{0.4pt}} + \frac{\qquad}{\rule{1.5cm}{0.4pt}} = 1$$

2. **Find** the values of *h* and *k*. The _____ (*h*, *k*) is _____ between the _____.

$$(h, k) = \left(\frac{\qquad}{\rule{1.5cm}{0.4pt}}, \frac{\qquad}{\rule{1.5cm}{0.4pt}} \right) = (\underline{\ \ }, \underline{\ \ })$$

3. **Find** the value of *b*, the distance between one _____ and the center (___, ___). Also, find the value of *c*, the distance between one _____ and the center (___, ___). Use the co-vertex (1, 4) and the focus (4, 3).

$$b = |4 - \underline{\ \ }| = \underline{\ \ } \quad \text{and} \quad c = |\underline{\ \ } - 1| = \underline{\ \ }$$

4. **Find** the value of *a*. Because the equation is for an ellipse, use $a^2 = b^2 + c^2$.

$$a^2 = b^2 + c^2 = \underline{\ \ }^2 + \underline{\ \ }^2 = \underline{\ \ }, \text{ so } a = \underline{\ \ \ \ }$$

The standard form of the equation is

$$\frac{\qquad}{\rule{1.5cm}{0.4pt}} + \frac{\qquad}{\rule{1.5cm}{0.4pt}} = 1.$$

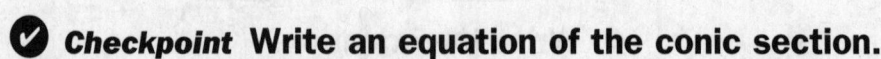

✔ *Checkpoint* Write an equation of the conic section.

3. Parabola with vertex at (−3, −1) and focus at (−3, 1)	4. Ellipse with foci at (−3, 0) and (−3, −6) and co-vertices at (−1, −3) and (−5, −3)

CLASSIFYING CONIC SECTIONS

If the graph of $Ax^2 + Bxy + Cy^2 + Dx + Ey + F = 0$ is a conic, then the type of conic can be determined by the following characteristics.

DISCRIMINANT	TYPE OF CONIC
$B^2 - 4AC < 0$, $B = $ ___ , and $A = $ ___	_____
$B^2 - 4AC$ ___ 0 and either _____ or _____	Ellipse
$B^2 - 4AC$ ___ 0	_____
$B^2 - 4AC$ ___ 0	Hyperbola

Example 5   *Use the Discriminant*

Classify the conic section given by
$3x^2 + 3y^2 - 5x + 6y - 1 = 0$.

Solution

The equation is written in the form $Ax^2 + Bxy + Cy^2 + Dx + Ey + F = 0$ where $A = $ ___ , $B = $ ___ , and $C = $ ___ .
Find the _____ .

$B^2 - 4AC = 0 - 4(\text{___})(\text{___})$

$\qquad\qquad = 0 - \text{___} = \text{_____}$

Because $B^2 - 4AC$ ___ 0 and ___ = ___ , the conic is a _____ .

✔ **Checkpoint** Use the discriminant to classify the conic.

5. $5x^2 - 3y^2 - 10x - 12y - 22 = 0$

6. $-3x^2 + 6xy - 3y^2 + 4x - y + 10 = 0$

Words to Review

Use your own words and/or an example to explain the vocabulary word.

Distance formula	Midpoint formula
Focus, foci	Directrix
Circle	Center
Radius	Ellipse

Vertices	Major axis
Co-vertices	Minor axis
Hyperbola	Transverse axis
Conic sections (conics)	General second-degree equation
Discriminant	

Review your notes and Chapter 13 by using the Chapter Review on pages 733–736 of your textbook.